Created and Directed by Hans Höfer

D0091854

INSIGHT GUIDES
San Francisco

Edited by John Wilcock

Managing Editor: Martha Ellen Zenfell

Editorial Director: Brian Bell

HOUGHTON MIFFLIN COMPANY

APA PUBLICATIONS

ABOUT THIS BOOK

Millions of visitors have been known to leave their hearts in San Francisco. "Baghdad by the Bay" is one nickname, but locals are more likely to refer to their hometown as "the City." For most Americans – even those who have never been here – San Francisco is their favorite place. And not just Americans. "A city of charming people and hideous buildings," observed the English critic Cyril Connolly almost half a century ago. "Yet San Francisco and its surroundings… probably represent the most attractive all-the-year-round alternative to Europe that the world can provide."

San Francisco lends itself particularly well to the approach taken by the 185-title award-winning *Insight Guides* series, created in 1970 by **Hans Höfer**, founder of Apa Publications. Each book encourages readers to celebrate the essence of a place rather than try to tailor it to their expectations and is edited in the belief that, without insight into a people's character and culture, travel can sometimes narrow the mind rather than broaden it.

Höfer

This new and comprehensively revamped edition was supervised by **John Wilcock** in California and Apa's American-born North American Editor-in-Chief **Martha Ellen Zenfell** in London. Zenfell and Wilcock, though 7,000 miles apart, have collaborated on a number of books, among them *Insight Guide: Los Angeles* and the best-selling *Insight Guide: California*.

Wilcock

Zenfell

Wilcock, a graduate of the *New York Times*' travel desk and subsequently author of books about more than a dozen countries, dates his acquaintance with California back to his visits while a columnist for New York's *Village Voice* and his editorship of the *Los Angeles Free Press*.

"I went up to San Francisco in the '60s to cover the Human Be-In in Golden Gate Park," he recalls, "and to me that seemed to be the beginning of a whole new world. It could only have happened here." Together with **Matthew Parfitt**, Wilcock is responsible for the history chapters and also the pieces on Hearst Castle, Herb Caen and cable cars.

Responsible for much of the writing, updating and editing was Silicon Valley-born **Jeffrey Davis**. His experience "working graveyard shifts at the local supermarket, by day as a reporter for *The California Aggie* (a campus paper at the University of California, Davis) and going to class sometime in between," preceded his editorial stints at *Harpers* and *Esquire* magazines in New York. Davis was eventually drawn back to the West Coast to work as an editor at San Francisco's *Mother Jones*.

Davis

Susan Richter, author of "The Gourmet's City," claims that her extensive background in the restaurant business supports her more artistic impulses. After being a waitress for many years, she hopes one day "to dine in some place better than the employee lounge." She has worked for the Sierra Club and *The New Republic*, and reported for the *Oakland Tribune* and the *Alameda Times-Star*.

Wine expert **Howard Rabinowitz,** author of "Literary San Francisco" and updater of the Chinatown and Japantown chapters, is a Hindi scholar and screenwriter. He has lived in the Bay Area for a few years and has no plans to quit. As Rudyard Kipling wrote a century ago, "San Francisco has only one drawback. 'Tis hard to leave."

Cunningham

The original *Insight Guide: San Francisco* was the combined efforts of a hard-working team headed by **Hilary Cunningham**, a Canadian who studied at New York University before transferring to Yale. The pioneering efforts of Cunningham's team can be felt throughout this new edition. Few places, however, change as fast as California and, to keep pace, most of the articles contained here are brand new – all written by Bay Area residents who not only know but also understand how San Francisco works.

Laura Jamison, who covers the Bay Area arts scene for the *SF Weekly*, was a natural choice to write our chapter on the same topic. Now an editor at *San Francisco Focus* magazine, she is also responsible for the chapters on Union Square, Mission, SoMa and North Beach. A former columnist for the *San Francisco Chronicle*, **Randy Shilts** ("The Gay Community") died of AIDS just as the revamp for this book was going to press. Shilts was a high-profile local figure and author of three groundbreaking books on gay culture.

Wagstaff

The essay "The Great Outdoors" is by **Sean Wagstaff**, who clocks in at the high-tech trade magazine *MacWEEK*. He windsurfs around San Francisco, kayaks and fly-fishes the Sierra rivers in summer, snowboards every winter weekend and somehow found time to write this article for us.

Pertersen

Journalist **Julie Petersen**, who lives in the heart of Silicon Valley, about which she writes for this book, grew up in a high-tech family that followed her father from one computer firm to the next. She now works on the staff of *Mother Jones*.

In the "Daytrips" chapter, Sacramento is covered by **Dennis Pottenger**, a former staffer on *Sacramento* magazine, who for the past 10 years has specialized in politics in the state capital. He once wrote a book about the San Francisco football team, the 49ers. About Sacramento he reports, paraphrasing the well-known saying, "Well, there is a *there* there, but it's just so hot sometimes that *there* means home with the air conditioning on at full blast."

A s well as the efforts of the new contributors, much of the work of the original team lives on – sometimes in words, and always in spirit. **Peter and Virginia Maloney** ("Northern Waterfront" and "Mansions") now live and work as writers in New York. **Philip Thayer** ("Golden Gate Park") is a dancer, poet, writer and New Yorker who regards the Bay Area as a second home, having spent several seasons with the Oakland ballet company. A big West Coast thank you, too, to **John Gattuso**, **Alice Scharper**, **Stephen Scharper**, **Patrick Finley**, **Michelle Quinn**, **Eric Szemes** and **Lee Foster**, all of whom made valuable contributions.

Thayer

Compiler of the updated Travel Tips section is **Priscilla Yamin**, who, in addition to working for *Mother Jones*, spent a year living in the Czech Republic where she co-authored *Prague Naturally*. **Steve Curley** also contributed to the research and updating.

In the London editorial office, **Jill Anderson** and **Lesley Gordon** guided the text through a variety of Macintosh computers, and **Pam Barrett** proofread and indexed the manuscript.

CONTENTS

TRAVEL TIPS

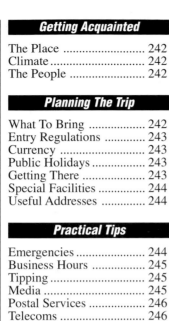

WELCOME TO SAN FRANCISCO

North Beach to Tenderloin, over Russian Hill,
The grades are something giddy, and the curves are fit to kill!
All the way to Market Street, climbing up the slope,
Down upon the other side, hanging to the rope;
But the sight of San Francisco, as you take the lurching dip!
There is plenty of excitement on the Hyde Street Grip!

Gellett Burgess, "The Hyde Street Grip,"
in *A Gage of Youth,* 1906

San Francisco wins visitors' hearts, straightaway and effortlessly. It is a pastel city for lovers and pleasure seekers, soft and feminine and Mediterranean in mood. Foghorns and bridges, cable cars and hills. Alcatraz and Fisherman's Wharf, Chinatown and North Beach – all invite feelings of fascination or enchantment.

San Francisco is comfortable with contradiction, jealously preserving the past and delighting in anachronism, yet always riding the latest wave of fashion, whether in *haute couture*, in gay and lesbian culture, or in computer chips. Haughty but humane, the city may fleece the tourist and celebrate wealth, but it maintained soup kitchens for the poor long before modern economics revived that custom elsewhere in the land.

The City by the Bay is what many call it and, although there must be scores of cities beside scores of bays, almost everybody knows that this particular reference is to San Francisco. It's a big bay, too, being 50 miles (81 km) around and crossed by no fewer than five bridges. One, the Golden Gate Bridge, is possibly the most famous bridge in the world, and as evocative of the city as the little cable car, Fisherman's Wharf and, yes, Tony Bennett's timeless song. Even before he left his heart here, San Francisco was virtually every American's favorite city – and that includes all the people who haven't even been here yet.

It's not hard to explain why this is so. To begin with, it's an enchantingly beautiful city, one of the most distinctive in the world with its gorgeous panoramas from 43 different hills, watery vistas, a verdant park that seems to go on forever and the mostly lowscale development dominated by old houses that delight the eye just as they did when they were built a century or more ago.

It's also a city with a strong sense of neighborhood, each with a distinct identity and yet overlapping and inter-relating so people mix and mingle and go through them instead of bypassing them on the highway when they want to visit some other part of town – which is a more familiar pattern.

Small as it is (pop. 730,000), San Francisco has many times

featured on the world's front pages: the discovery of gold, the 1906 earthquake and fire, the founding and first home of the United Nations, the Haight-Ashbury "commune" which became an international magnet for the 1960s hippies and the renowned attitude of tolerance which has served as a sort of metaphorical welcome mat for unorthodox lifestyles.

These days, the vast majority of San Franciscans are middle-class, ranging from the ambitious young professionals who have invaded the city's fashionable districts to the immigrant families who run neighborhood businesses. More than other people, all San Franciscans – from the richest to the poorest, from the hushed precincts of Presidio Terrace to the run-down projects of Hunters Point – are conscious of their stake in the city.

San Francisco's residents form a demographic bouillabaisse not found elsewhere on the North American continent. Although the descendants of early Italian, German and Irish families are still found in snug enclaves, their numbers have been greatly diminished over the past couple of decades by the lure of suburbia, with its cheaper and bigger houses.

Their place has been filled by an influx of Asian and Hispanic people, in recent years many of them Filipinos, the fastest growing minority; refugees from Southeast Asia; and both wealth and people from jittery Hong Kong. One consequence has been that the lively but small 23 square blocks of Chinatown haven't been able to absorb the new arrivals. So they have spread their cultures west through the avenues into the formerly all-white Richmond and Sunset districts.

Many of the city's new arrivals have also been homosexuals fleeing hometown disapproval for San Francisco's famed easy-going tolerance. During the past 15 years, San Francisco's gays have emerged from a guilt-ridden existence to play a major role in the city's political, cultural and economic life. They have even been elected to the 11-member board of supervisors, which governs the city along with the mayor. The police department actively recruits both gay men and women.

The city will welcome you, too, whatever your tastes and inclinations might be, and doubtless be everything you want it to be. You'll absorb the ambiance, be entranced by the sights, delight in the food and sleep well at night. You might even learn to appreciate the fog.

"The San Francisco fog has never been sufficiently glorified," wrote Arnold Genthe, in *As I Remember*. The fogs "come in, not an enveloping blanket but a luminous drift, conferring a magic patina on the most commonplace structures, giving them an air of age and mystery."

Genthe was writing in 1930, but the fog, of course, is still there. As you walk through the steep, charming and well-known streets, see if you agree.

Right, music soothes the savage streets.

par Franquelin d'après Choris.

Danse des habitans de Califo

20

Pl. III

Lith. de Langlumé r de l'Abbaye N. 4

à la mission de s^e Francisco.

For thousands of years before the Spaniards arrived, the Miwok, Ohlone and Wituk Indians, among others, occupied much of northern California, living in the kind of harmony with the land that the most ecologically-conscious can only dream of today. But once the Europeans arrived, their decline was assured. Regarding the tribes as little better than animals compared with "the people of reason" (themselves), within a century the avaricious newcomers scorned and virtually obliterated the culture and ravaged the environment. The city of San Francisco was built on greed and gold, which are often synonymous.

Early explorers: Exactly what Sir Francis Drake discovered in 1579 during his voyage around the world in the *Golden Hind* has never been established with certainty. Drake had a mission from Elizabeth I to "annoy" the Spanish provinces and had been obediently causing havoc up and down the west coast of Mexico. (Yet in his gentlemanly manner of operation, he had killed not one person.) Apparently Drake passed by the bay's entrance without venturing inside or even noticing an opening. But his log shows that he did anchor just north of the bay and sent several landing parties ashore. It seems that one of these groups left behind the small brass plate that was discovered only in 1936 near Drake's Bay.

It was rumors of riches that enticed the Spaniards from the beginning. The early explorers were seeking a Northwest Passage that would lead them to the Orient and its valuable spice trade. Hernando Cortés, the conqueror of Mexico, had ordered a series of expeditions up the coast of Baja California – at the time thought to be an island – but it was not until 1542 that Juan Rodriguez Cabrillo discovered the land to the north. Cabrillo even passed by these shores without noticing the immense natural harbor that is now San

Francisco Bay, but doubtless it was concealed in fog as it so often still is today.

Later, Gaspar de Portolá, on his northern expedition to find a suitable harbor, also missed its significance, thinking it to be an open gulf. But another explorer, Jose Francisco Ortega, reported it as "a great arm of the sea extending to the southeast farther than the eye could see." It wasn't, however, until the visit of Captain Juan Bautista de Anza six years later that a decision was made to build a mission here at Yerba Buena.

The mission, a little chapel with a thatch roof, was founded on October 9, 1776, by Fray Palóu. The chapel was named Mission Dolores after the nearby creek. Palóu acted for the renowned "Apostle of California," Fray Junipéro Serra, who was directly responsible for founding nine of the eventual 21 Californian missions, and personally baptized thousands of Indians. Presidios (garrisons), like the one nearby, were customarily built at strategic points to protect a mission against hostile tribes or foreign colonists.

Remote outpost: By the end of the century the population remained under 1,000. The garrison was strong enough to sustain attacks by hostile Indians but would have easily fallen to attacks from the sea had there been any. But northern California was still a remote outpost and held little appeal for foreign adventurers. Ironically, the Gold Rush that eventually ended the region's isolation might have come a century earlier if the Indians' discovery of the precious metal had been acted upon. Instead, the Spanish padres to whom it was shown advised silence on the matter, reasoning correctly that knowledge of its existence would bring an unmanageable influx of invaders.

By the end of the 18th century, however, foreign officials were beginning to show a discreet interest in the region. In 1792, the English sailor George Vancouver scouted the coast, bringing with him the first American visitor, John Green, to the shores of California. And the Russian trading post and garrison only 50 miles (80 km) to the north at

Preceding pages: a mission to convert. **Left,** Sir Francis Drake landed near San Francisco Bay around 1579.

Bodega Bay was engendering a certain nervousness on the part of the Californians. The Russians eventually left in 1841. By this time Mexico had declared its independence from Spain and the secularization of the missions had begun – a process that had been intended to turn over the land and livestock to Native American families but which mostly resulted in their further exploitation by enterprising new owners. Nevertheless, life in the area remained uneventful.

When a certain Captain Beecher visited this part of northern California in 1826, five years after Mexico had declared its independence from Spain, he noted among the

residents only ennui. "Some of them," he wrote, "were ingenious and clever men but they had been so long excluded from the civilized world that their ideas and their politics, like the maps pinned against the wall, bore the date 1772 as near as I could read forth fly specks." It wasn't until 20 years after his visit that the US flag was raised, the year (1846) that Samuel Brannan arrived with a group of 230 Mormons to colonize what was then renamed San Francisco. There was also some apprehension about the growing signs of interest by France and Britain in the American West and especially the value to a foreign power of San Francisco Bay, which an American diplomat, Waddy Thompson, described as "capacious enough to receive the navies of all the world."

But the immediate problem lay nearer to home. In May 1846, President James Polk engaged the United States in war with Mexico. Even before news of this declaration reached California, an independent group of nationalists at Sonoma, led by Ezekiel Merritt and William B. Idle, awoke the Mexican authority, General Vallejo, from his bed and obliged him to sign articles of surrender.

Their action had been encouraged by the presence of a US expedition led by a cartographer and explorer, John Charles Fremont. But as he declined to allow the rebels to raise the Stars and Stripes, they created a new flag depicting a grizzly bear racing a red star – the Bear Flag, as it became forever known. Accepting his acclamation as President of the Californian Republic, Fremont led a mission to capture the state capital at Monterey but found Commodore John Sloat had sailed from Mazatlan and arrived there first. Whatever Mexican resistance there had been crumbled quickly. All over California, groups raised the Stars and Stripes and claimed the territory.

Discovery of gold: One week before the signing of the Treaty of Guadalupe in January 1848, which ended the war and ceded California to the United States, James Marshall, contractor of a mill he had just built for John Sutter, discovered gold in the Sierra Nevada foothills. Sutter was an immigrant from Switzerland, whose 49,000-acre (19,800-hectare) Sacramento Valley ranch had been granted to him by the Mexican governor of California. He tried to keep the find a secret, but the news, of course, changed the nature of this peaceable pastoral region forever. By the end of May the word was all over California: the editor of the *Californian* announced the suspension of his newspaper because his entire staff had quit.

"The whole country from San Francisco to Los Angeles and from the sea shore to the base of the Sierra Nevada," he wrote, "resounds with the sordid cry of gold! GOLD! GOLD! – while the field is left half-planted, the house half-built and everything neglected but the manufacture of shovels and pick-axes…" Before the year was out more prospectors had arrived from Oregon, Mexico, Peru and Chile.

The early arrivals made instant fortunes from merely washing the abundant nuggets out of a stream or scraping the gold dust from easily accessible veins in the rock. It was estimated that the area was yielding as much as $50,000 worth of the precious metal each day. But as the risks increased, the supply dried up and prices of everything skyrocketed. The real necessities of life were buckets, shovels, rockers, dippers, pans. Miners mostly lived in tents, sleeping on blankets atop pine needles, but for those who needed a roof overhead, the rental of a hut in town cost $3,000. It wasn't long before those who serviced the prospectors grew considerably richer than most of the laboring class. Levi Strauss arrived from Germany to sell tents but ended up turning his supply of canvas into durable trousers. In 1850 a gold digger wrote home: "You can scarcely form a conception of what a dirty business this gold digging is… A little fat pork, a cup of tea or coffee and a slice or two of miserable bread form the repast of the miners."

Paid on delivery: Women understandably were in short supply. Hundreds of prostitutes would board ships in Mexico and South America knowing that their fares would be paid on arrival by captains selling them to the highest bidder. In his book *Madams of San Francisco*, Curt Gentry points out that although speculators tended to import large quantities of anything saleable, sometimes the market would be glutted and the speculators out of pocket. "There was safety in the importation of women," he explained. "They might become spoiled but nobody ever found it necessary to throw one away."

In 1854 the Board of Aldermen – Canute-like – outlawed brothels which had become, wrote B.E. Lloyd, "the curse-mark of San Francisco's brow." But, although red lights twinkled outside almost every house on such streets as Kearny, Stockton and Grant just north of Market, the behavior of their occu-

pants was discreet. "The madams spent thousands of dollars furnishing their places to look just right, down to Old Masters on the walls and bookshelves filled with good books that were never read," wrote Charles Lockwood in *Suddenly San Francisco:* "The low class brothels, on the other hand, were anything but safe, discreet and elegant."

Hookers, prospectors, merchants and adventurers alike – all seemed to regard San Francisco as their personal mecca. It had become a city in which unprecedented numbers of people thought they saw their future. In later years, Edwin Markham, comparing the city to Venice and Athens "in having

strange memories" said it was unlike the other places "in being lit from within by a large and luminous hope."

Already in debt and lacking funds to keep law and order, much less provide shelter or health care for the newcomers, San Francisco cast around for a way to raise funds. The city came upon the idea of a steep tax on gamblers, of whom there seemed to be an unlimited supply. "Gambling saloons glittering like fairy palaces… suddenly sprang into existence, studding nearly all sides of the plaza and every street in its neighborhood," a historian recorded. "All was mad,

Left, the 19th-century Presidio. **Right**, an early photograph of Mission Dolores.

feverish mirth where fortunes were lost and won on the green cloth in the twinkling of an eye." As much as $60,000 was bet on the turn of a single card.

Floating jail: The new license fees paid for policemen and the upkeep of a brig – moored at Battery and Jackson streets – used as a city jail. Virtual anarchy ruled the streets, through which roamed gangs of hoodlums, some operating with almost military precision. The depredations of one group known as the Hounds were so outrageous that one day a group of citizen volunteers armed themselves, rounded up the criminals and tried and sentenced them (although they were

regular law and order regained command.

By this time the gold was beginning to peter out, but dating from this time are the endless disputes over water rights (which continue to this day) when miners whose claims were staked far from stream beds collaborated to build ditches funnelling water from sources whose "riparian rights" (i.e. ownership of the adjoining land) were in conflict with "appropriation rights."

The introduction of hydraulic mining bringing streams of water to bear on hillsides intensified the problem. The extensive network of canals and flumes which eventually brought water a long way from its origi-

soon released for lack of enough facilities in which to confine them). Two years later, in 1851, by which time almost a dozen daily papers were operating, the citizens once again took control by forming a 200-member Committee of Vigilance. "Whereas… there is no security for life and property," they declared they were "determined that no thief, burglar, incendiary or assassin shall escape punishment either by the quibbles of the law, the insecurity of the prisons, the carelessness or corruption of the police or a laxity of those who pretend to administer justice." This group tried and hanged a trio of burglars before

nal source came to be worth more than the claims it served, but the conflicting arguments over who had a prior right to the water were never solved.

California as It Is and as It May Be, Or, A Guide to the Goldfields was the title of the first book to be published in San Francisco (in 1849). In it, author F.B. Wierzbicki wrote that the city looked like it had only been built to endure for a day, so fast had been its growth and so flimsy its construction.

"The town has led the van in growth… there is nothing like it on record. From eight to ten thousand may be afloat on the streets and hundreds arrive daily; many live in shanties, many in tents and many the best way they can… The freaks of fortune are equally as remarkable in this place as everything else connected with it; some men who two years ago had not a cent in their pockets, count by thousands now…"

For most of the '49ers (as the Gold Rush miners were called), the town was rough, ready and expensive. Eggs from the Farallone Islands sold for $1 apiece. Real-estate speculation was epidemic. Each boatload of '49ers represented another batch of customers. As the city burst from the boundaries of Yerba Buena Cove, "water lots" sold for crazy

blocks at a time, but each was followed by sturdier rebuilding.

By 1854, with a library, churches, schools and theaters among the many substantial stone or brick buildings, and horse-drawn streetcars traversing the now-tidy streets, it was becoming clear that the Gold Rush was coming to an end. Immigrants were still arriving, along with boatloads of supplies that could no longer be paid for, but shops and businesses were going bankrupt and the streets were filling with penniless and now jobless ex-miners. About the only people still sitting pretty were the gaming bosses whose money had thoroughly corrupted the

prices on the expectation they could be made habitable with landfill. Much of today's downtown San Francisco is built on landfill.

Fire hazard: A major hazard was fire in hastily-built San Francisco, where most buildings were constructed of wood and cloth and where ocean winds constantly fanned the flames of wood-burning stoves and oil lamps used for heating and light. Half a dozen major conflagrations broke out between 1848 and 1851, each of them destroying several

Left, San Franciscan hopefuls try to strike it rich. Above, a quiet moment in a Gold Rush boomtown.

city government. The gunning down of James King, a prominent editor whose *Evening Bulletin* had targeted police and the courts, brought a revival of the vigilantes. It was a controversial move that aroused many critics, but it did serve its purpose in banishing from the city most of the undesirable elements. Within months it was disbanded and electors had voted in a new city government.

Whatever chance California had of becoming placid was swept away in 1859 by yet another torrent of riches flowing down the Sierra slope. This time it was silver, not gold, that geared up the rush.

ON STONE BY F. PALMER,

Clarkes Point.　　　　Rincon Point.　　　　　　　　　　　　　　Happy Valley.　　Long Wharf (building.)

Entered according to Act of Congress in the year 1851

VIEW OF SAN FRA

TAKEN FROM TELEGRAPH HILL, APRIL 1850, BY Wm B. M^c

Published by N. Currier, N.Y.

Office of the District Court of the Northern Distr.t of N.Y.

(building.) Appollo Warehouse   Niantic Warehouse   Sansome St   LITH. & PUB. BY N. CURRIER, 152 NASSAU ST. COR. OF SPRUCE N.Y.   Portsmouth Square

CISCO, CALIFORNIA.

RIE, DRAUGHTSMAN OF THE U. S. SURVEYING EXPEDITION.

NO B. McMartrie, San Francisco

One of the most comfortless outposts of the Gold Rush had been centered around Nevada's Sun Mountain on the dry eastern slope of the Sierra near Lake Tahoe. There was a little gold up in the Virginia Range, but eking a living out of the area's irritating bluish clay was wicked work. In June 1859 a sample of that "blue stuff" found its way to Melville Atwood, an assayist in Grass Valley. Atwood found an astounding $3,876 worth of silver in that sample of ore.

At first it appeared that the Silver Rush would mimic the Gold Rush of a decade earlier. "Our towns are near depleted," wrote one spectator. "They look as languid as a consumptive girl. What has become of our sinewy and athletic fellow citizens? They are coursing through ravines and over mountaintops," looking for silver.

Silver Rush: One of the athletic young men who rushed up to the Virginia Range was Mark Twain. In his marvelous book *Roughing It* he describes how he and his fellow almost-millionaires "expected to find masses of silver lying all about the ground." The problem for Twain and the thousands like him was that the silver was in, not on, the steep and rugged mountains. And getting it out was not a matter of poking and panning.

The Silver Rush, it turned out, was a game for capitalists, men with the money to dig tunnels, buy claims, install the expensive machinery and mills that transformed the blue stuff into cash. They were men like William Ralston of the Bank of California in San Francisco, and the four legendary "Bonanza Kings" – James Flood and William O'Brien, former saloon-keepers; and James Fair and John W. Mackay, old miners – whose Consolidated Virginia regularly disgorged $6 million a month.

As usual, the treasures of the Comstock

Preceding pages: an early view of San Francisco. **Left**, the 1870s brought violent discrimination against Chinese immigrants. **Right**, the domination of the "Big Four" railroad barons was a target of protest for the press.

Lode (named for an old-timer who, in traditional fashion, ended up broke) flowed downslope from the boomtown of Virginia City to San Francisco. By 1863, $40 million of silver had been wrestled out of the tunnels in, around, and through Sun Mountain. Two thousand mining companies traded shares in San Francisco's Mining Exchange. Fortunes were made and lost in moments as rumors of bonanza or borasca (profitless rock) swept into town. At one time, more speculative

money was wrapped up in Comstock mining shares than existed in real form on the whole of the Pacific Coast.

The Comstock lasted until the 1880s, plumping up California's economy with the $400 million the Virginia Range yielded. In San Francisco, Billy Ralston, the Comstock's greatest mine owner, had taken over as the city's top booster.

Ralston poured his Comstock money into a myriad of grand schemes: he built the Palace, America's largest city hotel; he bought sugar refineries, lumber, stage and water companies; and as the 1860s drew to a close, he happily prepared for what he and his fellow plutocrats thought would be the capstone to the state's greatness – the long-awaited completion of the trans-continental railroad which had been foreordained by the building of California's first railroad, the 22-mile (35-km) Sacramento Valley line in 1856.

Another successful mineowner, George Hearst poured some of his millions into a newspaper, the *San Francisco Chronicle*, turning it over to his son, William Randolph in 1887. Thus was the beginnings of what became the largest publishing empire the world had known up to that time.

By the time of his death in 1951, William

Randolph Hearst had extended his empire to more than a score of daily papers (including two New York papers and two Chicago papers), 14 magazines in the US, and two in England, 11 radio stations and five news services employing a total of 38,000 people. Hearst served two terms as congressman for California but was beaten in his runs for governor, mayor and president. His personal spending was said to run to $15 million a year, of which at least $1 million went on art and antiques, the bulk of this destined for his hilltop ranch at San Simeon, south of San Francisco. He also owned a million-acre

(400,000-hectare) estate at Chihuaha in Mexico, St Donat's Castle in England, the 67-acre (27-hectare) estate Wyntoon in northern California, and commercial and residential property in various US cities.

Hallidie's cable car: An efficient transport system was one of San Francisco's earliest achievements, with half a dozen different companies operating horse-drawn services by mid-century. But the hills were steep and often slippery and watching a horse fall down on one of them, pulling the carriage after it, was credited with inspiring Andrew Hallidie with the idea for the cable car. The fact that the London-born Hallidie operated a factory that manufactured wire rope which could be installed as an endless belt under the hills and be used to pull up the cars was obviously a help, and by 1873 Hallidie's cable cars were operating on a 2½-mile (4-km) route along Clay Street.

The rush for gold had added a new urgency for contact between the east and west coasts. In addition to those in search of the gold itself were hundreds who sought to become part of the boom by shipping supplies, and although regional railroads were an actuality, trans-continental lines were still in the future. It was not until 1853 that the Federal government allocated funds for the study of feasible routes with California's gold boom making the state a top contender for the terminus over previously favored Oregon.

Meanwhile, there were the clipper ships, elegant replacements for the sturdy vessels that in the days when reliability was more important than speed took six or eight months to get from Boston to San Francisco. In the year 1849, after President Polk had declared that "the abundance of gold in (California) would scarcely command belief" almost 800 ships set off on the lengthy journey from the East Coast. But starting with Donald McKay's *Flying Cloud* in 1851, a trim, fast clipper could make such a journey around Cape Horn in 90 days – and pay for itself in the freight charges on a single run. Within a dozen years, 50 steamers out of San Francisco were carrying passengers and freight not only up and down the coast but as far away as China and Australia.

"When this bay comes into our possession," Secretary of State John C. Calhoun had predicted in 1844, "there will spring up the great rival of New York." Before the end of the century the port, with its easy access to Arctic waters, was to become the whaling capital of the world.

Concurrent with the development of clippers – and by 1860 their era was over – was the growth of the overland stage. Spurred mostly by the need to deliver the mails, it was financed initially by regional postmasters. For a brief period, the glamour of the Pony Express (relays of boy jockeys, unarmed, dodging Indian ambushes) captured the public imagination, but the intervening Civil

upon securing California's place in the Union, at last stirred itself. In the winter of 1862, the Pacific Railroad Act granted vast tracts of western land, low-interest financing and outright subsidies to two companies – the Central Pacific, building from Sacramento, and the Union Pacific, building from Omaha. In 1869 the rival companies met for a "joining of the rails" at Promontory, Utah, and in 1876 the Southern Pacific line connected San Francisco and Los Angeles.

In his widely-read book *Progress and Poverty*, Henry George, a journeyman printer and passionate theorist, had warned that the increasing dominance of the railroads would

War also brought the telegraph system and sending $5 letters lost favor. It was to be another half century before, on January 25, 1915, a month before the Panama Pacific International Exposition opened, San Francisco's Thomas Watson received the very first transcontinental phone call – from Alexander Graham Bell himself.

Plans for a railroad linking the coasts had been floating around for many years. When the Civil War broke out Congress, intent

Left, William Randolph Hearst. **Above**, Market Street in 1865.

prove to be a mixed blessing. He predicted that California's immature factories would be undersold by the eastern manufacturing colossus and that the Central Pacific's ownership of vast parcels of land along its right-of-way would drive prices of much-needed agricultural land shamefully high. George even saw the racial tensions that would result from the railroad's importation of thousands of Chinese laborers. "Crocker's Pets," as they were called, flooded the state's job market in the 1870s and became the targets of bitter discontent.

George's prophecies began coming true

with the arrival of the first train. In San Francisco, real-estate dealing of $3.5 million a month fell to less than half that amount within a year. "California's initial enthusiasm soon gave way to distrust and dislike… an echo of the national conviction that the railroads were responsible for most of the country's economic ills" was the assessment of historian John W. Caughey in his book *California*. "The railroad became a monster, the Octopus. It was a target for criticisms by all those made discontented and bitter by the hard times of the seventies."

The genius of the Central Pacific was a young engineer named Theodore Dehone Judah, builder of the Sacramento Valley line, whose partners unfortunately were uncommonly cunning and ruthless men.

Charles Crocker, Mark Hopkins, Collis Huntington and Leland Stanford, who became known as "The Big Four," had been lured west by the Gold Rush. They were Sacramento shopkeepers when they invested in Judah's scheme. Shortly after Congress dumped its largesse in their laps, they forced Judah out of the Central Pacific. He died, aged 37, in 1863, still trying to wrest control from his former partners.

The Central Pacific made the Big Four almost insanely rich. The government's haste to get the railroad built, and Stanford's political maneuvering, made the Central Pacific the virtual dictator of California politics for years. Between them the railroad barons raised private investment, earned government subsidies, acquired bargain-priced land, imported cheap "coolie" labor from China, and by their exploitative and monopolist practises became multi-millionaires.

Bribery and corruption: As the biggest landowners and biggest employers, the immensely rich railroad barons were able to manipulate freight rates, control water supplies, keep hundreds of thousands of acres of productive land for themselves and subvert politicians and municipal leaders. It was to be many years before state regulation of the railroads became the norm rather than the other way around. In the beginning, at least, carping at the Big Four's use of the railroad's treasury as a kind of private money preserve was a game just for malcontents and social-

ists. In the mahogany boardrooms of San Francisco's banks, on the editorial pages of its newspapers and, in the overheated stock exch-ange, up and down Montgomery Street, the verdict was unanimous. The new railroad would bring firm and fabulous prosperity to the state of California.

In April 1868, five years after construction had begun on Sacramento's Front Street, the first Central Pacific train breached the Sierra at Donner Pass. On May 12, 1869, the Golden Spike was driven at Promontory Point, Utah, and the coasts were linked. "San Francisco Annexes the Union," read one San Francisco headline. But the rush of prosperity failed utterly to materialize.

In the winter of 1869–70 a severe drought crippled the state's agriculture. Between 1873 and 1875 more than 250,000 immigrants came to California. Many were factory workers and few could find work: the "Terrible '70s" had arrived. For William Chapman Ralston, these years were a great calamity. As the head of the Bank of California in San Francisco, the former Comstock mining tycoon had presided over the endless boom mentality that was a legacy of the Gold Rush. But, by the mid-1970s, the booms had given way to the full bloom of depression.

On "Black Friday," April 26, 1875, a run on the Bank of California forced it to slam shut its huge oaken doors at Sansome and California streets. Driven into debt by Comstock mining losses and by the failure of the railroad to bring prosperity, Bill Ralston drowned the next day while taking his customary swim in the bay.

End of an era: William Chapman Ralston's death signalled the end of California's booming affluence. Those hurt most by the great shrinkage of capital in the 1870s were the state's working people. During the gold and silver rushes California's laborers had enjoyed a rare freedom to move easily from job to job and to dictate working conditions. Now, however, with massive unemployment, unionization began to take hold. For the next 60 years, California would suffer recurrent bouts of labor strife.

Right, end of an era: an abandoned miner's shack in Northern California.

Long before the new century San Francisco had become California's most prosperous center, a city of 27,000 buildings, a place whose 1,700 architects were perfecting the "tall, narrow rowhouse with vertical lines and a false front to make the house look more imposing," noted a book by the city archivist. These characteristically Victorian and Queen Anne-style homes, or those of them that survived the 1906 fire, still predominate in at least half a dozen neighborhoods today.

A geologist named Andrew Lawson had discovered and named the San Andreas Fault a dozen years previously, yet, despite two earthquakes in the 1890s, there had been very little notice taken. When the Big One arrived – at 5.16am on Wednesday, April 18, 1906 – there had been scant warning except for the strange nervousness of dogs and horses on the previous evening.

Fire and rubble: The fire, following an 8.25 Richter-scale earthquake, destroyed 28,000 buildings over an area of more than 4 sq. miles (10 sq. km). It killed 315 people; the bodies of 352 more were never found. The city had experienced many earthquakes before but none on this scale and in a city that was home to more than 40 percent of the state's population (it is now less than 4 percent) the effect was cataclysmic. Only an unearthly low rumble preceded fissures opening up and spreading wavelike across the city. Rails were twisted and snapped; streets turned to rubble and church bells jangled chaotically. In 48 seconds it was over, but the city lay in ruins.

With its alarm system destroyed, the Fire Department lacked coordination. When the brigades did arrive they found mangled mains lacking any water supply. The situation was worst in the area south of Market Street where skilled demolition work might have prevented the fire from spreading. Experts

were lacking and improvisations by the inexperienced commandant of the Presidio, Brigadier General Frederick Funston, who had leaped in without authority to fill the vacuum, served only to destroy scores of beautiful mansions along Van Ness Avenue and to spread the fire still further.

Hundreds were dead or still trapped in smoking ruins, 500 city blocks were leveled and a handful of people had been shot or bayoneted by Funston's inexperienced mili-

tia who had poured into the streets to keep order and prevent looting.

Golden Gate Park became the home of as many as 300,000 people for at least the next few weeks. Cooking inside the tents was banned, sanitation was rudimentary, water was in short supply and rats (and the threat of the bubonic plague) a lingering menace.

But there was a will to recover. A Committee of Forty on the Reconstruction of San Francisco was formed to define the tasks to be done and A.P. Giannini's tiny Bank of Italy, making loans to small businesses intent on rebuilding, was at the forefront of

Preceding pages: aftermath of the 1906 earthquake. **Left,** the opening of the Panama Pacific Exposition, 1915. **Right,** a cartoonist ponders the effects of the next big quake.

those determined to revive the city's fortunes. The bank was later to become the Bank of America, the country's largest. Aid poured in from all over the world, $8 million worth within the first few weeks. Even the much-reviled Southern Pacific Railroad pitched in generously, freighting in supplies without charge, offering free passage out of the city and putting heavy equipment and cranes to work on clearing up the debris.

Two events in successive years held great significance for San Francisco: the first was the opening of the Panama Canal in 1914, which cut days off the ocean route from the east while making the long journey around

Major labor troubles typified the Depression years and those which followed, culminating in the General Strike of 1934 when the International Longshoremen's Union immobilized traffic in the port. During one demonstration, two strikers were killed and 100 people – police and strikers – were injured.

In 1933, the year that Alcatraz Island became the site of what was for 30 years to be America's most-famous prison, ground was broken for the Golden Gate Bridge, although it wasn't dedicated until four years later, six months after the even longer (4½-mile/7-km) Bay Bridge joined San Francisco to Oakland. Only a few weeks before the Golden Gate

Cape Horn obsolete. Then, on January 25, 1915, only a month after San Francisco's Thomas Watson received the very first transcontinental phone call, from Alexander Graham Bell himself, the Panama Pacific International Exposition opened in the city.

During the year that the exposition was open, 19 million visitors came to marvel at the latest fashions and inventions. The distant war in Europe had few repercussions in the Bay City beyond boosting industry, manufacturing and mining, with a consequent steep drop in employment when World War I came to an end.

ceremony, 10 workmen had died when their scaffold collapsed. Two years later, the city celebrated the opening with the Golden Gate International Exposition, which was attended by 17 million people.

The bridge, more than any other single image, has been responsible for the romantic vision the city retains in the national psyche. "To pass through the portals of the Golden Gate" wrote Allan Dunn, "is to cross the threshold of adventure." And Gene Fowler asserted: "Every man should be allowed to love two cities; his own and San Francisco." It is not surprising that the founders of the

United Nations came here in 1945 after World War II was over, for their first conference. But even with the thousands of new workers to staff the wartime factories and the bustling port, as well as numbers of servicemen who had remained behind when the war was over, the city's population was still only 700,000 – less than half that of its rival 450 miles (725 km) to the south. (By 1990, in fact, its population of 724,000 was even less than that of the Silicon Valley "capital" of San Jose, with 782,000, and for the first time, whites numbered less than 50 percent).

Nevertheless, the war had a tremendous impact on the local economy – "as great as

behind barbed wire and under military guard. Americans of Japanese heritage were estimated to have lost $365 million in property from having to sell their homes at under market prices at this time.

In the 1950s, the city was the birthplace of a new cultural renaissance beginning with what local columnist Herb Caen termed "beatniks." Led by writers Allen Ginsberg (*Howl*) and Jack Kerouac (*The Dharma Bums*) and supported by Lawrence Ferlinghetti of North Beach's City Lights Bookstore, the Beats exemplified a life style centered around poetry readings, marijuana and dropping out of the mainstream – a

any event since the Gold Rush," wrote historian Oscar Lewis. And even before the war, San Francisco, with its obvious ties to Oriental ports, had begun to harbor a large component of Asian immigrants. At least 110,000 *Nisei* (second-generation Japanese) had been unfairly rounded up and sent to detention camps in the xenophobic early days after Pearl Harbor.

Although accused of no crime they lived

Left, the Golden Gate Bridge was dedicated in 1937. **Above**, Janis Joplin performs in the Polo Fields, Golden Gate Park, 1967.

potently attractive lifestyle which came to have wide appeal and soon brought a stream of youthful admirers to the coffee houses of North Beach and, in the following decade, to the streets of the Haight-Ashbury district.

Over on the Berkeley campus of the University of California the locus of dissent was the Free Speech Movement, which kept up a steady assault against racism, materialism and what the students regarded as the stifling effects of the "multiversity" itself, and its aid and encouragement to the Vietnam war machine. Anti-war protests, which eventually spread around the world, which began here, for all intents and purposes, with the writers and protesters clustered around Max Scherr's *Berkeley Barb*, which was one of America's five earliest "underground" papers. Scherr, a bearded radical who had previously operated a bar called Steppenwolf, took to the streets himself to sell his paper which, at its peak, reached a circulation of 100,000 – an astonishingly high figure for a newspaper that was still largely put together by a group of amateurs in a crowded kitchen.

Stimulated by the burgeoning rock music scene and steered by underground newspapers, thousands of gaudily dressed hippies

– successors to the Beats – descended on Golden Gate Park the first day of January 1966 to celebrate what was termed a Be-In. Among those who addressed the 100,000-strong gathering were Ginsberg, psychedelic drug guru Tim Leary ("Turn On, Tune In, Drop Out"), Mario Savo and other representatives of the Free Speech Movement from Berkeley, plus a daredevil parachutist who dropped from the clouds into the center of the gathering.

The resultant worldwide publicity made Haight-Ashbury irresistible to disaffected kids from all over the world, substantial numbers of whom began to clog San Francisco's streets, with predictable results. The euphoria was short-lived and within a year it was all over, with begging, drug dealing and exploitation by greedy landlords the most notable side effects. It was from the Haight-Ashbury district that the notorious murderer Charles Manson recruited some of his most earnest disciples.

Tolerant: Nevertheless, the hippie movement and the New Left helped to change the American lifestyle, and nowhere more than in San Francisco, whose heterogeneous population – 46 percent white, 29 percent Asian, 14 percent Hispanic, 11 percent black – is generally regarded as being more tolerant than that of other cities.

Gay men and women (*see pages 63–66*) are commonplace here (as, sadly, is a high incidence of AIDS victims) and most variances from the currents of mainstream America are accepted benignly. This part of the state is the center of the country's ecology movement, home to such groups as the Sierra Club, Friends of the Earth and the whale-savers of the Greenpeace Foundation. Towns such as Petaluma have passed no-growth ordinances and San Franciscans have fought long and hard against "Manhattanization". The battles are not always peaceful: in 1978, San Francisco mayor George Moscone and Harvey Milk, an openly homosexual city official, were murdered in City Hall by a redneck.

Although the center of the state's power has moved south towards Los Angeles, California in general is on the leading edge of the future. With the high technology of nearby Silicon Valley and San Francisco's acknowledged lead in such emerging developments as Virtual Reality, northern California is still a significant player. Simultaneously it shares with the rest of the state a fascination and involvement with consciousness expansion, Eastern philosophy and exploring new lifestyles. New Yorkers sometimes scornfully claim to be too busy *living* their lives to have time to think about how to improve them. But are the lifestyles that Californians are trying to improve, the lifestyles that others will be living next?

<u>Left</u> and <u>right</u>, dream weavers.

PEOPLE

No city invites the heart to come to life as San Francisco does. Arrival in San Francisco is an experience in living.

— William Saroyan

"Typically atypical" is one way to describe the constantly changing San Francisco culture, for the city boasts a rich and diverse community, a melange of ethnicities, drawn by the city's natural beauty and breathtaking environs. San Francisco has known such diversity for a century and a half, since its time as a Gold Rush seaport, when author Henry Dana was overwhelmed by the mix of peoples walking the wild city's streets.

Today, to live in San Francisco is to be swallowed up in its cultural variety, and to enjoy the benefits of both urban and country living. Only minutes away are some of the most scenic parklands and dramatic cliffs, soaring down to the bay and the Pacific Ocean. This is an infinitely habitable city, small enough in which to feel comfortable, and yet large enough to create excitement and the sense of true urban vitality.

Human landscape: The ethnic mix that has characterized San Francisco's human landscape contributes to its unique standing among North American cities. Tourists from every corner of the northern hemisphere pour into this urban gem, and quickly have the sense that they are somewhere other than the United States mainland.

The sun-bleached hillside houses rising from the turquoise bay remind one of the Mediterranean; the bustling open shops and incense-laced air of Chinatown could easily be mistaken for a slice of downtown Beijing; and what's more, the serenity of a Japantown tea service mirrors that of its counterpart across the Pacific.

So whether one thinks of San Francisco as a smorgasbord or a bouillabaisse, the most enduring impression to be had of this city is

one of overwhelming diversity – there is no denying the fact that San Francisco is cosmopolitan and dynamic.

The numbers: San Francisco is the nation's 13th largest city, with its 725,000 people fitting snugly into 47 sq. miles (120 sq. km). According to the 1990 census, 46 percent of the city's population is white, 29 percent Asian (more than half of which are Chinese), 14 percent Hispanic, and 11 percent black. In recent years, the city has also drawn record

numbers of Filipinos and Southeast Asians, as well as new arrivals from Hong Kong.

The city also boasts a high number of young singles – "Yuppies" in recent parlance – and between 1980 and 1990, the number of single people between 25 and 34 years of age increased dramatically, and keeps rising. At the same time, only 20 percent of San Francisco households include children, fewer than one-fifth of adults under 45 own their own home, and nearly 100,000 people – almost one in seven residents – live with a friend, lover, or roommates.

San Francisco is a highly decentralized

Preceding pages: a smokeless-free zone; Chinese New Year; hot dog and hairy master. **Left,** a ferry tale. **Right,** black and proud.

city where many of its inhabitants secure themselves from generation to generation in cozy neighborhood enclaves where they maintain separate and distinct cultures and identities. Separate though they are, each culture seems – on the whole – untiringly tolerant of the others.

No better example of such tolerance can be found than among San Francisco's thriving gay and lesbian population – according to most estimates, about one in five city residents is gay – which crosses all those ethnic divisions, and which wields considerable political power within the city.

The individual histories of each group

shed light on the unique history of California. For example, the great California Gold Rush of the late 1840s brought together some of the most diverse groups of society.

Until the '49ers came, as historian James Adams notes, "every American frontier had been settled by agriculturalists for the most part. There had been a marked uniformity of social and intellectual life on all of them. But here, every type of citizen of every social grade or profession came, not to hew forests, farm and make homes, but to get as rich as possible as quickly as possible." San Francisco became a boomtown literally over-

night. Indeed, 20 years after the Gold Rush, one observer remarked that most likely one out of every 10 San Franciscans had "worked the mines." By 1851 the population of San Francisco jumped from 1,000 to 40,000 in three years – a staggering spurt of growth for this budding frontier town.

Every state, nation and race was represented in the Gold Rush migration. In 1850, Mexicans, Irish, Germans and French made up four-fifths of the foreign-born population of San Francisco.

Chinese: By 1851 there were 25,000 Chinese working in California mines, the majority of them settling later in San Francisco. These Chinese fortune seekers shared a common dream that *Gum San*, the Gold Mountain, would provide them healthy fortunes with which they could return home and rejoin their anxious families. The first Chinese men to come to San Francisco and northern California during the Gold Rush were called "coolies" – workers willing to do hard labor for significantly lower wages than whites. This term came from the Chinese phrase *ku li*, meaning "bitter strength."

Wherever new gold strikes were made, Chinese workers formed communities. In San Francisco they lived in crude, segregated barracks in a section soon known as Chinatown, which provided goods and services, often at cheaper prices than their white competitors could, to both the Chinese and non-Chinese population. Space was precious. San Francisco landlords added on verandas and makeshift back rooms to already dilapidated wooden buildings. The community began to grow and thrive.

Entertainment in the form of opium, for which 25¢ would buy enough for 12 pipes, was popular until declared illegal in 1906. Music halls and theaters sprang up and the greatest New Year's celebrations took place in February, in accordance with the Chinese calendar. Chinese restaurants, then as now, were popular with Chinese and non-Chinese patrons. In the 1860s, as the Gold Rush was dying out, so many Chinese miners got jobs on the railroads – at half the pay of whites – that eventually they formed 90 percent of the Central Pacific's workforce. One newspaper of the time reported that 20,000 lbs (9,000 kg) of bones were collected from shallow graves along the tracks where Chinese workers had died. The bones were sent home to China for burial.

Chinese labor filled many jobs until various exclusion laws forced them out, after which other Asians began to take their place. Anti-Chinese sentiment became widespread late in the century, and resulted in such violent events as the one in 1869 in which a Chinese crab fisherman in San Francisco was branded with a hot iron. As a result of this backlash, by 1900 Japanese workers were underbidding Chinese in the canneries.

From 1890 to 1940 the Chinese, both idea of whether they would be allowed to enter the city. Many Asians, primarily Chinese and Japanese, were turned back and had to board ships for the long journey home. To this day, one can see the inscriptions and poetry etched into the concrete walls of the barracks on Angel Island. Much of this discriminatory legislation was eradicated in the 1940s. And in subsequent years, as immigration quotas have been relaxed, entire families have arrived in San Francisco to make new lives for themselves.

Chinatown, one of the city's major tourist attractions, is very much more than a place for sightseeing. The Chinese community is

locally and throughout the United States, faced harsh discrimination. Laws were created which prohibited them from marrying non-Asians, becoming citizens, holding skilled jobs and owning property. When San Francisco's immigration station on Angel Island was opened in 1910, it had separate facilities for Asians. Conditions were similar to prisons of the day, with new arrivals subjected to humiliating physical examinations and long months of waiting without any

Left and **right**, nearly 30 percent of San Francisco's population is Asian.

one of the most important segments of the population, wielding an increasing amount of political power and making valuable cultural contributions to the city.

Japanese: Despite protests against their immigration, the number of Japanese in the US increased from 6,000 in 1900 to 25,000 a decade later. Most of these immigrants settled in California, with a large number choosing San Francisco. Trade unions in the city protested against the hiring of Japanese workers and, after the great earthquake of 1906, many fled south to Los Angeles.

Like many of the Chinese who call the city

home, the Japanese-American community in San Francisco draws its cultural strength and power from its own history on the borders of the United States. While some fought during World War II on the side of the United States against their mother country, thousands were detained in concentration camps. Reparations from the United States government 40 years later did little to erase the bitter memories, but went a long way towards securing a permanent place for the Japanese in American culture. Today, roughly 12,000 Japanese live in San Francisco, most in the area called Nihonmachi, or Japantown.

Filipinos: The first Filipinos to come to the

US mainland were students, who arrived between 1903 and 1910. Although expected to return to their country after their studies, many remained. The Philippines had been under the American flag since the end of the Spanish-American war, so they came to the US without restriction, but their status was ambiguous. A second wave, many of whose members had been laborers in Hawaii, arrived in the 1920s, at which time California farmers hired contractors to recruit Filipino laborers. Often they were treated with the same anti-Asian sentiment that had been faced earlier by the Chinese and Japanese.

After 1946, when the Republic of the Philippines was established, strong economic and military ties to the US continued and the immigration quota was raised. Revised immigration laws in 1952 brought another wave of Filipino immigration and recent census figures show the Filipino community to be among the city's fastest-growing "Asian-Pacific" immigrant groups.

Lacking the regional and family organization of the Chinese and the Japanese to establish settlements, Filipino immigrants, many from remote islands, finally found unity through the American labor movement. They ultimately merged with Mexican-American union members to form the United Farm Workers. More recent arrivals from the Philippines have tended to be professional people and students, who come for specialized training in such fields as engineering and medicine.

Koreans and Vietnamese: Until 1970, Korean immigration to the San Francisco Bay area was slight, and the Koreans, unlike their Chinese and Japanese counterparts, tended to disperse among local populations rather than form tight enclaves. The Koreans were different from other Asian groups in that they often arrived in the United States with large sums of capital to start businesses, while many Southeast Asians and Chinese work in the US, often for below the minimum wage, in order to save up enough money to start their own business.

Now refugees from Kampuchea, Vietnam and Laos are settling in San Francisco in record numbers and predictably facing some discrimination. Recently, there have been some clashes in the Bay Area among Vietnamese fishermen and local white fishermen, who feel threatened by the newcomers. Although some laws regarding the use of certain types of nets have been established (laws aimed at inhibiting Vietnamese fishing) a number of strong-advocate legal groups have emerged to serve the interests of the Vietnamese people.

For the most part, however, Southeast Asians are overcoming the tremendous culture shock that they encounter when they arrive in the US. Indeed, Asians across the city are gradually coming to be seen as the "model minority" because of their exceptional scholastic achievements.

Italians: San Francisco's most legendary Italian might be Domingo Ghirardelli, who brought chocolate to the city one year after another Western treasure – gold – was discovered in 1848. But before there was gold and chocolate there was one man, Pietro Benzi, who had settled in the drowsy little village of Yerba Buena in 1840, when there were no more than a handful of Italians living in what was then called Alta California. Genoese sailors had been trading along the western shore for years, but the remote towns and harbors contained little to interest the worldly seafarers.

and Venetians all took the grueling five-month journey from the old world to the new, only to discover that the stories they had heard of striking it rich with gold nuggets were mostly just that – stories.

Still, California was a land rich in possibilities. The soil was fertile, the bay was filled with fish, and the town was starved of commerce. For a diligent people accustomed to a life of hard work and saving, San Francisco was as close to *paradiso* as they would ever come. They stayed.

By the 1860s, the Italians had created a strong presence in North Beach, side by side with Irish, Germans, Chileans and Yankees.

When gold was discovered in the Sierra foothills, the situation quickly changed and, of the Italians, it was the Genoese who were the first to settle into the "promised land" beyond the Golden Gate. Within months, tales of streets paved with gold spread throughout the old country, and people of many northern Italian provinces soon followed the example of their pioneering cousins. Rural Ligurians, Luccans, Florentines

Left, king takes bishop. **Above**, wedding party in the park.

The new San Franciscans called their relatives over, and whole families – sometimes entire villages – were reconstituted in their New World *colonia.*

Although the community gave the appearance of solidarity, provincial differences survived intact from the old country. Italians of different regions spoke dialects, followed their own customs and were loyal to opposing political powers.

And, of course, the battles that rocked the newly unified Italian nation were fought with equal vigor in the New World. In their own quiet way, debates raged within the

Latin Quarter between Republicans and Royalists, Free Masons and Papists.

It was only natural that Italians of different regions earned their livings in distinct ways as well. The sea-faring Genoese stuck to trade and the fishing industry; Ligurians grew and sold produce, and the others opened shops or established businesses.

In the 1880s a second wave of immigrants arrived, this time from southern Italy. As in the old country, Sicilians were considered second-rate citizens by the northerners who called them *terrone* (dirt-eaters).

Largely unskilled and often less sophisticated than their sea-going cousins, Sicilians and succeeded in winning the respect of the city as a whole. A.P. Giannini brought financial power to the common folk with his Banco d'Italia, an enterprise some people disparaged as "that little dago bank in North Beach." The name was later changed to the Bank of America, and Giannini's bank became one of the largest financial institutions in the world.

Mexicans: In the first 30 years of the 20th century, nearly 10 percent of the population of Mexico migrated to the southwestern United States, with Texas and California receiving the largest number. In California their numbers went from 8,000 to 370,000,

did what they had always done – hard manual labor. As an island people, however, they were able fishermen and by the turn of the century, they had displaced the Genoese from Fisherman's Wharf and filled the bay with their colorful *felucce*. To this day it is the Sicilian parishioners of Saints Peter and Paul who carry the image of *Maria Santissima del Lume* on a platform of flowers from the church to the wharf, where a priest conducts the Blessing of the Fleet.

There were, however, a number of *prominenti* who distinguished themselves from the anonymous faces of North Beach with most of them recruited to harvest cotton, cantaloupe and lettuce crops. Working the fields until the harvest was over and then returning across the border to their families, the migrants' transient status often rendered them a semi-homeless community.

Settling in colonies or *barrios*, where cheap rentals were available but where there were no zoning requirements – no sewers, no paved roadways or street lighting – they would often succumb to illnesses such as tuberculosis. The late Hispanic activist Caesar Chavez, well known leader of the United Farm Workers Union, lived in such a *barrio* in Santa Clara county just 50 miles (80 km) south of San Francisco.

Declining farm prices in 1929 coupled with opposition to Mexican laborers brought about attempts to impose a tax on new immigrants, but at that time there were fewer than 100 people patrolling the border and the majority of Mexicans entered illegally, simply by climbing over a fence. During the 1940s, "enforced rotation" of migrant workers and the mass deportation of unemployed aliens was suggested. But in the early 1990s, the makeup and psychology of San Francisco's large colony of "illegal" Mexican immigrants was greatly changed by a huge

who were barred from public schools. He had to teach in these schools until replacements could be found. In the city, black settlers took action to secure their civil rights. A Franchise League was formed to campaign for the repeal of a law forbidding blacks the right to testify in trials involving whites. Five hundred white San Franciscans signed the petition in 1860, and by 1863, the campaign had succeeded.

Following World War II, the tremendous influx of blacks from the South into the Bay Area to work in shipyards and defense industries during the war helped to create a housing shortage in San Francisco. Japanese

federal amnesty program which allowed many thousands to apply for "legal" immigrant status. It has lifted the dread of deportation from an entire generation.

African-Americans: Thousands of free blacks were among the '49ers who made their way to California in search of instant riches. One such black pioneer, J.B. Sanderson, became famous for starting schools in San Francisco for poor Indian, Asian and black children

people, returning from their long internment, came back to find they could no longer afford homes.

In the 1940s, the black population of San Francisco increased elevenfold to 45,000. Most of these migrants came from Louisiana, Oklahoma and Texas – the same states from which whites had fled during the Dust Bowl years – heading for the urban centers of the West Coast, where the majority of the thriving war industries were now located.

In San Francisco, many black migrants lived in housing projects in areas like Hunters Point and the Fillmore District, where

Left, crowds at Candlestick Park. **Above**, San Francisco once had one bar for every 100 inhabitants.

they were charged high rents for dilapidated Victorian dwellings. Shortly after the Watts riots in southern California in 1965, a smaller uprising took place in San Francisco's Hunters Point district. When the black ghettos could no longer be ignored by the city, job training programs were instituted and new businesses were established. The Office of Economic Opportunity and other agencies came in to help provide skills and advice. Hunters Point began receiving $3 million a year from the federal Model Cities Program.

Today, the black population of San Francisco has dropped to 76,000, or 11 percent, with most of the departed moving to the suburbs that have begun to push the Bay Area's outer limits into the San Joaquin Valley, the wine regions of Sonoma and Napa counties, and south from San Jose and the Peninsula.

City dwellers: When the *San Francisco Chronicle* columnist Alice Kahn wrote in the early 1980s about Young Urban Professionals, giving them the decidedly unsophisticated acronym of "Yuppies," she could not have realized that the name would catch on so quickly and spread not only across the United States, but also the entire world. In San Francisco there are Yuppie enclaves, most notably in the Marina section just west of Aquatic Park and Fort Mason and extending to the Presidio.

Despite their overwhelming diversity, San Franciscans all live with the knowledge of one thing: the inevitability of another big earthquake. "San Francisco is a mad city, inhabited for the most part by perfectly insane people," Rudyard Kipling once observed. Many natives feel proudly that history has proved him right.

Back in 1906, for example, San Francisco was considered a "city of sin" by most Easterners. But San Franciscans had already stopped paying attention to such arbitrary judgments about their city, and went about their daily business as usual. Nor did they pay attention to the rumors of impending disaster. In *Zadikiel's Almanac* for 1906 the following prediction was made: "In San Francisco Mars and Saturn are on the fourth angle, or lower meridian. In the vicinity of that great city underground troubles –

probably a serious earthquake – will be destructive about Christmas day or the latter half of February. The winter will be stormy and cold."

San Francisco's winters, however, were normally cold and stormy; earthquakes were nothing to get excited about. The city experienced them regularly, but they had caused little damage. Only a few people still remembered the big quake of 1868; the city (whose 1906 population of 450,000 exceeded that of Los Angeles) was booming and prosperous.

When the big one came on April 18, the earth shook and rolled all along 192 miles (309 km) of the California coast from Point Arena to the Pajaro Valley in Monterey County. In San Francisco, which had no closing laws for bars and restaurants – unlike its southern neighbors – many people were still entertaining. According to historian John Kennedy, some people insisted afterward that a spirit of foreboding had lain under the evening's "feverish excitement, a haunting, unvoiced feeling that somehow tonight was San Francisco's last night to celebrate."

The city rebuilt itself slowly, and to many it seemed that the destruction had given San Francisco an opportunity to make over the city's poorly designed street system and reorganize the neighborhoods. The city's population, which had dwindled to 110,000 after the earthquake, gradually regained its former prosperous proportions.

Back to the future: What does it mean to live in San Francisco, with its history of the 1906 quake and devastating fire? Most people live in this city because they are drawn to it; they feel an affinity with its numerous and awesome hills, its neighborhoods, the San Francisco Bay, and with its unique culture. Most San Franciscans have a good idea where they'd like to be when the Big One strikes – nobody wants to be downtown, and nobody wants to be away from their homes. Being outdoors in an open space – in Golden Gate Park, for instance – would be ideal. Some people want to be in an airplane or on a boat. The unavoidable fact is this: San Francisco – the fault line that it is built on – is due for more quakes. It's just a matter of time.

Right, placard protest.

They've rioted in the streets, refurbished entire neighborhoods of once-decaying Victorian homes, wielded the most powerful voting bloc in local politics, accepted high government posts in national politics, built a substantial business community and, altogether, given San Francisco its current international reputation as the world's gay mecca. The brash emergence of the city's out-front, unabashed and sometimes volatile gay community undoubtedly represents the most significant sociological development in San Francisco since the early days of the beatniks and the hippies.

No one knows the exact number of gays living in San Francisco, although city officials speculate endlessly. But there are at least 100,000 in this city of 725,000.

Like nearly every aspect of San Francisco history, the transformation of the Gold Rush town into a homophile Oz grew from most unlikely and improbable beginnings.

It started in the waning days of World War II. The US military began systematically purging its ranks of gays, booting out suspected homosexuals at their point of debarkation. For the massive Pacific theater of the war, this meant San Francisco.

The purges created an entire class of men who had been officially stigmatized as homosexuals. Unable to return home and face inevitable shame, they stayed in the Bay Area, socializing in discreet bars or, more often, at intimate soirées. Another migration of professional gays came during the early 1950s in the heyday of the anti-communist McCarthy era, when the federal government drummed thousands of homosexuals out of government jobs.

Local authorities, meanwhile, did not take much of a liking to the idea of gays grouping in the bohemian bars of North Beach. They treated any gathering of more than a few dozen men like an armed insurrection. Bar raids, mass arrests and harsh prosecutions of

men and women accused of frequenting "disorderly houses" became common.

Activist origins: By 1960, gays began moving toward an open campaign for civil rights, a course of action unthinkable a few years before and unprecedented in American history. Ultimately, gays can credit such institutions as the US military establishment and the San Francisco Police Department for this, since the political activism was created largely in response to anti-gay excesses.

It all started humbly enough in 1955 with the formation of the US's first lesbian group, the Daughters of Bilitis. Back then the notion that homosexuals could band together in pressure groups, just like normal people, was considered novel. But it caught on. Cadres of politically active gays soon formed, with such non-threatening names as the Society for Individual Rights and the Mattachine Society, whose then-radical publication timidly asked whether homosexuality was a "disease or way of life" and whether gays should be rehabilitated or punished.

In 1961, José Sarria, a prominent female

Left, glad to be gay. **Right**, city official Harvey Milk was assassinated in 1978.

impersonator who was sure he was neither diseased nor in need of rehabilitation, got so irate over police raids on his Black Cat bar that he took off his dress and high heels and donned a three-piece suit to run for the Board of Supervisors, San Francisco's version of a city council. Sarria polled a then-astounding 7,000 votes and clued the fledging gay groups to the fact that their future power would lie in the ballot box.

Liberal candidates for the Board of Supervisors were politely seeking gay endorsements by 1964 without seeing their careers destroyed by pious moralists, a breed in short supply in San Francisco anyway. When the

influential minority group in town. Studies have shown that, proportionately, gays tend to vote in larger numbers and give more money to political candidates than their heterosexual counterparts.

Even as Feinstein campaigned at the Society for Individual Rights, the hippie counterculture was in full bloom in the Haight-Ashbury neighborhood. This provided a fertile territory for the Gay Liberation Movement that was sweeping west from New York City on the heels of the leftist anti-war movement.

It didn't take long for some of the flower children to question whether the do-your-

1969 board election came along, so did an attractive 35-year-old political newcomer named Dianne Feinstein. Feinstein, who would later be mayor from 1978 to 1988 and then a US Senator in 1992, campaigned aggressively among gays and later credited the margin of her landslide city-wide victory to gay ballots.

With that, the dam broke and politicians started courting gay voters with the enthusiasm once reserved for organized labor or the Chamber of Commerce. Within a decade, most pundits would estimate that one in four of the city's voters was gay, the single most

own-thing hippie ethos might mean more than simply wearing love beads, growing long hair and swallowing LSD. It might even mean accepting the tinglings of taboo sexuality. Slowly, a few dozen, then a few hundred, gay hippies moved over the hill from Haight Street to Castro Street, a nearby Irish-American enclave that was well on its way to going to seed.

The native working-class Catholics were terrified at the "gay invaders," as they called them, and many panicked, moving out. They left behind a huge, if somewhat dilapidated, stock of quaint 1880s Victorian homes for gay gentrification. The area quickly evolved into the first neighborhood in the nation which was literally owned and run by gay people, for gay people.

City Hall drama: Castro Street rapidly became the embodiment of the gay drive for acceptance, and in late 1975, gay votes elected George Moscone, the first mayor wholly sympathetic to gay voters. Two years later, neighborhood voters elected Harvey Milk to the Board of Supervisors. Milk, a Castro Street camera shop owner and gay activist who organized the area's merchants group, became the first openly gay city official to be elected in American politics.

Moscone in City Hall. The city reeled in shock at the crime and a mixed crowd of 40,000 people again marched the familiar path from Castro Street to City Hall, silently bearing lighted candles.

Six months later, when a jury decided to imprison double-murderer White for only five years, another even rowdier mob marched on City Hall, this time sparking the massive gay "White Night" riots which gained worldwide attention and headlines. Dan White, paroled in 1985, eventually killed himself. Ironically, this happened in the same year that *The Life and Times of Harvey Milk* won an Oscar for the best documentary.

While gays surged to the forefront of the nation's social agenda, Castro Street echoed with the chants of angry demonstrators who massed around the gay bars and marched to City Hall a mile away.

A series of traumatic historical events interceded in the late 1970s to add even more drama. In 1978, former Supervisor Dan White, the city's most anti-gay politician, gunned down Supervisor Milk and Mayor

Left, gays participate in a fund-raising tricycle race. **Above**, lesbians on wheels; Halloween bash at a Castro Street bar.

Such an outburst in other cities might have strained public acceptance of homosexuals, but this wasn't the case in San Francisco. The sheer volume and diversity of the gay population had ensured a legitimacy that no single event, however scandalous, could possibly undermine.

Entering the mainstream: The gay population is fairly happily dispersed among several major neighborhoods around the city. The sprawling Castro district today features the Young Urban Professionals, a decidedly non-hippie generation of prepped-up, well-heeled "Yuppies." In the South of Market gay enclave, buckled around Folsom Street, is a fiercer-looking bohemian set with a penchant for motorcycles, chains, black leather and public displays of dominance or submission. Young gay transients in tight blue jeans hustle unabashedly on Polk Street and on the corners of the seedy Tenderloin district, while an affluent pocket of three-piece-suited gay business executives is perched comfortably on the breast of very, very proper Pacific Heights.

The continuing presence of gays in such large numbers has created a city in which, more than any other, gays have melded into the mainstream. For years the city has had gay and lesbian supervisors, police officers, congressional aides and bureaucrats, as well as judges on the Municipal Court. Gains for which gays once struggled are slowly becoming a matter of course.

Calm: These later years have also brought a significant calming effect on the once-turbulent gay community. Angry rhetoric has cooled as activists who once railed against the establishment have become a part of the establishment themselves.

The advent – and ravaging effects – of AIDS has no doubt been the most important catalyst in transforming gay culture in recent years. For those in the gay community, living constantly with the deaths of friends and lovers has become, in some ways, a new way of life. The once-lusty nightlife has been toned down, and conventional values on dating and courtship are being reasserted. Nevertheless, there are still enough revelers remaining on the scene to give the city some of the wildest, most colorful gay bars anywhere on earth.

The raucous marches have thinned, as there are fewer and fewer local injustices at which mass anger could be directed – whatever the situation in other parts of the world. The experience of San Francisco in the past two decades has illustrated the great irony of the American gay rights movement. Once the major goal of that movement is achieved and discrimination is all but eliminated, the entire issue of whether one is gay or straight seems no longer to be an issue.

<u>Right</u>, dancin' in the street.

There is no lack of artistic enterprise in the San Francisco Bay Area; in fact, it's nearly impossible to go a day without rubbing elbows with an artist, poet, actor or writer – or at the very least, an extremely well-informed critic. While traditional artistic forms such as opera, symphony and ballet are well-respected and hold a firm place in the city's cultural history, the Bay Area has really built its reputation as a breeding ground for experimental, and often outrageous work.

Artists of all media and inclinations have always flocked to San Francisco to break new ground – but not to become stars. Conventionally, new forms and movements come to life here, then travel to Los Angeles and New York to be marketed; this holds true in theater, visual arts and the music industry. Some historians may trace this boundless tolerance for new, wild creative ventures back to the city's Barbary Coast era, but it's more likely due to the national upheaval of the 1960s, when San Francisco became the quintessential counterculture city. San Francisco's tolerance seems inexhaustible: nothing, it appears, is too outrageous, too outlandish, too different.

In recent years, the radical climate and lower rents of such East Bay towns as Oakland and Berkeley have made those areas home to artistic communities, too. There, as well as in the city, African-American, Asian-American and Latin American artists have made biculturalism an integral part of their work, and correspondingly, an integral part of Bay Area culture. The influence of Pacific Rim countries is also growing rapidly, although as a world port San Francisco has always felt the presence of these cultures.

Visual Arts: San Francisco is proof that a young city can create a formidable reputation for itself if it's willing to put up the cash. The first group effort to bring visual art to the forefront of the city's culture happened in

Preceding pages: pretty as a picture. **Left,** opera houses appeared in the 1850s. **Right,** opera is often heard at Caffe Trieste.

1871, when 23 visual artists formed the San Francisco Art Association, exhibiting in a loft above a market. By the 1890s art had become a social concern, and a rich patron donated a Nob Hill palace to the Art Association to better display its work.

The flamboyant neo-Egyptian Exhibition Hall, built for 1894's Midwinter International Exposition in Golden Gate Park, evolved into the De Young Museum. Its permanent collection boasts important works in the Col-

onial American tradition, as well as the California School of Painting, characterized by the works of Thomas Hill, Alfred Bierstadt and William Keith. These landscapists specialized in gargantuan mountain gorges, vast Yosemite landscapes and natural light.

In 1915, the huge Panama-Pacific International Exposition brought paintings and sculpture to San Francisco and local artists discovered and adopted elements of French aestheticism. Bernard Maybeck's Palace of the Legion of Honor, devoted primarily to French art, opened in the 1920s.

The San Francisco Museum of Modern

Art, which in the following decade became the second in the country dedicated to modern art, houses a fantastic permanent collection, the best on the West Coast. Included are works by Henri Matisse, Andy Warhol, Francis Bacon, Vasily Kandinsky, Joan Miró, Frida Kahlo, Jackson Pollock, Jasper Johns, and Diego Rivera. The state-of-the-art building is a pleasure to walk around, with or without the interactive audio tour.

San Francisco was the center of a northern California strain of the Arts and Crafts Movement, which blossomed in both Europe and the United States. Many of the handicrafts, such as baskets and glasswork, as well as the

dark-wood furniture, can be seen in San Francisco's museums.

Money, climate and the University of California at Berkeley brought Diego Rivera, Clifford Still and Mark Rothko to San Francisco. Public murals and abstract expressionism became regional traditions. In answer to abstract impressionism, David Park and Elmer Bischoff spearheaded a counter-movement called Bay Area Figurative, but it is almost impossible to find a single indigenous artistic strain here. Taste among the pioneers leaned toward vulgarity; money from the Gold Rush helped San Fran-

cisco produce the most extravagant collection of bar-room nudes this nation has ever seen. But that's a genre that had no progenitors, and the few movements that San Francisco can call its own seem to have little, if any, historic precedent.

Some of history's most influential photographers have based themselves here, including Ansel Adams, whose dramatic black and white photos of majestic Yosemite landscapes have become familiar images worldwide. Adams started the first professional photography courses at California School of Fine Arts (now San Francisco Art Institute) in 1946. Edward Weston, Imogen Cunningham and Dorothea Lange also worked and lived here. Today, the Ansel Adams Center, as well as the privately owned Fraenkel Gallery, regularly exhibit some extraordinary work.

Knowledge and respect for wood, clay, stone and cloth are also a tradition in this region. Carpenters, designers and printmakers abound, as do potters and jewelry artesans. Peter Voulkas, Robert Arenson and other ceramists are world renowned.

Music and opera: San Francisco was a young city that loved making merry, so it's no surprise that music was an important element in its social life. What seems incongruous is that a passion for opera sprouted alongside the music halls and cabarets. Almost as soon as the initial wave of newcomers flooded into the city in the 1850s, opera houses appeared. Several operas ran simultaneously, and each performance was the subject of much critique and discussion. Fire brigades escorted their favorite divas to performances, while European troupes made San Francisco a regular stop on their tours. On Christmas Eve, 1910, one of the largest crowds in the city's history assembled in front of the Chronicle building to hear a renowned soprano sing Verdi's arias.

The tradition continues. "The San Francisco Opera," reported the *New York Times*, "has won a reputation as second only to the Met in this country." Likewise, in the scale of social events, opening night of the opera season in San Francisco is second only to the Academy Awards in Los Angeles each year. In the Bay Area, a metropolitan area one-third the size of New York, there are no less than seven full-scale opera companies. Every fall, Free Opera in the Park, a much anticipated event, takes place in the bandshell in Golden Gate Park. Die-hard opera fanatics arrive at 10am to hear the rehearsal before the 2pm concert – and really, can one get enough of listening to Pavorotti for *free*?

Symphonic music made its splash in the 19th century via the talents of Fritz Scheel, who later founded the Philadelphia Orchestra. Under Pierre Monteux, the San Francisco Symphony, founded in 1923, became one of the major orchestras in America. Along with the opera and the ballet (also

served here. The San Francisco Chamber Orchestra, Oakland Symphony and other highly polished groups play music ranging from baroque to Bartok.

In the 1950s, composer Darius Milhaud came to Mills College in Oakland and Roger Sessions arrived at the University of California at Berkeley, inspiring a whole generation of musicians and composers. The Kronos Quartet, an innovative, punky-looking yet lofty-sounding group, is a particular point of pride amongst the city's residents. *Rolling Stone* magazine has called them "Classical Music's own Fab Four."

The region's earliest musical invention

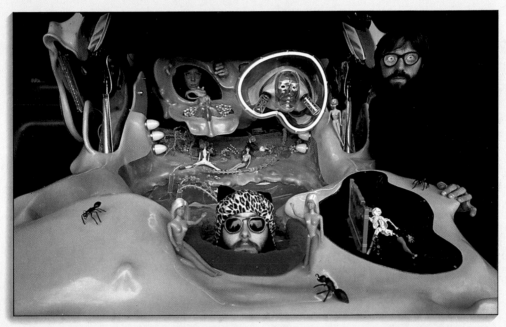

more than 50 years old), the symphony is the only one in the country subsidized by public money and San Francisco recently redistributed its wealth to include experimental, ethnic and alternative arts.

The breadth and variety of classical music in this town is fairly astonishing; there are more concerts per capita here than in any other city in the country, a phenomenon described by one critic as an "unreasonable profusion." Chamber music, too, is well-

Left, SFMOMA's Matisse, *La fille aux yeux verts*. **Above**, artists ponder the true meaning of life.

was the minstrel show. The honky-tonk reached its apotheosis on the Barbary Coast, and the folk-music revival of the 1950s flourished here. Out of this openness to popular forms and divergent lifestyles emerged the cultural revolution of the 1960s – free love, drugs, a new kind of rock 'n' roll. It all took root and flourished in San Francisco like in no other city.

Hippies poured in by the busload to hang out in the Haight-Ashbury district, drop acid, and participate in one of the most noteworthy social movements of this century. The concerts and light shows held at the Fillmore and

Avalon Ballroom auditoriums became the standard for rock concerts. Groups like The Grateful Dead, Jefferson Airplane, Janis Joplin and Credence Clearwater Revival regularly appeared in these venues and at open-air concerts in Golden Gate Park.

This legacy of rock has not been lost on the current generation, and a plethora of clubs give young groups a lively, well-attended atmosphere to jam. Well-known hip-hop groups and rappers have emerged out of Oakland and San Francisco, and the Bay Area is home to a thriving jazz scene.

Literati: More than a century ago there were already a score of local periodicals asserted that Californians believed that "a man who has served a lifetime as a dramatic critic on a New York paper may still be incompetent but a California critic knows it all, notwithstanding being in business most of his life or a plow-artist on a ranch."

Criticism – of society at large as well as of the arts – was expected to be rigorous. In that era, the population consisted largely of independent laborers, tradesmen, and entrepreneurs of all kinds, which made San Francisco a city sympathetic to the plight of the worker, and much of the city's literature reflects socialist leanings.

Henry George's *Progress and Poverty* was

serving a minuscule but dedicated readership of 100,000. In the 1860s, the bylines of some of the most important writers of the time appeared in these journals, including Mark Twain, Bret Harte and Ambrose Bierce. With their disdain for the affected gentility of the East Coast and their fervent appreciation for the free-thinking west, these sharp-tongued raconteurs and essayists paved the way for a tradition of social criticism, satire and general ideological rambunctiousness that continues to characterize both social and artistic movements locally.

During his tenure in the city, Mark Twain a treatise on the rights of all people to the use of the earth; Frank Norris, a University of California at Berkeley graduate, portrayed his anti-capitalist sentiments in *The Octopus* and *McTeague* (which were set in San Francisco); Jack London, an ardent socialist who grew up around the canneries of Oakland, devoted most of his work to proletarian themes.

In a later epoch, another famous San Francisco writer, Dashiell Hammett, was targeted by the unscrupulous, red-baiting House Un-American Activities Committee in the 1950s for his reported association with communists. He was subsequently jailed, and his career ruined.

At about the same time, the Beat poets, possibly one of the most notable literary movements to come out of San Francisco, based their writings on a lifestyle. Jack Kerouac (author of *On The Road*) used the word beat – from beatitude – to describe those like himself who were into poetry, jazz, eastern philosophy and wanderlust. Poets read their verses in smoke-filled coffeehouses to the sounds of then-emerging be-bop jazz.

"San Francisco," wrote Robert Louis Stevenson, "keeps the doors to the Pacific."

In the past 30 years a wealth of Eastern thought and teaching has passed through these doors with Zen Buddhism being the aspect of the Beat movement perhaps most specific to the Bay Area. The writings of Alan Watts in the 1960s did much to popularize the tenets and practices of Zen. Many local writers have sojourned in Asian countries. Translators, schools and bookstores devoted to Eastern philosophy are scattered throughout the Bay Area, and the

Left, Japanese drum troupe. **Above**, performance by one of the Bay Area's theater groups.

largest Zen monastery in America can be found nearby in Carmel Valley.

While San Francisco lacks the publishing clout of New York, it has always been a maelstrom of literary activity. Bookstores are especially plentiful and authors continue to find the Bay Area a good place to find inspiration. Wallace Stegner made his home here until his recent death, and Pulitzer-prize winning poet Czeslaw Milocz lives in the East Bay. Punk writer Kathy Acker, whom William Burroughs has called a "post-modern Colette," moved west from New York City to work and teach literature at the San Francisco Art Institute. The Bay Area's considerable women's community has given rise to poet Adrienne Rich, Chicana playwright and poet Cherríe Moraga and many feminist erotica writers. Internationally known writers Amy Tan (*Joy Luck Club*), Alice Walker (*The Color Purple*), Armistead Maupin (*Tales of The City*) and Anne Rice (*Interview With A Vampire*) all have lived in San Francisco, and most have used it as a backdrop.

In recent years, this legacy of poetry readings, combined with a passion for that budding theatrical genre, the solo show, has given rise to an art form called Spoken Word. Avant-garde poets mount a stage in a hip, sometimes techno, club atmosphere, giving as much attention to their delivery as text. The writers (ranging from hip-hop to epistle-style prose) and their reverence for technology set this movement off from the poetry readings of a previous generation.

Theater and dance: San Francisco has a long, although mightily varied, theater tradition. In the Barbary Coast era, cabaret held sway as the principal form of theater. Later, in the second half of the 19th century, melodeons (theater-bar-music halls) began to proliferate. Both the love of bawdiness and the love of musical theater lives today: the Shorenstein-Hayes' Best of Broadway series imports large-scale musical productions from New York each season, and burlesque has given way to a sublimated form of porn that populates the North Beach and Tenderloin neighborhoods. The most socially acceptable of these is Finocchio's, a long-standing female impersonator venue that folks of all ages, genders and classes attend, and the Mitchell Bros, a vestige of the sexual revolution that attempts to rise above common sleaze – though in the end, it's still porn aimed at the straight male.

A more serious theater tradition harkens back to the turn of the century, when San Francisco regularly hosted traditional stock companies from England as well as other parts of the States. Edwin Booth, John Drew, Ethel Barrymore, Sarah Bernhardt played many times in San Francisco. After the 1906 earthquake leveled the town, money for reconstruction went first to symphonies and museums, only later to theater.

San Francisco expatriates: Herbert Blau and

Jules Irving founded New York's famed Actors Workshop in 1959 on the premise that theater belonged to actors and directors – *not* to producers and promoters. It was that philosophy, combined with the generosity of philanthropic foundations, that created a boom in the 1960s. Theaters began developing new work and/or actors rather than simply staging New York productions that came to town. The most notable of these was, the American Conservatory Theater (ACT), at that time led by Bill Ball, a visionary who helped create the model for regional theaters throughout the country.

From the start, ACT had a penchant for Moliere and other classical European works. Other regional theaters, however, took the plunge into the work of developing young writers. At The Magic Theatre, for instance, a brilliant young playwright named Sam Shepard began a career that has eventually made him one of the world's best-known contemporary dramatists.

The Eureka Theatre, Asian-American Theatre Company, and Berkeley Repertory Theatre have also provided a forum for new playwrights. David Henry Hwang (author of *M. Butterfly*), for instance, first produced his plays at AATC. In recent years, unfortunately, a sluggish economy, the loss of principal artistic visionaries and a changing arts community has caused some of these establishments to put on fewer plays or to fold.

Stand-up comedy is another long-standing San Francisco tradition that took off in the 1960s and '70s, when people such as Lenny Bruce, Robin Williams and Lily Tomlin rose from small comedy clubs in North Beach to national recognition. That legacy, combined with the economics of producing full-scale theater, led to the birth of the "solo show" in the 1980s. The one-person show has since evolved into a recognized theatrical genre, and San Francisco's "Solo Mio Festival", held every September, is partly credited with creating the demand.

Just about every theatrical form imaginable can be found in San Francisco, from agit prop to Shakespeare, to avant-garde experimental work. Every political and cultural group is also represented, including gays, African-Americans, and feminists. Modern dance, influenced by world cultures, has also taken off in San Francisco. The Margaret Jenkins Company and Oberlin Dance Collective paved the way for the adventurous works of Joe Goode Performing Group and Contraband. Berkeley's Zellerbach Hall has become a regular stop for the best touring dance companies in the world.

Although public funding isn't as ample as it once was, the arts in San Francisco forge ahead on shoestring budgets, strong artistic vision and an inspiring legacy.

Left, brush strokes. **Right**, love conquers all.

A bronze plaque in Union Square's Burritt Alley, just off Bush Street, reads: "ON APPROXIMATELY THIS SPOT, MILES ARCHER, PARTNER OF SAM SPADE, WAS DONE IN BY BRIGIT O'SHAUGHNESSY." The memorial doesn't mention the classic detective story *The Maltese Falcon* or its author, but leaving the alley and walking toward Powell Street, the mystery is solved as you pass "Dashiell Hammett Street" on the right. Don't be surprised if you cross paths with other literati as you stroll around the city. In 1988, the San Francisco Board of Supervisors gave the go-ahead to a plan proposed by the celebrated City Lights Bookstore to rename 12 streets for prominent writers and artists who lived and worked in San Francisco.

They could have added dozens more. From the Gold Rush days through the Beat era and the more recent past, San Francisco has spawned its own writers and drawn others from points north, south and east. Even today, in the neo-Beat cafés of the Mission district and North Beach, you can hear poets spouting their rhythmic verse with passion at open-mike readings.

What is the special appeal of this place for would-be wordsmiths? In part, its vital literary scene is self-propagating; a rich past, as well as books by and about San Francisco's writers, inspires others who would follow in their heroes' footsteps. What's more, with its jumble of ethnic neighborhoods spilling over into one another, San Francisco is alive with languages and cultures. It's a welcoming and romantic literary breeding ground, offering the golden promise of the West.

Mark Twain's Gold Rush: "San Francisco is a truly fascinating city to live in... The climate is pleasanter when read about than personally experienced," wrote Mark Twain in his 1871 memoir, *Roughing It*. Twain, born Samuel Clemens, headed west from Missouri in 1861, following his brother Orion, who was a newly appointed secretary to the

Governor of the Nevada territory. When Twain's dream of striking it rich in the gold mines didn't pan out, he took to writing humor and travel pieces for Virginia City's *Territorial Enterprise* newspaper, and fast became a celebrity throughout the West. His travels continued westward, and for two years, 1864 and 1865, Twain worked in San Francisco, covering the police, fire, and theater beats for the *Morning Call* newspaper, before writing more customary lampoons and commentaries for the *Golden Era* and the *San Francisco Chronicle*. Today, the *Chronicle* is home to a more recent San Francisco literary figure, longtime columnist Herb Caen (*see page 85*).

Jumping frogs: You won't find many traces of Twain's brief stint here, but it was a crucial time in his development as a writer. While in San Francisco, he first began using the pen name "Mark Twain." He also achieved his first literary success here, writing the *Notorious Jumping Frog of Calaveras County*, his first short story, based on a tall tale he heard in a saloon in the town of Angels Camp. An annual jumping-frog contest held there every Spring pays homage to the story.

Other Gold Rush literary figures include Bret Harte (who befriended Twain during his brief stay) and Ambrose Bierce. Like Twain, Harte was a contributor to the *Golden Era*. He was also the most popular – and best paid – Western writer of his day. In 1870, Harte was earning $10,000 a year from the *Atlantic Monthly*, contributing a story to every issue. Bierce, author of the flawlessly cynical *Devil's Dictionary* – he defined birth as "the first and direst of all disasters" and a bride as "a woman with a fine prospect of happiness behind her" – as well as acclaimed short stories about the Civil War, was perhaps the first recognized columnist in American journalism. His Sunday column, "Prattles," which appeared in William Randolph Hearst's *Examiner*, skewered any and all forms of pomposity with a fierceness that earned him the nickname "Bitter Bierce."

Preceding pages: coffee and sci-fi at the beatnik haunt Vesuvio. Left, City Lights Bookstore.

(He stipulated to his editors that his column appear exactly as written.) It is impossible to say when Bierce died; in 1913, he went off to Mexico as a war correspondent to follow bandit Pancho Villa, and never returned.

Robert Louis Stevenson is honored by several monuments in San Francisco, despite spending less than a year in Northern California. In 1879, he traveled from his native Scotland in pursuit of Fanny Osbourne, a married woman with whom he had fallen madly in love in France. Trying unsuccessfully to support himself with his writing he spent several impoverished months living in a rented room at 608 Bush Street, waiting for

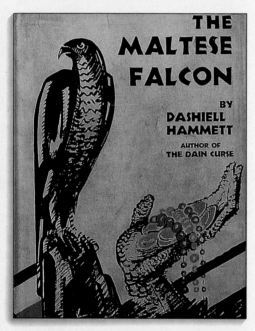

THE
MALTESE
FALCON
BY
DASHIELL
HAMMETT
AUTHOR OF
THE DAIN CURSE

Mrs Osbourne's divorce to be finalized. Afterwards Osbourne and Stevenson were married and sojourned in Napa Valley, where Stevenson recuperated from tuberculosis.

Although Stevenson didn't write his major works until after his return to Scotland in July 1880, a monument dedicated to him in the northwest corner of Chinatown's Portsmouth Square depicts the *Hispaniola*, the galleon featured in his classic pirate novel, *Treasure Island*. The inscription below the ship is taken from his "Christmas Sermon." Stevenson often came to Portsmouth Square to write and to watch the ships.

Born in San Francisco in 1876, Jack London maintained close ties with the Bay Area throughout the course of his short, celebrated life. In *Martin Eden* (1909) and *John Barleycorn* (1913), London recalls the Oakland waterfront beside which he grew up. At the age of 14, he bought a sloop, the *Razzle Dazzle*, and became an oyster pirate along the shoals of the San Francisco Bay. Although he was so accomplished that he was known as the "Prince of the Oyster Pirates," the following year London had a change of heart and went to work as a deputy for the Fish Patrol.

London traveled everywhere, across the US and Canada, on a sealing schooner off the Japanese coast and, in 1897, to the Klondike with the Gold Rush. After each adventure, he came back to Oakland. Returning from the Klondike with scurvy, London began to write about his experiences on the rugged Alaskan frontier. *The Son of the Wolf* (1901), his first collection of short stories, brought him immediate success and he continued writing in this vein, producing a collection of acclaimed, best-selling novels.

London's Oakland: Apart from the plaque at 605 Third Street marking his birthplace, there are few Jack London landmarks in San Francisco itself; most of his family's homes were destroyed in the fires following the 1906 earthquake. The city of Oakland renamed its waterfront shopping plaza Jack London Square in 1951. There you'll find Heinhold's First and Last Chance Saloon, an actual haunt from London's waterfront days. Supposedly, London sealed the purchase of his first sloop here. Several houses in which he lived can still be found in East Oakland, among them 575 Blair, in the Piedmont hills, where in 1903 he wrote his most popular novel, *The Call of the Wild*.

Two years later, London and his wife Charmain moved north to a ranch (dubbed "Beauty Ranch") in Glen Ellen, in Sonoma's wine country. At the then-incredible cost of $70,000, London built his dream home, Wolf House, only to see it burn down on August 23, 1913 – the night before he and his wife were to move in with all their belomgings. Since 1959, the ranch has been open to the public as Jack London State Historic Park.

The estate houses his widow's formidable collection of memorabilia; a short path from the house leads to the ruins of Wolf House and the grave where London's ashes were buried after his death in 1916.

Although Gertrude Stein was born in Allegheny, New York in 1874, the Steins moved west to Oakland in 1880 and she grew up there, before going east in 1891 to study at Radcliffe and Harvard, and eventually, in 1901, continuing on to Europe where she remained an expatriate for years. In 1934, Stein and her companion Alice B. Toklas revisited the area during a US lecture tour. She is still remembered in Oakland, not

delphia. At 14, he dropped out of high school to help support his family, and shortly afterwards joined the Pinkerton Detective Agency. Many of the shady characters in his fiction were based on characters he encountered in his five years as a Pinkerton man.

In 1921, Hammett moved to San Francisco to marry Josephine Dolan. Although they had planned to return east, they stayed on, living in rented flats. By day, Hammett wrote advertising copy for Samuels Jewelers at 865 Market (still in business), and by night he wrote his own detective fiction.

Hammett created an indelible character in Sam Spade, the cynical gumshoe disap-

always fondly, for having written "There is no *there* there" about the city, in her 1937 memoir, *Everybody's Autobiography* .

New-style detective: Dashiell Hammett lived in San Francisco from 1921–29, during which time he created such books as *Red Harvest* and *The Dain Curse*, a hard-boiled style of novel writing that redefined the American mystery story. Born in Maryland in 1894, Hammett was raised in Baltimore and Phila-

pearing into a foggy San Francisco night. Aficionados of *The Maltese Falcon* can still stop in at John's Grill, at 63 Ellis (between Powell and Stockton streets), which is one of the stops in summer on a weekly tour of Hammett sites. Established in 1908, John's is one of the only two restaurants mentioned in the novel that is still open for business. Its second-floor Maltese Falcon Dining Room is filled with Hammett memorabilia.

In the mid-1950s, the writing emerging from the cafés of North Beach commanded national and international attention as the arbiter of a cultural revolution. The "Beat

Left, an early edition of *The Maltese Falcon*. **Above**, Jack London's First and Last Chance Saloon in Oakland.

Generation" had been first defined on the East Coast a decade earlier, with Jack Kerouac, Allen Ginsberg and John Clellon Holmes experimenting with spontaneous writing based on the rhythms of jazz and be-bop. But it wasn't until Kerouac and Ginsberg came west in 1954 and 1955, encountering writers Lawrence Ferlinghetti, Gary Snyder, Michael McClure and others, that the Beats galvanized a literary movement.

It came together in San Francisco on October 7, 1955, at a poetry reading at the Six Gallery, an artists' cooperative. Organized by Kenneth Rexroth, the "Six Poets at the Six Gallery" reading featured Rexroth, Snyder,

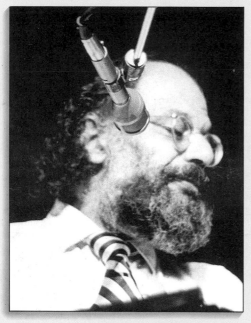

McClure, Ginsberg, Philip Whalen and Philip Lamantia and introduced the first public reading of Ginsberg's incendiary poem, "Howl." Kerouac recounts the event in his novel *The Dharma Bums*.

The poem created a sensation when it was published in 1956 and was immediately confiscated by US Customs officials as "obscene" literature. Ferlinghetti's City Lights Bookstore, the first paperback bookstore in America, and the publisher of *Howl & Other Poems*, was brought up on criminal charges. The ensuing trial (which City Lights won) brought the Beats to national prominence, as

did Kerouac's book *On The Road*, published in 1957. Many quintessential Beat hangouts, such as the Co-Existence Bagel Shop and The Place, are long gone, but some remain. City Lights at 61 Columbus (just up from Jack Kerouac Street), in the heart of North Beach, carries a wide range of Beat writings. At 255 Columbus, Vesuvio Cafe, which opened in 1949, still retains the Bohemian feel it had in the 1950s. Welsh poet Dylan Thomas favored this bar when in San Francisco. Caffe Trieste, at 606 Vallejo, continues to be a favorite among writers. On Saturday mornings, you can often hear live opera performances.

The '60s and beyond: As the beatniks gave way to the hippies, so were the Beats followed by The Merry Pranksters. Led by Ken Kesey, author of *One Flew Over The Cuckoo's Nest,* the Pranksters were early experimenters with hallucinogens and organized several massive LSD-tinged gatherings, or "Acid Tests," among them the legendary Trips Festival in January 1966. Held at Longshoreman's Hall in Fisherman's Wharf, the event reportedly drew 20,000 adventurous souls. Tom Wolfe's *The Electric Kool-Aid Acid Test* recounts the Pranksters' exploits in detail.

At the same time, San Francisco was also home to *Rolling Stone* magazine and its infamous correspondent, Hunter S. Thompson. Thompson lived in the Haight-Ashbury district during the mid-60s when he was researching *Hell's Angels*, his off-kilter look at the motorcycle gang.

In the 1970s, playwright (and now movie star) Sam Shepard produced his influential plays *Angel City* and *Curse of the Starving Class* at the Magic Theater, currently housed at Fort Mason. Armistead Maupin, a North Carolina native who relocated to San Francisco in 1971, offered a serial called "Tales of the City" in the *San Francisco Chronicle* beginning in 1976. Detailing the lives of young gay and straight San Franciscans, the series was embraced by the public and published in several volumes of best-selling books. It was later popularized as a BBC television series.

<u>Left</u>, the Beat goes on: Allen Ginsberg.

MR SAN FRANCISCO

It was the *New York Mirror's* Walter Winchell who invented the so-called "three-dot" style of journalism once ubiquitous in American newspapers, but for a generation Herb Caen has been its most famous practitioner. For thousands of San Franciscans, his column is the first thing they read each day and when he shifted from the *San Francisco Chronicle* to the rival *Examiner* (and back again in 1958) tens of thousands of fans are said to have moved with him.

Although Caen maintains he still doesn't know what makes a good item, others have pinpointed "his outstanding ability to take a wisp of fog, a chance phrase overheard in an elevator, a happy child on a cable car" as major ingredients. Caen says he owes some of his style to an early news editor who admonished him to "be entertaining" because he was easily bored and had "a very short attention span."

He defines a great column as "twenty-four short, snappy items" which can be as varied as an offhand comment about a landmark city building infiltrating its elevators with recorded music, to somebody's recollection of a woman gushing to T.S. Eliot in London about what a wonderful party they were attending and the poet's rejoinder: "Yes, if you can see the essential horror of it."

Answering one of his critics who accused him of writing "the same column every day" about a city that had died long ago, Caen remarked, "That's accurate. But I'm trapped in this persona I've created... this late version of a Walter Winchell spin-off... it just keeps going along."

Born in Sacramento in 1916, he wrote his first column, Raisin' Caen, for the student paper while at high school and apart from his 3½-year stint in the army, has churned out five columns a week for over half a century. He still types on an old Royal typewriter and usually answers his own telephone, leaving an assistant to deal with the hundreds of weekly tips from an army of faithful readers and fans.

He strings around 1,000 words together daily with such subheads as "Bay City Beat" or "Caenfetti." His half-century spent documenting the minutiae of what he once termed "Baghdad by the Bay" not only makes him San Francisco's supreme chronicler but also gives his opinions a sort of timeless credence. Comparing *The New*

Yorker, under its new editor Tina Brown, with the older version, for example, he remarked offhandedly that he had been a subscriber since 1936 – two years before he began his *Chronicle* column – and added about the glitzier magazine, "There's a hole in there where a soul used to be."

Interviewing him almost a decade ago, magazine writer Ken Kelley observed that in no other American city does a columnist wield such great influence anymore. Caen feels that he didn't get noticed "until I started writing these sort of love poems to San Francisco. I hadn't realized the depth of narcissism in this city... I got this huge reaction to either my bad poetry about the fog coming in through the Golden Gate or the old San Francisco stuff which I used to dig out of old

books and papers... To this day people aren't that crazy about the gossip or the political stuff – they like the sentimental stuff the best... (especially) this 'old San Francisco stuff.' Part of it is synthetic after all. Nostalgia is a bad reporter." Caen's nostalgia columns appear in the paper's Sunday edition.

When defining today's typical San Francisco resident, Caen said that it would be somebody who lives in Novato (a neighboring suburb) "or somewhere he can afford the rent. A typical San Franciscan is either an old guy like me who can afford to go on living here or some kids who double or triple up in some place where the rents haven't gone out of sight." ∎

It's not that other cities are behind, it's just that when it comes to food, San Francisco has always been slightly ahead of the competition. Consider this: San Francisco once boasted the only restaurant in America serving pizza; opened the first Chinese and Japanese restaurants in the West; gave rise to that nebulous culinary catch-all, "California cuisine." So – when you bite into an avocado and shrimp sandwich in a Jersey diner, or munch a "Chicago" or "New York" style pizza, or "do sushi" in downtown LA, just remember: they ate it here first.

With over 3,000 eating and drinking establishments in San Francisco – more per capita than anywhere else in the world – and a compact array of ethnic neighborhoods spilling over into one another, it's no surprise that the spirit of innovation has made San Francisco a city renowned for its food.

It has always been this way, or so it seems. Even at the time of the Gold Rush in 1848, which forever changed the face of the West, San Francisco was nothing but a transient, shanty town, filled with houses made of paper and men with dreams of gold. Populated by hotel-dwellers and apartment renters, none of which had kitchens, eating out became a tradition by necessity.

Maritime marketing: This legacy began long before California's fertile Central Valley had been tilled for its produce. Vegetables and fruits were shipped in from the Sandwich Islands, apples and pears from Chile, and basic necessities, such as butter and eggs were shipped around the Horn from the Atlantic Coast. So much shipping of food, just to please the palates of the city's denizens.

Perhaps the noblest practice in the city's memory is the "free lunch" saloon. In even the simplest corner grocery or "bit" saloon, hard-working clerks and brokers could, for the meager price of a mug of beer, feed on an impressive array of cheese, bologna, dried beef and pickles.

In the more elegant saloons adorned with crystal chandeliers and mahogany tables, brandy-sipping bankers and merchants were offered a more elaborate spread. On the ground floor of the Palace of Fine Arts, a free lunch at the Lick House included pig's head, crab salad, terrapin stew, Holland herring and smoked salmon.

There were, of course, plenty of places for

those who struck it rich on gold to spend their new fortunes. The Poulet d'Or, the city's first French restaurant, opened in 1849, and was soon renamed "The Poodle Dog" by miners who couldn't cope with the French vowels. Young men-about-town and their female companions could feast on good French cuisine in curtained and cushioned booths and discreet upstairs bedroom suites.

American Paris: By the turn of the century, the city became known as the "American Paris." When the 1906 earthquake leveled San Francisco, some muttered that perhaps the city was getting its just desserts and prophesized that this would teach it to adjust to a more modest appetite.

They were wrong, of course. Amidst the rubble, restaurateurs set up trestle tables and served meals. Dinner over, they set about the business of rebuilding. The rest of the country soon learned that it took more than an earthquake to dull the appetites of San Franciscans. The theory held nearly a century later. After the disastrous fire that swept through the Oakland hills in 1991, some of the Bay Area's finest restaurants once again pulled together in a charity effort to ensure that the devastated property owners were, if still homeless, at least well fed.

have since added the newest options to the city's international variety of dishes.

Historical appetite: Word of the culinary riches soon whet the appetites of food connoisseurs the world over, who were drawn to the intrigue of the American Paris. Once in San Francisco, visitors could sample and purchase – as they still can today – Crab Louis salad and fresh petrale sole from the dockside stalls of Fisherman's Wharf; Italian gnocci and oven-fresh *foccacia* bread from the tiny storefronts of North Beach; armsful of French bread; warm tortillas and chili-laden *salsas* from the bustling Mexican Mission; and Thai fish cakes and Chinese pot

If the 1906 earthquake failed to turn the city sober and serious, Prohibition made another attempt. With one bar for every 100 inhabitants, San Francisco may have been the most bibulous city in the States. When alcohol was outlawed, people shrugged their shoulders and said, "We might as well eat."

The early ethnic diversity of the city gave San Franciscans plenty of fare to choose from. Mexican missionaries were joined by scores of Chinese, French and Germans who arrived in the city in 1848 – enticed by the Gold Rush, but who remained to cook. Vietnamese, Thai, and Cambodian immigrants

stickers from Clement Street, deep in the heart of the Richmond area.

In 1935, after a trip to San Francisco with her companion Gertrude Stein, Alice B. Toklas recalled her adventures in her cookbook: "In San Francisco we indulged in gastronomic orgies. Sand dabs meuniere, rainbow trout in aspic, grilled soft-shell crabs, paupiettes of roast fillets of pork, eggs Rossini and tarte Chambourde. The tarte Chambourde had been a specialty of one of the three great French bakeries before the San Francisco fire. To my surprise, no one in Paris had ever heard of it."

While the unique French tart may have been news to Parisians, it could not have surprised long-time San Franciscans, raised on such a cross-cultural stew. They began to feel that they ate so much sushi and pasta and *dim sum* and pâté that they began to regard and reinvent these favorites as part of their native cuisine.

Fueled by the culinary riches of the world, local chefs rebelled against the antiquated notion that French food belonged only in French restaurants, Chinese in Chinese restaurants, and so on. Experimentation became the *notion d'jour*, and over the years, the mixing and melding of international ingredients – along with a decidedly Western touch – gave rise to a culinary revolution. Chefs aren't fond of the term, but for better or worse, the food media deemed the result "California cuisine."

Berkeley bites: The gourmet "revolution" was happening all over San Francisco, but nowhere with more passion than across the Bay Bridge in nearby Berkeley, where eclectic cuisine was introduced most dramatically. In 1971, Alice Waters opened Chez Panisse (1517 Shattuck Avenue). Waters set out with no formal training, just a year spent abroad experiencing European food. To Waters, freshness became the highest virtue and foods were cooked simply to foster their natural flavor.

Chez Panisse opened as a typical French bistro. Frustrated by an inability to get quality goods as they did in France, Waters began encouraging local purveyors to come to her door. Farmers grew special vegetables to complement a specific dish and raised hand-fed livestock and poultry according to careful specifications. Small-time fishermen sold her their catch and, for the first time in years, local oysters were farmed.

Armed with these local ingredients, the Panisse kitchen went to work. The result? The strictly French food became less "French," and the menu suddenly offered dishes like ravioli made of potatoes and garlic, or a simple grilled lobster.

The response was so overwhelming that

Left, dining amongst the rubble of the 1906 earthquake. Right, seminal sour dough.

Waters opened a second café upstairs, The Cafe at Chez Panisse, where she offered a similar cast of fresh dishes, though on a more modest scale. Acme bread and Provencal olives greet diners as they choose from the internationally intertwined daily selections such as haute cuisine pizzas, Cajun rabbit stew or Indian-style chicken.

As Waters-trained chefs began to branch out on their own, taking the Chez Panisse philosophy to other restaurants, the public watched with interest. In few other cities, with the possible exception of Paris, do restaurant-goers elevate chefs to celebrity status, tracking their careers from one restau-

rant to the next, as they do in San Francisco.

Perhaps the most noted Chez Panisse graduate is Jeremiah Tower, who opened his own restaurant, Stars (750 Redwood Alley) in 1983. Modeling it after a great Parisian café, Tower's American brasserie appeals to the taste of gourmets as well as those in search of an after-work beer, serving everything from five-course meals to champagne and oysters, to pizza and hot dogs.

For a combination of quality and glitz, few chefs have received more notoriety than Wolfgang Puck. Best known for his Los Angeles restaurant Spago, Puck brought his name up the coast to San Francisco's Union Square to open Postrio (545 Post Street). The multi-level, art gallery-style dining room is packed seven days a week from breakfast to supper. See-and-be-seen locals, celebrities and tourists flock to the trendy eatery to taste, among other fare, the designer pizzas that made Puck famous down south.

Another landmark of the new cuisine lies north across the Golden Gate. Nestled in a stand of redwoods in Marin County, a renovated Victorian now houses the Lark Creek Inn (234 Magnolia Ave, Larkspur). The brainchild of proprietor and chef Bradley Ogden, Lark Creek has mastered the marriage of

ture from the formal, haute cuisine of the 1980s. The latest wave of gourmet San Francisco restaurants seem more lively and cheerful than those of the past, with a culinary eye toward heartier fare. New restaurants are succeeding with moderate prices while not straying from the quality ingredients that gave the food its distinction.

Located South of Market in a renovated 1910 warehouse, Lulu (816 Folsom) has been bustling since early 1993. From the French-Italian Riviera-style menu, Lulu encourages its patrons to eat family-style, to pick a number of dishes for the table and share them with their companions. With a

ambiance and cuisine. Ogden is originally from Michigan, and his menu seems like a tribute to home cooking – Yankee pot roast, roasted chicken, suckling pig – all cooked in a brick, wood-burning oven.

Ogden's restaurant in the country proved so successful that he moved his Midwestern sensibility-style cooking to the city. One Market (1 Market Street), near the northern waterfront, offers rustic fare similar to that at the Lark Creek Inn, yet with an urban touch and downtown convenience.

Ogden's move to One Market is a recent trend in California cuisine – a marked depar-

casual atmosphere, modest prices and impeccable food, the restaurant is one of San Francisco's places to see and be seen.

Bix (56 Gold Street), tucked in a Financial District alley, is a 1940s neo-deco supper club that has been a favorite among San Franciscans for years. The bustling bar, featuring a jazz pianist and torch singer, provides the perfect backdrop for sipping martinis and Manhattans, or enjoying uptown-style California cuisine. It would seem impossible for the food at the Cypress Club (500 Jackson Street) to match the intrigue of the voluptuously draped, futuristic decor.

Yet, by adding an element of design to classic San Francisco fare, the elegant Cypress Club succeeds in pleasing the chaotic downtown crowd.

Even carnivores can appreciate the strictly vegetarian cuisine at Green's (Fort Mason, Building A), which harvests its own vegetables. The Chez Panisse-trained chef takes her inspiration from many places, offering grilled marinated tofu, linguini with wild mushrooms, and salad made with feta cheese and sprinkled with flowers. Surprisingly elegant, the spacious, waterside restaurant is especially spectacular at sunset.

If you're inclined to a subdued atmos-(777 Sutter Street), a few blocks off Union Square. A flowered fabric tent, wicker lamps and an enormous floral bouquet in the room's center set the stage for the Provencal cuisine. The four- or five-course prix fixe or à la carte menu changes nightly.

For the seafaring: "Fisherman's Wharf" is something of a gimmick. Generations of San Franciscans have always known that the city's finest fresh fish come first to the doors of two venerable restaurants, Sam's (374 Bush Street) and Tadich's (240 California Street). Lines have stretched outside their doors at mealtime for the past century. Today, a more contemporary seafood-craving

phere, and willing to pay prettily for the pleasure, Masa's (648 Bush Street) is considered the standard by which all other restaurants are judged. The elegant decor and china plates and crystal wine glasses signal an evening of nouvelle French cuisine. Reservations are accepted three weeks in advance – and an entire night's seating is likely to be booked by 11am. If it *is* booked, give consideration to the venerable Fleur de Lys

Left, Stars is an American brasserie. <u>Above</u>, celebrity chef Wolfgang Puck's restaurants and fame have crept up the coast from Los Angeles.

gourmet crowd is flocking to Aqua (252 California Street) just a couple of doors down in the heart of the financial district.

The need for brevity excludes many of the other 3,000 establishments where you can eat, drink and be merry in San Francisco. But if you're looking for a place to dance off your dinner, Harry Denton's is the perfect spot. The rugs here are rolled up, literally, at 10.30pm when the waterfront dining room is transformed into a dance club. If you're lucky, Harry himself – one of San Francisco's quirkiest and most popular restaurateurs – will be in town to dance on the bar.

VIRTUAL REALITY AND SILICON VALLEY

Though you won't find its name on any map – and its exact location is disputable – Silicon Valley definitely exists, and to trace its history is to trace the evolution of contemporary culture. This valley, which stretches about 20 miles (32 km) from the lower San Francisco peninsula to San Jose, nurtured many of the technological advances that have shot the world into the electronic age. Having exhausted the frontier they settled, the valley's inventive minds have turned to creating their own horizons.

Silicon Valley embodies the very definition of high-tech America, but with a new Californian state of consciousness. Endowed with the enterprising spirit of pioneers, it is a place where international giants in the electronics and computer industries got their first break in suburban garages, and where futuristic dreams are manufactured into reality.

Palo Alto, home to Stanford University, lies at the heart of this region both as a physical intersection and high-tech magnet. The valley is bounded to the east by the bay and to the west by the mountains thrust up by massive land shifts along the San Andreas fault. Traversed by US 101 and pinched off by the foothills just beyond San Jose, it spreads north toward San Francisco, consuming a number of small cities in its wake.

High-tech: An estimated 7,000 high-tech businesses dealing in everything from microscopic transistors to networked computer systems are located here. The valley embraces nearly 15 cities, including Mountain View, home of the United States Navy's Moffett Field and NASA/Ames Research Center, a revitalized San Jose (now America's eleventh largest city) and several suburban communities like Cupertino and Sunnyvale, which have grown so densely populated that it's nearly impossible to tell where one begins and the other ends. Industrial office parks and silicon chip factories

now dominate where acres of fruit orchards once blanketed the land. At intervals along this major highway tiny orchards peek from between rows of identical tract houses – reminders of the region's rural roots.

Before the silicon chip existed, this land was known as Santa Clara Valley. It was first settled in the mid 1800s, not by fortune seekers of the 1849 Gold Rush but by farmers who found wealth in the area's rich soil. In 1851, the first significant contribution to

the future incarnation of the valley was made when Stanford University was established by railroad tycoon Leland Stanford near Palo Alto. The high-tech atmosphere of the area was further cultivated by Palo Alto native Lee DeForest, who in 1906 invented a three-element vacuum tube that provided the spark for the development of electronics. A marker in front of his former residence at 913 Emerson Street commemorates the house as the "birthplace" of this industry.

In the early years, America's brightest technical minds migrated to Stanford's engineering school to study radio, the valley's first

Left, "virtual reality" drinks at a local nightclub.
Right, the microchip originated in California's Silicon Valley.

high-tech industry. When they finished school, they stayed – and a thriving radio, telephone, and telegraph industry emerged. In 1938, two Stanford students living at 367 Addison Street – David Packard and William Hewlett – founded what would one day be one of the world's high-tech corporate giants: Hewlett-Packard. That house is now a state historical monument.

With World War II, San Francisco also became the center of West Coast military activity. From Highway 101 near Mountain View, you can see the empty hull of a dirigible hangar marking Moffett Naval Air Station. In 1940, NASA (National Aeronautics

and Space Administration) leased space at Moffett. This facility, NASA/Ames Research Center, was for many years the focus of the country's astrophysical research, and still houses the world's largest wind tunnel. Ames became a touchstone not only for the electronics and engineering communities of Silicon Valley, but an early testing ground for the exploration of the latest Silicon Valley frontier – "Virtual Reality."

In 1956, valley native William Schockley returned home after receiving the Nobel Prize for developing the electronic transistor. He intended to build an empire, but the eight young engineers he had hired all left to form the Fairchild Semiconductor Company. It was here that Bob Noyce, in 1959, developed the miniature semiconductor set into silicon that would forever change the face of bucolic Santa Clara Valley. Noyce, known to many as the father of Silicon Valley, founded Intel – where the microprocessor was developed – in 1968, foreshadowing the personal computer revolution.

One discovery begat another. Along with Intel and Fairchild, companies like Advanced Micro Devices and National Semiconductor grew to be internationally known magnets of high-technology. Those companies, in turn, brought exponential population growth to the valley.

The 1970s was the decade of the Silicon Valley rush. The electronics industry was flourishing and the time was ripe to apply the new technology. In 1972, Nolan Bushnell founded Atari in yet another garage – this one at 3572 Gibson Avenue in Santa Clara. Bushnell created the world's first videogame, called Pong, or electronic ping-pong. Simple though it was, it ignited the modern video-game craze. More important, high technology had finally found a way into people's living rooms, not just into industrial mainframe computers.

Atari – and several other valley companies that followed – gave the average American family their first of many brushes with technology. In just a decade, Atari grew from a counter-cultural garage brand to a small high-tech empire, eventually to be owned by Warner, one of America's largest entertainment giants.

In the hands of a new generation, the shape of high-technology was molded in new ways during the late 1970s and early 1980s. Teenage techno-jocks hooked on video games began fiddling with chip boards and microprocessors to see what they could do. In the last of the great valley garages – at 2066 Crist Drive in Cupertino – Steve Jobs and Steve Wozniac turned out their first micro computer. In 1982, the two formed Apple. A legend was born, and the personal computer revolution began. Now a sprawling green glass and stucco complex, Apple's headquarters (still located in Cupertino, but now at 20525

Mariani Avenue off Highway 101) is one of the few companies that allows visitors past the front door.

Obsolete but influential: During the 1980s, personal computers replaced video games as the entertainment of choice. Atari became extinct, like many Silicon Valley giants before and after it, but not without launching the careers of a new generation of explorers. What would be next? In Atari's Sunnyvale research laboratory, engineers were beginning their advance on the next high-tech frontier that would fascinate the modern world. Researchers worked on a new kind of computer game that seemed to create a new

house. Point your finger toward the ruby and you swoosh down inside of it and everywhere you look, red light glows. Point down and you are at the base of a column, point left and you pass unscathed through the marble walls to find yourself standing on an oriental rug which moves endlessly like a motorized kaleidoscope. Welcome to the fantastic world of Virtual Reality.

This strange realm is a comparatively recent step in the evolution of computer-generated graphics. Rather than simply viewing graphics on a flat screen, Virtual Reality users immerse themselves in a completely artificial environment, which has approxi-

dimension in which humans and computers could coexist. Some called it "electronic LSD," others simply regarded it as another of the valley's undiscovered technological wonders. Most know it as Virtual Reality.

Imagine you fly with your fingers. When you point up, you rise high above trees, clouds, above a towering white marble pillar with a huge red ruby beaming like a light-

Left, Steve Wozniac was co-founder of Apple Computer. **Above**, the engineering department of Stanford University spawned some of the best brains in the business.

mately the look and feel of real life.

Gearing up for the experience requires looking like a creature from outer space. One essential is the video-goggle, or head-mounted display, inset with two miniature liquid crystal screens. The views of the two screens are slightly different, producing the 3-D effect of normal vision. The headset also senses the movements of your head and reports this information back to the computer. The computer then creates moving images on the screens that mimic your shifting point of view. Also essential is a way of navigating your way through this world.

This is done by a "data glove," laced with sensors that measure finger movements.

The glove commands the computer to move or stop, and can also mimic the actions of picking up an object, opening a door or throwing a ball as they happen (or are dramatized) in real life. Body suits – as sensitive to movement as data gloves – come next.

Inner space: Imagine that a good computer programmer can build you any world you want, no matter how fantastic, unreal, exotic, or mundane. You can live in a multiple-story mansion, walk on Mars, fly around in a molecule or take a virtual-tour of the whole of San Francisco.

all came together. NASA/Ames Research Center in Mountain View was the first site of a fully functional Virtual Reality testbed. In typical valley fashion, a group of America's foremost researchers – many of them natives of the area – assembled to manufacture the future. Ames Research Center concentrated on developing more useful applications for the technology, particularly in the areas of space exploration. Among other achievements, researchers hoped to develop Telepresence, a device through which an earthbound person could control a robot located in space – or on another planet.

NASA/Ames Research Center soon

The possibilities are endless – but realities are slow to follow. The American media quickly dubbed this infinite supply of computer-generated hallucinations "electronic LSD" – in some ways a fitting name for an experience that emanated from the San Francisco Bay Area with its hippie counter-culture history. The hype and hysteria thrust Virtual Reality into underground pop-culture.

Various scientists, computer programmers and theorists across the country were independently developing and perfecting specific components of Virtual Reality, but it was in Silicon Valley in the late 1980s that it

launched more Virtual Reality ventures, including VPL Research of Redwood City. Every legend has its hero, and Virtual Reality has Jaron Lanier. As the chief executive of VPL, Lanier embodied the spirit of Silicon Valley at its most eccentric. The youthful, dreadlocked zealot embraced both the usefulness and high-entertainment value of Virtual Reality. His company did much to launch the private exploration of virtual worlds. As a result VPL became the principal suppliers of Virtual Reality headsets and gloves to companies around the world.

The total cost for a VPL system can easily

reach $300,000, but the race is on to develop affordable VR tools – playthings for every household. Like so many Silicon Valley pioneers, however, Lanier's VPL was ill-fated. Its foreign parent-company scooped up all the patents and kicked employees out on the streets. In its place, several new companies in the Bay Area (some started by former VPL employees) have sprung up to carry on the research. Jaron Lanier still remains a local techno-saint.

Worldwide applications: The Virtual Reality research that started in Silicon Valley touched off a budding industry around the world. In Tokyo, the Matsushita Electric Works uses

make it, streamlining the building process and saving thousands of dollars in time-wasting, costly mistakes.

The medical establishment plans to employ Virtual Reality in the preparation for rare surgical procedures and for medical training. And drug researchers are using the new technology to develop better pharmaceuticals and to increase the efficiency and safety of the development process. But in the end, it will probably be the entertainment value of Virtual Reality that will drive full-scale development by private corporations. There's big money to be made in the international entertainment industry, the kind of

Virtual Reality to assist customers in building the kitchen of their dreams. Prospective buyers wearing headsets can try out different floor-plans, rearrange appliances at whim and even resize the cabinets. In London, Virtual Reality is being used to train drivers of public transportation vehicles. In a similar fashion, VR can also be a design aid in everything from shoes to houses to cities. Designers can view their product before they

Left, Apple's modern headquarters are still located in Cupertino. **Above**, hackers and phreaks, challenging computing's certainties.

money needed to continue important research in all applications of Virtual Reality.

Silicon Valley continues to mutate. Speculation has mounted about whether it has passed its prime. But with so many companies, it's hard to believe this area will be a ghost town soon. Regardless of its future, this technological Mesopotamia has provided the tools for a new generation – computers, software programs, and a staggering array of electronics. The techno-trailblazers who live here have moved on to conquering virtual worlds, ensuring an endless supply of new "valleys" and, perhaps, new civilizations.

California could be a dozen states, each with its own outdoors personality, its own climate, its own natural wonders. For many Californians, the outdoors is synonymous with activity. It's a big state, the theory goes, and you'll have to keep moving to see it.

While breathtaking scenery and solemn serenity intrude on every scene in California, this outdoors tour of the state adopts the native philosophy: that is, go where you like, but *do* something when you get there. The naturalist John Muir once sat transfixed by the "window to the Heavens" he found in the high Sierra – to get there, he walked. Today, millions of tourists arriving in the dusty heat of July experience the awesome beauty of Muir's Yosemite Valley through the greasy windows of a tour bus – a dull, forgettable experience.

Mountain high: California has high mountains – the Sierras – that run the length of the state like a spine, north to south, separating forest from desert. Thickly forested on the shoulder, as bald as a cue ball on top, polished smooth by the moving glaciers of the last ice age, the Sierras are rich in strange, beautiful geology: the giant, batholith, granite domes of Yosemite National Park, Kings Canyon and Desolation Wilderness, with names like El Capitan and Half Dome; the cores and flows of extinct volcanoes with names like Devil's Postpile and Valley of the Moon.

In the north, the Sierras of Tahoe and Yosemite give way to the foothills where gold sometimes still generates a rush; the hardened ponderosa of pine, madrone and manzanita fall away to the lush, irrigated oasis of the San Joaquin Valley, the low rise of the coastal mountains, then the cool Pacific Ocean. In the valley, through a break in the Coast Range, the Sacramento River and its hundreds of tributaries form a delta that drains through the San Francisco Bay.

There are many ways to enjoy the outdoors of California: the drive along the high

winding, seaside cliffs of Highway 1 is spectacular in any part of the state. But to experience California as natives do, you'll do well to elevate your heartbeat – walk, roller-skate, ride a bike, paddle a kayak, climb a 2,000-ft (610-meter) granite face, or "catch a wave." California is rife with outfitters, schools, clubs, rental shops, guides, resorts – and even tour buses – that specialize in outdoor adventure.

The Central Coast: "The coast" begins roughly at Point Arena, 100 miles (160 km) north of San Francisco, encompasses the huge natural harbor of San Francisco Bay, includes the coastal mountains that form – among other things – the hills of San Francisco, extends down through Half Moon Bay and Santa Cruz, includes the teeming marine environment of Monterey and Carmel, and follows the sheer, rugged cliffs of the coast through Big Sur.

San Francisco lured early arrivals with the shelter of the San Francisco Bay, a huge natural harbor that is home to myriad bird life, a noisy colony of sea lions that has taken residence at Fisherman's Wharf, island wildlife sanctuaries, and fascinating tidal marshes.

The parks and grassy hills near the city are oak and scrub on one side, redwood coastal forest on the side facing the sea. In the days of sail the bay provided a much-needed respite from the fierce prevailing winds that blow out of the northwest virtually all summer long. Although a bane to old-time ships, it's a boon to modern sailors. Sailing craft of every description crowd the vast bay on weekends. Surfers race the swells under the Golden Gate Bridge, and float like butterflies off the beach at Crissy Field, one of the world's greatest urban windsurfing spots.

Just north of the Golden Gate Bridge, opposite San Francisco, the Marin Headlands and Mount Tamalpais are considered the birthplace of mountain biking. Miles of scenic trails are perfect for this bouncy form of cycling, and the bikes share the trails with hikers and equestrians.

Some 30 miles (48 km) north of the bay's

Preceding pages: the California coastline. **Left,** the rugged cliffs of Big Sur.

northernmost tip, in the valleys of Napa and Sonoma at the heart of California's wine country, cyclists take long tours on the rolling hills that wind past scores of vineyards. In the forest slopes above Sonoma, rainy spring days are the occasion of one of California's strangest migrations: thousands of red-bellied salamanders literally come out of the woodwork, and make their way to the stream beds where they spawn. Often in sight of vineyards and wineries, the Russian River and Cache Creek are popular rafting and canoeing streams.

Monterey: Traveling south from San Francisco, the best course is on Highway 1 along

upwind, is a carefully protected nursery for the giant, billowing elephant seals, most noted for the male's ability to inflate its prodigious fleshy nose, and the fact that the male is often five times the size of the females in its harem.

While the seals themselves are of no bother to boardsailors and surfers, this is the one area in California that's truly a lunch counter for the great white shark. One attack a year is the norm, but few are fatal. Actually, the sharks are under far more predatorial pressure than the surfers and windsurfers; biologists fear that the prehistoric fish are being hunted to extinction out of misplaced fear

the coast. All the way to Santa Cruz the coastline is a rough jumble of broken cliffs and long, misty beaches. Surf fishing is popular here, as is hang gliding and surfing. Along this stretch you're likely to see hundreds of windsurfers braving the cracking swells and blowing sands of Gazos Creek, Scott Creek and Waddell Creek. Waddell is considered one of the best windsurfing spots in the country and top sailors are often spotted jumping waves and pulling spectacular aerial maneuvers with names like "killer loop" and "cheese roll." This despite the fact that Ano Nuevo State Park, a mile or two

and misunderstanding, with disastrous consequences to the marine ecology.

Monterey Bay is the setting of some of America's most noted literature: the writing of John Steinbeck, who, among other things, wrote about Cannery Row. The Canneries were there for a singular reason: the great schools of sardines that once teemed in Monterey Bay. These fish were the base of a food chain that included vast schools of salmon, ling cod, and other game fish. Whaling was also once part of the local fleet's calling. There are still massive schools of squid, and, as a result of careful breeding, the sardines are beginning to return, too. Flocks of shorebirds and great numbers of sea lions and seals are only the most visible signs of life in this region.

A popular pastime in Monterey is to rent easily-paddled, open-topped kayaks called "Scuppers," and to paddle out to the local kelp beds. The kelp, which ranges all along the coast, forms fantastic underwater forests; scuba diving is extremely popular in Monterey and all along the coast to the south. The kelp is long and spindly at the base and stretches up to form thick mats at the surface. Divers swim through these forests for sightings of California's territorial ocean

backs with an infant sleeping on their belly, lolling about the water fastidiously cleaning their fur, or happily munching a shellfish as a sunbather might float on her back in a pool.

For those who prefer their ocean taken from shore, the Monterey Bay Aquarium has among its collections a life-size living kelp bed you can view from several levels. Just south of Monterey, the town of Carmel is an exquisite cypress-grove that leads to spectacular shorelines. Nearby Point Lobos is an underwater marine sanctuary. Visitors must make reservations to dive here, and are not permitted to harm any marine life. Driving south, the road climbs away from the ocean

goldfish, the Garibaldi, ling cod, many types of rockfish, and others.

Where the divers and kayakers converge at the surface, both are likely to encounter one of California's most delightful wild animals, the sea otter. The otters were once hunted for their fur. But the animals, which survive on abalone and urchins plucked from the bottom, are too winsome and intelligent to have escaped the sympathy of animal lovers. The creatures are often seen floating on their

Left, sailing the bay. Above, Mount Diablo is located near the Berkeley hills.

to become a breathtaking drive along high seaside cliffs. There is little coastal access along this route. But along the way, travelers will eventually come to Big Sur, a huge wilderness in the coastal mountains.

Northwest Coast: This California coast is somberly beautiful: long, empty beaches littered with driftwood, rugged sea cliffs, sawmills and fishing towns, and forests that come to the edge of the ocean cliffs. Swimming is none too inviting here – the sky is usually gray and the water is a constant 50°F (10°C) – but you can enter the surf with a wetsuit. Surfing has a loyal following, particularly at the point breaks of river mouths and harbors. The waves here are powerful and dangerous and no place for the novice. Undertows and rip tides are also common, demanding caution.

Cold-water diving gear (a 7-mm wetsuit, hood, booties, fins, mask, snorkel, and 20 lbs/9 kg of lead to sink all that neoprene) equips you to hunt for abalone. These giant mollusks are a delicacy, but prying them off the rocks at depth is not for the casual swimmer. Sometimes, at low tides, a wader may find a legal-sized "ab" in a tide pool.

Fishing abounds on the coast. You can cast from rocks or piers, or embark on a "party

confluence near sea level of the Sacramento and San Joaquin rivers. Like many huge river mouths, the Sacramento Delta has been turned into an agricultural bonanza. The river here is freshwater, but strongly affected by the tides. It winds through the delta in a thousand tiny threads, like lace. Each of the islands in this web has been walled off by levees and turned to farmland. Many farmers reach their homes by small bridges and roads; others are forced to ride ferries.

The entire delta was once an endless marsh, but now that it is under more regular control, it is only the out-of-the-way corners that teem with waterfowl. One of California's

boat" to probe the depths for salmon, ling cod, rockfish and other denizens of the deep. Unusual, chilling sport can be had pursuing surf smelt. The fisherman uses a big triangular net on a frame. Plunging the net into oncoming breaking waves, the fisherman is soaked completely. The nets are available for rent; the smelt, sometimes caught by the bucket full, are deep-fried and eaten whole.

The Sacramento Valley: If you leave San Francisco on a freighter traveling east, heading inland toward the source of the muddy water that flows into San Francisco Bay, you will enter a wide twisting delta formed by the

great adventures is a trip on the delta in a rented houseboat, for which you are advised to bring or rent a waterski boat, and bring along every form of watersports equipment that can be mustered.

The delta is the only ready outlet for most of the rivers that run out of the Sierras and into the huge bowl lying between the foot of the Sierras and the coastal range. This entire valley was mostly marshland when Europeans first saw it. Alternately flooded and baked, it teamed with bear and elk as well as ducks, geese and other water-loving birds. Settlers quickly drained the land for farms.

The Sacramento River is by far California's largest. Its tributaries include most of the west slope of the Sierras, and while it travels through foothills, farmland and, ultimately, into San Francisco Bay, its water is a hotly contested commodity. A major dam, Shasta, at the northern end of the state, is the first plug in the Sacramento's flow. Other dams block the progress of most of the other rivers that end up in the Sacramento. Along the way, this huge river is the source of all kinds of wild scenery. People have been known to canoe it, swim it, drive boats up and down its length, and even to spend long hours on hot summer days floating in it,

hills, ponderosa, alpine meadows and granite domes. The sky here is clear and brilliant, the rivers steep and serious.

The pioneer conservationist John Muir, one of the co-founders of the Sierra Club, once wrote: "Well the Sierra be named, not the Snowy Range, but the Range of Light." A wilderness trail of several hundred miles bears John Muir's name, as do a vast wilderness and a college of the University of California. Any visitor to these beautiful mountains will find a deep spiritual connection with Muir's writing.

Yosemite, now a national park, was Muir's chief inspiration, a wondrous collection of

nestled in the tube of a truck tire.

The Sierras: The Sierra Nevada range is 400 miles (643 km) long. It peaks at the summit of Mt Whitney, 14,490 ft (4,416 meters) which is less than 100 miles (160 km) as the crow flies from the lowest point in the lower 48 states, Death Valley (150 ft/45 meters below sea level). This gives some idea of its severity; an imposing wall facing east. The west slope, however, is a different story. This is a long, sloping Sierra of foot-

Left, elk once roamed the Sacramento Valley.
Above, Cathedral Rocks, Yosemite.

granite domes and towers thousands of feet high, as sheer as if they had been lopped off with a knife. It was actually ancient glaciers that carved out the bowl of Yosemite, Touolumne (pronounced *Too-all-o-me*) and the other spectacular canyons of the region. The polished granite and the rarefied air lend a feeling of crispness and clarity found in few other places.

In summer, the high season, avoid the crowds and buses of Yosemite Valley, however tempting. Opt instead for a visit to the remoter locations of the park, perhaps not as spectacular, but more scenic, without the bumper-to-bumper cars. Or set your sights on one of the other Sierra wonders.

Incidentally, the Merced and Touolumne rivers that run though Yosemite Valley and Hetch Hetchy, respectively, become torrential whitewater rapids just downstream from the park entrance. Both rivers are frequented by commercial river companies, and the Touolumne River, a gorgeous wilderness whitewater, has protected national status as a Wild and Scenic River.

A good distance north of Yosemite, almost due east of San Francisco and Sacramento, is the sapphire of the Sierra, Lake Tahoe. This has the distinction of being the largest and most scenic lake in two states (it is split down the middle by the California-Nevada state lines), tucked in the bowl formed by high alpine peaks, redwood groves and pine forests. Tahoe is part outdoors playground, with the state's best snow sports, golfing, horseback riding, waterskiing and so on, depending on the season, and part tourist park, with many boutiques, casinos (on the Nevada side) and cheap hotels.

Choice sports: Tahoe has two outdoors seasons: summer, when waterskiing on the lake is king; and winter (November through early May in good years) when the snow pack leads to cross-country and downhill skiing. Snowboarding is the favorite sport of the young; telemark or back-country skiing, whereby you climb a mountain on skis and ski down, is also gaining favor.

The ski areas that attract the most tourists, Squaw Valley on the North Shore, and Heavenly Valley at the South Lake, are huge, full-featured resorts. Squaw has a giant hotel, an Olympic history, an ice skating rink on top of the mountain, a bungee jumping tower and a golf course. Heavenly is similar. Many smaller areas, with names like Kirkwood, Homewood, Sugar Bowl, North Star and Donner Ridge, are friendlier spots to ski, though the sheer vertical drops are not as great. In the summer, adventurers can carry mountain bikes on the lifts of many ski areas, exploring the vast alpine network of trails, some with a bird's-eye view of Tahoe.

<u>Right</u>, naturalist John Muir called the Sierras the "Range of Lights."

It's the hills more than anything that offer San Francisco's visitors such a variety of vistas. On foot they're a chore to climb but by bus, auto or cable car, every trip is an adventure and the resultant views, the glimpses of the bay, make it all worthwhile. Which is not to say there isn't a lot to see at sea level too.

For a city just a few miles wide and long, San Francisco covers a great deal of terrain – natural and social – offering visitors seemingly endless options. At least a dozen distinct neighborhoods are tucked within the narrow city limits, surrounded by truly stunning natural beauty. It is a city of genres – a place in which encountering the haphazard energy of an ethnic community, the impressive arrogance of an elite neighborhood, and the irresistible tackiness of a tourist trap merges into a chaotic, but never dull, portrait.

From the rich living atop Nob Hill to the homeless in the Tenderloin, San Francisco offers a vast social and topographical chasm to explore, observe, and experience. Inevitably, however, the city is an encounter with people – of all shapes, sizes and persuasions – who express their idiosyncrasies in unabashed and unusual ways. San Francisco is a *bricolage* of cultures – seemingly ad hoc, yet somehow hanging together with a sense of permanence.

It is virtually impossible, then, to figure out exactly what one will find in San Francisco. But a healthy spirit of adventure, whether subtle or reckless – along with a comfortable pair of sneakers – is a prerequisite for a visit to this city.

There are always some wonderful surprises awaiting those who choose to venture off the beaten path. On the following pages, we hope to lead you in the right direction in terms of what to see and do, but don't take our word for it. See and do for yourself.

In the following sections, San Francisco is mapped out as a series of neighborhoods full of sights, experiences and activities. While not *all* of what is available in San Francisco is covered here, what is presented reflects a combination of the city's popular and out of the way offerings. The Northern Waterfront, North Beach, Chinatown, SoMa, Union Square, Japantown, the Castro and Mission neighborhoods, as well as Golden Gate Park are represented as worthwhile areas to visit.

For travelers interested in other parts of northern California, a final section explores some of the best day trips that can be made while visiting the city.

Preceding pages: bridging the gap; Alcatraz island from Russian Hill; mansions in Pacific Heights; Transamerica Pyramid at night. **Left,** San Francisco's many towers.

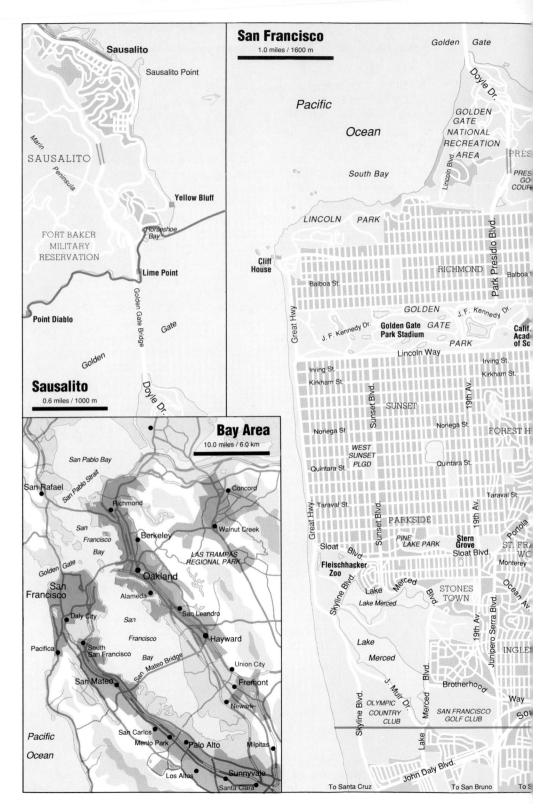

Sausalito

Sausalito Point

SAUSALITO

Marin Peninsula

FORT BAKER
MILITARY
RESERVATION

Point Diablo

Yellow Bluff

Horseshoe Bay

Lime Point

Golden Gate Bridge

Golden Gate

Sausalito
0.6 miles / 1000 m

Doyle Dr.

San Francisco
1.0 miles / 1600 m

Golden Gate

Doyle Dr.

Pacific

Ocean

South Bay

GOLDEN GATE NATIONAL RECREATION AREA

Lincoln Blvd.

PRES

PRES
GO
COUR

LINCOLN PARK

Cliff House

Balboa St.

Park Presidio Blvd.

RICHMOND

Balboa

GOLDEN

Great Hwy.

J. F. Kennedy Dr.

J. F. Kennedy Dr.

Golden Gate
Park Stadium

GATE

PARK

Calif.
Acad
of Sc

Lincoln Way

Irving St.

Kirkham St.

Sunset Blvd.

SUNSET

19th Av.

Irving St.

Kirkham St.

FOREST H

Noriega St.

WEST SUNSET PLGD

Noriega St.

Quintara St.

Quintara St.

Taraval St.

Great Hwy.

Taraval St.

Sunset Blvd.

PARKSIDE

19th Av.

Portola

Sloat

Blvd.

PINE LAKE PARK

Stern Grove

Sloat Blvd.

ST. FR
WO

Fleischhacker Zoo

Skyline Blvd.

Lake
Lake Merced

Merced

Blvd.

STONES TOWN

Monterey

Ocean Av.

19th Av.

Lake

Merced

J. Muir Dr.

Merced Blvd.

Juninero Serra Blvd.

Brotherhood

INGLE

OLYMPIC
COUNTRY
CLUB

Skyline Blvd.

Lake

SAN FRANCISCO
GOLF CLUB

Way

So

John Daly Blvd.

Bay Area
10.0 miles / 6.0 km

San Pablo Bay

San Rafael

San Pablo Strait

Richmond

Concord

San
Francisco
Bay

Berkeley

Walnut Creek

LAS TRAMPAS
REGIONAL PARK

Golden Gate

Oakland

San
Francisco

Alameda

San Leandro

Daly City

San

Francisco

Hayward

Pacifica

South
San Francisco

Bay

Union City

San Mateo

San Mateo Bridge

Fremont

Newark

San Carlos

Menlo Park

Palo Alto

Milpitas

Pacific

Ocean

Los Altos

Sunnyvale

Santa Clara

To Santa Cruz

To San Bruno

To S

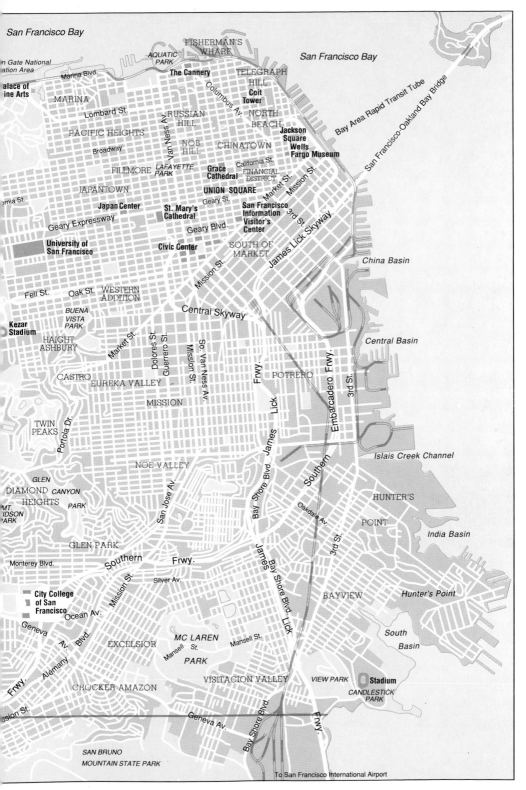

San Francisco Bay

FISHERMAN'S WHARF

AQUATIC PARK

The Cannery

TELEGRAPH HILL

San Francisco Bay

n Gate National ation Area

Marina Blvd.

alace of ine Arts

MARINA

Coit Tower

Lombard St.

RUSSIAN HILL

NORTH BEACH

Bay Area Rapid Transit Tube

PACIFIC HEIGHTS

NOB HILL

CHINATOWN

Jackson Square

San Francisco-Oakland Bay Bridge

Broadway

Wells Fargo Museum

California St.

FILLMORE

LAFAYETTE PARK

Grace Cathedral

FINANCIAL DISTRICT

JAPANTOWN

UNION SQUARE

Market St.

Mission St.

Japan Center

St. Mary's Cathedral

Geary St.

San Francisco Information Visitor's Center

3rd St.

China Basin

ornia St.

Geary Expressway

Geary Blvd.

University of San Francisco

Civic Center

SOUTH OF MARKET

James Lick Skyway

Fell St.

Oak St.

WESTERN ADDITION

Central Basin

BUENA VISTA PARK

Central Skyway

Kezar Stadium

Market St.

Dolores St.

Guerrero St.

So. Van Ness Av.

Mission St.

Frwy.

POTRERO

3rd St.

HAIGHT ASHBURY

CASTRO

EUREKA VALLEY

MISSION

Lick

James

Embarcadero Frwy.

Islais Creek Channel

TWIN PEAKS

Portola Dr.

NOE VALLEY

Bay Shore Blvd.

Southern

HUNTER'S

GLEN

DIAMOND HEIGHTS

CANYON PARK

San Jose Av.

Oakdale Av.

POINT

India Basin

MT. IDSON ARK

GLEN PARK

Southern

Frwy.

3rd St.

Hunter's Point

Monterey Blvd.

Silver Av.

James

Bay Shore Blvd.

BAYVIEW

South Basin

City College of San Francisco

Mission St.

Lick

Geneva

Ocean Av.

Av.

Blvd.

EXCELSIOR

MC LAREN

Mansell St.

Mansell St.

VIEW PARK

Stadium

Alemany

Mansell St.

PARK

CANDLESTICK PARK

Frwy.

CROCKER AMAZON

VISITACION VALLEY

ssion St.

Geneva Av.

Bay Shore Blvd.

Frwy.

SAN BRUNO MOUNTAIN STATE PARK

To San Francisco International Airport

121

NORTHERN WATERFRONT

The picture is now a pretty one down at the water's edge, San Francisco's historic northern waterfront, where the city and the bay have their most dynamic meeting. Once a working port and industrial district, today the waterfront, from Fisherman's Wharf to the Embarcadero Center, is still a good place for fishing and sailing. But as over 10 million visitors a year can attest, the waterfront has become a magnet for shopping, dining, and seeing art and theater.

Disastrous as the October 1989 earthquake that struck the San Francisco Bay area was, there are those who felt they could see a silver lining. For among the material casualties of the 7.0 quake was the Embarcadero Freeway – a main traffic artery into San Francisco that had hugged the city waterfront like a giant fence. It was severely damaged and had to be demolished, opening up previ-

Left, a panhandling welcome. **Below**, Ghirardelli Square.

ously obscured views of the northern waterfront and restoring one of the world's most famous ports to its stately grandeur. For years the elevated highway's critics had tried to get it removed and here, at one stroke, nature had done the job for them.

When the freeway came down at last, longtime *San Francisco Chronicle* columnist Alice Kahn announced: "The Ferry Building has been liberated! You can see it! Beyond, the pier buildings curve in a gracious line like bridal attendants posed for a wedding picture."

On the waterfront: Alongside hundreds of sailboats and the ferries packed with tourists and commuters alike, San Francisco's maritime history is moored here along the waterfront. An historical waterfront retrospective starts at the **Hyde Street Pier**, where several venerable ships are open to public inspection.

Built in 1890, the steam-driven *Eureka* ferried people between San Francisco and Tiburon before the bay had bridges. The *Alma*, a scow-schooner, hauled hay, produce and lumber around the bay, while the *Eppleton Hall*, built in England in 1914, traveled as far as Panama. The *C.A. Thayer*, a wooden-hulled schooner, was a lumber ship that worked the California coast. Its last captain captured its final voyage on film, which can be seen during the tour.

The *Balclutha*, last of the square-riggers to work the salmon trade, is also here, having moved from her long-time berth at Pier 43. Built in 1886, the *Balclutha* made 17 trips around the Cape, was shipwrecked and served a brief stint as a movie star before her final voyage in 1930.

Right next to the Hyde Street Pier, **Pier 45** remains a working pier, as the all-too-fishy odors will readily confirm. Here, fishermen depart each day before dawn and return with sand dabs, scallops, Dungeness crabs and sea bass. The corrugated metal sheds lining the docks are **Fish Alley**, where the catch of the day is packed, ready to be sold. The *Pampanito*, a 300-ft (90-meter) sub-

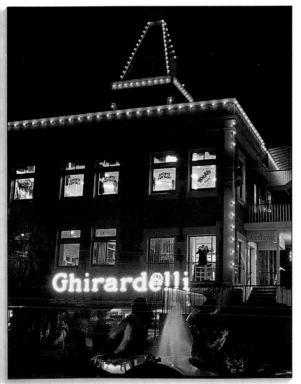

marine that played an active role in World War II, is also berthed on Pier 45 and open to the public.

If you've missed out in some way on San Francisco's seafaring lore, stop by the **National Maritime Museum** on Beach Street, an Art Deco structure that bears a remarkable resemblance to a boat. Inside are intricate model ships, a maritime library and all manner of ocean-going memorabilia.

The **Ghirardelli Square** clock tower stands as a signpost to the Fisherman's Wharf area. Occupying the entire block bounded by North Point, Polk, Beach and Larkin streets, Ghirardelli Square is an always-bustling retail center geared toward the city's visitors. Its imposing red brick structure was originally a wool factory that produced Civil War uniforms.

Before there was gold in California, however, there was chocolate. In 1849, Domingo Ghirardelli's factory opened just 13 days prior to the discovery at Sutter's Mill in the Sierra foothills. So much chocolate was made here between 1893 and the early 1960s that some maintain that chocolate still oozes from the old walls when it rains.

Although the original Ghirardelli chocolate vats – and working factory – have moved to San Leandro in the East Bay, Ghirardelli still offers daily tours and chocolate-making demonstrations. And if you don't have a sweet tooth, the square has over 70 other restaurants and shops as well as a spectacular view of the bay. The Kite Shop, for example, has just about every imaginable object that can be tied on a string. Folk Ark International has handicrafts from the world over, and other shops feature goods from Greece, France and Ireland.

The Ghirardelli courtyard shelters 120-year-old olive trees as well as a stage for comics and street performers. Many careers have been launched here, including that of actor Robin Williams. Wednesdays are audition nights, the time to catch the newest talent. For more seasoned fare, try **Cobb's Comedy**

The city by the bay.

Club, a stand-up comic showcase.

For those with an appetite for drama, the **Waterfront Theater**, home to the **Pocket Opera** (whose repertoire includes children's and contemporary works) is an entertaining spot.

Next to the maritime museum at the end of the Hyde Street cable car line is **The Cannery** on Leavenworth Street. This beautiful old fruit-packing plant, built at the turn of the century, was saved from the wrecking ball in 1967 when it was converted into a lavish 3-story shopping complex housing more than 40 shops and restaurants with varied cuisine. It offers splendid views. To the west, old Fort Mason was converted into a cultural center, one of whose major attractions is the **Mexican Museum**, a showcase for Mexican and Chicano art.

If the wharf triggers an impulse for angling, you can charter a fishing trip at Miss Farallones or sign up at any of the boats that offer day trips for salmon fishing, halibut, or other varieties, depending on the season. If you are a less active sailor, board a **Red and White Fleet** ferry headed across the bay to Angel Island, Alcatraz or Tiburon. Departures are from the pier near Pier 43.

An appetite for fruits of the sea can be satisfied in more passive fashion by strolling down **Jefferson Street** where sidewalk vendors boil and steam shellfish all day long. (The nearby **Bourdin Bakery** sells excellent sourdough bread to complete your picnic.)

The streets of Fisherman's Wharf are honeycombed with gift shops and restaurants where the food can be as superb as the views. **The Bay Company** is a souvenir center as well as a helpful source of tourist information. For Christmas in July, shop at The Incredible Christmas Store. Things get even more bizarre at **Ripley's Believe It or Not**, and **The Guiness Book of World Records Museum** challenges everyone's notions of the possible.

The 45-acre (18-hectare) **Fisherman's Wharf Complex**, built in 1978

Outdoor dining.

on the site of an abandoned cargo pier, from timber salvaged from other wharves, is today the most visited place in the city. Hundreds of sailboats and yachts berth here and two garden parks provide plenty of room for picnicking.

Like the street artists in Ghirardelli Square, Pier 39 has a few ocean-going performers of its own. In recent years, the pier has become second home to a gang of more than 400 boisterous sea lions, drawn, apparently, by a bumper harvest of the bay's spawning herring – a sea-lion favorite. Fifty or more sea lions took up residence on the boat docks next to Pier 39, from which they made nightly fishing forays into the bay. The concept had legs – or fins. Within a year, the population grew to nearly 400.

Old-time merchants sometimes complain about their noisy neighbors – their untidy toilet habits and strong halitosis (a result of their fish diet) don't make them popular up-close – but they never forget that it's the sea lions – and not the merchants – that so many of the tourists come to see. Away from the wildlife at Pier 39, you can get even closer to the water with a **Blue and Gold Fleet** Bay Cruise. Luxury yachts are also available for hire. Here, too, is the **Eagle Cafe**, a venerable waterfront eatery, which was moved intact to the second floor of Pier 39 when waterfront renewal threatened.

Center Stage is an outdoor venue for street performers. Indoors, **The San Francisco Experience** packs the tumultuous history of the city into a half-hour film, using 35 computerized projectors. Children will adore the high-tech fun at **Funtasia**, a video arcade carnival, and everybody has a chance to be a star at **Music Tracks Recording Studios**, where you can sing it your way.

The speciality Left Hand World, one of about 100 in the complex, features everything from measuring cups to fountain pens for the left-handed. And **Magnet P.I.** boasts the largest assortment of handmade refrigerator magnets in the world. Before leaving the area you might like to head a couple of blocks up Hyde Street to the famous **Buena Vista** café where you can sit and sip an Irish coffee, (which was invented here) while watching the cable cars turn around.

The Embarcadero: From Fisherman's Wharf the waterfront wraps around the bay, curving under **Telegraph Hill** to the **Embarcadero** at a point where the bay is obscured mostly by warehouses. (The best approach is via Market Street.) Most of the land here was reclaimed from the sea. Condominiums, restaurants and shops close to downtown and the Financial District give the area its economic vitality.

An essential part of this scheme is the **Embarcadero Center**, a massive retail and office complex. Restaurants and upscale shops abound: Barra of Italy features designer clothing, and The Nature Company has toys that range from giant inflatable iguanas to kaleidoscopes. The area also has chic restaurants such as the Fog City Diner or the Waterfront Restaurant, both offering spectacular views of the East Bay. There is nightly live music and dancing at Pier 23, at the restaurant of that name.

The heart of the Embarcadero, however, is the **Ferry Building**. Built around the turn of the century, it survived the earthquake of 1906 with no more consequence than a stopped clock – the first time it had ceased to tick. The 230-ft (70-meter) tower is a near copy of the campanile of Seville's Cathedral. Before the construction of the bay bridges, the Ferry Building was the second busiest passenger terminal in the world. Ferries still carry commuters to Tiburon and Sausalito, providing an inexpensive way to spend an afternoon on the bay. **Covarrubias' mural**, preserved from the 1939 Golden Gate International Exposition, colorfully lines the ramp leading to the **World Trade Center**.

The western end of the waterfront is dominated by the **Presidio**, a park cum military base best explored by car. From Union Square, bus No. 28 goes through the Presidio to the beginning of the 2-mile (3-km) long **Golden Gate Bridge**.

ALCATRAZ

For decades, hundreds of prisoners tried to escape Alcatraz island by attempting the treacherous, 1½-mile swim to San Francisco. Today, hundreds of triathletes swim the same course in about 25 minutes, while hundreds of thousands of tourists each year visit "the Rock."

Surrounded by frigid waters and the swift currents of San Francisco Bay, the 22½-acre (9-hectare) Alcatraz island was once home to the most notorious criminals of the century, including infamous Chicago mob boss Al Capone and "Machine Gun" Kelly. Set in the middle of one of the world's most beautiful harbors and accessible by ferry, this remote hump of rock remains one of the city's most popular tourist attractions.

Just a half-mile north of Alcatraz is idyllic Angel Island (also accessible by ferry), where picnickers spend sunny afternoons on the beaches and surrounding hills. To the west, the crimson-colored span of the Golden Gate straddles the bay and the entrance to the Pacific. San Francisco's cityscape looms from the south. Those views never escaped the prisoners. "Machine Gun" Kelly summed it up: "There was never a day when you didn't see what you were missing." On New Year's Eve, prisoners rattled their tin cups at the stroke of midnight.

Alcatraz was christened *La Isla de los Alcatraces* (Island of the Pelicans) by Spanish explorers in 1775. Its strategic position in the middle of the bay made it ideal for use as a defensive and disciplinary facility, and by the mid-1800s US Army soldiers stood guard on the island's rocky bluffs. The first military prisoners to serve time in the concrete cell block were, ironically, those who helped build it in 1912.

In 1934, in the wake of the Prohibition-induced nationwide crime waves, the Federal Bureau of Prisons decided on Alcatraz as the ideal facility to house its most hardened criminals. That year, 1,953 – including Al Capone – were rounded up and sent to the Rock. Alcatraz offered just three privileges for the best-behaved inmates: a recreation yard, a library, and/or a factory job.

The cells at Alcatraz were designed for maximum security. They are just 5 ft by 9 ft (1.5 meters by 3 meters), and the inmates spent 16 to 23 hours a day in them. All privileges, even the right to work, had to be earned by good behavior. Infractions of the rules were punished by confinement in the Segregation Unit, otherwise known as solitary confinement, where even light could be denied to an inmate.

The solitary life of a prison inmate was conveyed to a wide audience in *The Birdman of Alcatraz*, a movie starring former circus acrobat Burt Lancaster. Based on the life of Bob Stroud, who spent his 53 years of incarceration studying the science of birds, and eventually became a world authority, the film gained Oscar nominations for Lancaster as well as Telly Savalas and Thelma Ritter, in supporting roles.

No one was ever executed at Alcatraz, and over a period of 30 years, it proved to be escape-proof, despite the best efforts of canny prisoners. The most ingenious plot involved three men who, after tricking guards into thinking they were asleep, slipped off the island on a makeshift raft – made of smuggled raincoats and life jackets. They were never seen or heard from again. In all, five escapees are still missing, believed to have drowned. In 1961, faced with soaring costs, Attorney General Robert Kennedy ordered the penitentiary closed.

Daily tours begin with a 12-minute ferry ride from Fisherman's Wharf. ■

Left, inside the prison. **Right**, one of several guard towers.

129

TRIES

NEL 1956

ESSO

NORTH BEACH

"Little City" is what Italian immigrants called this hilly area of San Francisco when they settled here 100 years ago. Situated below Telegraph Hill's odd-looking Coit Memorial Tower, North Beach is – loosely speaking – the neighborhood found between Washington Square Park and Broadway.

On one end, at **Washington Square Park**, you'll find Saint Peter and Paul Church, a picturesque cathedral that is still a favorite setting for traditional Italian weddings. On any given Saturday, you're likely to see yards of white silk billowing in the breeze and dapper, olive-skinned young men in tuxedos. Oblivious to the festivities only yards away in the square, an elderly Chinese woman may practice *Tai Chi*. Down on **Broadway**, scantily clad female barkers prepare to chat up sailors, tourists and other lonely hearts to entice them into their sex clubs.

Java and jive: Although no trend or event could ever dilute North Beach's Italian flavor, a fascinating history of literary figures, comedic celebrities and strip joints has added immeasurably to the neighborhood's great color. The Beat poets once gathered here for java and inspiration; a young Woody Allen and Bill Crosby had their taste of the limelight at Enrico's Hungry I; and Carol Doda and Magnolia Thunderpussy bared their considerable physical attributes to enthusiastic audiences.

In recent years the Italians and other longstanding communities of Irish, Basque and Mexican families have been joined by Asian ethnic groups. In addition to the Chinese, who now make up most of North Beach's population, the latest wave of new arrivals have been young professionals. Now they have discovered North Beach, the skyrocketing value of real estate has priced some long-time residents out of homes their families have been in for generations.

Today, North Beach is a delightfully diverse neighborhood; stop in at any café and you may find yourself sipping espresso among elderly Italian men in fisherman's caps, playing cards and exclaiming in their native tongue; scruffy poets scrawling verse in their notebooks; or stylishly dressed Beautiful People who seem constantly to be posing for invisible cameras.

Oddly enough, this strongly family-oriented ethnic neighborhood has always drawn free-thinkers, artists, poets and cultural rebels of every kind. At the turn of the century, Frank Norris, George Sterling and other members of San Francisco's literary vanguard gathered here, just as boomtown writers Mark Twain and Bret Harte did decades before them. In the 1950s, the renowned Beat generation, led by Jack Kerouac and Allen Ginsberg, found North Beach's plentiful coffeehouses the perfect environment for their poetry readings. Columnist Herb Caen nicknamed these goateed, finger-snapping poets dressed from head to toe in black, "beatniks."

The notion of sexual freedom found fertile ground in North Beach, and in 1969 Carol Doda, along with many other well-endowed exhibitionists, began dancing topless. In the 1970s the punk movement found a home here in clubs like Mabuhay Gardens and the Stone. The **Stone** continues to showcase some of today's hardcore rock bands.

Early history: Before the Gold Rush, North Beach was the home of Juana Briones and her family, who built their adobe house in 1836 near the intersection of Powell and Filbert streets. Señora Briones operated a small *rancho* on the outskirts of the village, then called Yerba Buena, supplying fresh meat and produce to passing ships, and occasionally giving shelter to a deserting sailor.

When gold was discovered in the Sierra Mountains in 1848, thousands of immigrants poured into Yerba Buena Cove in one of the wildest booms ever to hit the West. A huddle of shantytowns, whorehouses, saloons and gambling halls quickly sprouted up along Broadway, and on Pacific near Kearny and Montgomery streets. This was the infamous Barbary Coast, named for the equally unsavory pirate headquarters in North Africa. The term *shanghai*, the practice of drugging a sailor's drink and sending him off to work on an undermanned ship, came from this squalid bit of civilization. For more than 60 years, this area's notorious reputation thrived and grew.

Settlers began pouring into San Francisco, squeezing into the valley between Russian and Telegraph hills toward the northern shore, from which North Beach takes its name. In those days, the bay reached as far inland as Francisco Street to the north and Montgomery Street to the south, before landfill extended the area to accommodate boatloads of new San Franciscans, many of whom had just deserted ships. Now, entire city blocks stand on land that was once a harbor in which sailors left ships to rot while they went off to strike gold.

When fires swept through the district after the earthquake of 1906 devastated most of the city, the Italians on Telegraph Hill who were trapped without water reportedly fought the blaze with buckets of "dago red," the neighborhood's local vintage. For many months, the homeless occupied Washington Square as survivors set about the long and arduous task of reconstruction, but within a year North Beach was almost completely rebuilt, becoming one of the first districts in the city to recover from the earthquake.

Most homes, built without the benefit of architects, took on variations of a simple Edwardian style. Many buildings have since been renovated, some being given an Art Deco stucco finish during the 1930s, but for the most part the homes in North Beach remain unadorned two- or three-story wood frames with bay windows and back alleys. Both the buildings and their layout give North Beach the feel of a European *quartiere*, an intimate enclave of simple **Pizza to go.**

homes sheltered from the towering modern architecture located only a few blocks away.

A good place to start a tour of North Beach is far from the usual tourist attractions in the area of the old Barbary Coast, just south of Broadway in a part of town now called **Jackson Square**. The name is deceptive: you'll find no square here, just as you'll find no beach in North Beach, no telegraph on Telegraph Hill. What can be found, however, are a few vestiges of the Barbary Coast and a handful of beautifully restored buildings that survived the wide-spread destruction of 1906. It's a good place for the intrepid to take a stroll, but only in the day time; leave your cameras behind.

Modern Sodom: It was a vast market place of flesh and liquor where sailors and miners found fleeting pleasures, fast money, and just as likely, a violent end. Second to gambling, shoot-outs were the favored participant sport, and fortunes often rode on the wink of an eye. An infamous band of Australian convicts called the "Ducks" terrorized local shopkeepers for a period, until a group of vigilantes hunted them down with a kind of rough justice (*see page 145 for the full story*).

Most businesses in the Barbary Coast made their money trafficking in human bodies; either selling sex to '49ers or selling kidnapped sailors to the captains of hell ships. Both enterprises turned over high profits, and local politicians were more than happy to turn a blind eye in exchange for a piece of the action. A red light burned on almost every block, signalling both high class "parlors" and squalid "cribs," where prostitutes worked in rooms barely big enough to fit a bed into.

In the worst cases, Chinese girls were bought as slaves and made to work until they became sick or died. Hell ships came to these wharves in search of sailors for brutal voyages around the Cape or "Shanghai journeys" to the Far East. Hundreds of hapless men who dropped

Italians called North Beach "Little City."

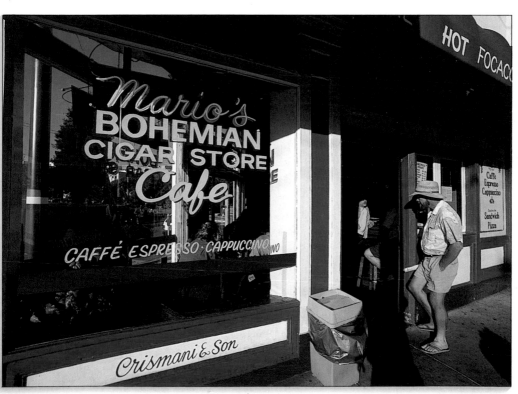

into local watering holes were kidnapped – or "shanghaied." Wily madams and saloon-keepers drugged the sailors with "Mickey Finns" or simply knocked them over the head, sometimes spiriting them away through trap doors built just for that purpose.

It is ironic that the birthplace of such unparalleled vice is now one of San Francisco's quieter neighborhoods. The Barbary Coast was almost completely destroyed in the fire of 1906, and although whoring and gambling continued for many years, neither pastime ever regained its original momentum. Renamed Jackson Square, the area is now home to architectural and interior design showrooms, most of them wholesalers which are not open to the public. But several buildings survived the flames, and many of them have been very well-preserved.

Travelers with an interest in urban restoration might check out the 700 block of **Montgomery Street**. Notable here is the impeccably restored **Belli Building**, the **California Steam and Navigation Building**, the **Ship Building** and the **Melodeon Theater Building**, all of them built in the late 1850s or 1860s. Around the corner, at Jackson Street and Hotaling Place, you will find the **Hotaling Warehouse**, a whiskey distillery which was immortalized by the Charles Field verse:

If, as they say, God spanked the town
For being over-frisky,
Why did He burn His Churches down
And spare Hotaling's whiskey?

West coast Broadway: Traveling north on Montgomery and then west on Broadway toward **Columbus Avenue**, the scene changes dramatically. These two blocks of Broadway were San Francisco's "great white way," a now somewhat faded assemblage of video parlors and strip joints offering the standard variety of commercial vice. Sleazy bars, watered-down liquor and live sex acts abound here. Long gone are the days when Carol Doda made "silicon" history. Sitting topless on a piano, she was

San Francisco's diminishing porn district.

lowered onto the stage, much to the delight of the audience who got a chance to see what implants are all about.

The great white way experienced a face-lift of sorts in the 1950s and onward, when such figures as Barbra Streisand, Johnny Mathis and Lenny Bruce plied their trades in the area's nightclubs, but elements of the "sleaze factor" still remain.

Strip joints, however, are struggling against the advent of videos and 1-900, numbers which allow porn consumers more anonymity. The Condor, for example, a long-standing landmark in North Beach, which was famed for the enormous neon woman attached to its facade, recently reopened as a benign, and rather colorless bar.

North Beach is a splendid place for people-watching, both because the population is so diverse and because the many coffee houses along Columbus Avenue provide perfect ringside seats. Proprietors leave windows open on warm days so that patrons can sit in the fresh air and bright sunlight and take in the vibrant street life.

On the other side of Union Street lies Washington Square Park, an expansive plot of grass that offers a delightful spot for a picnic. Molinari's Delicatessen at 373 Columbus, just across from **St Francis Church**, sells inexpensive chianti and the makings of a do-it-yourself Italian sandwich.

If you'd rather sit down to lunch in a more conventional manner, stop in at **Little Joe's**, 523 Broadway. This boisterous restaurant has large, family-style tables, ample counter seating and an open kitchen where chefs whip up tasty and reasonably priced pasta and seafood dishes. Heed the sign at the door: "Rain or shine there's always a line." Little Joe's is just as popular as it claims to be, so be prepared to wait your turn, especially on a weekend. Don't be discouraged from checking it out, though; the line moves quickly.

The intersection of Broadway, Columbus and Grant, marks the meeting

North Beach's Little Italy.

place of at least four distinct neighborhoods. To the southwest, Chinatown sprawls out in a confusion of bright lights and narrow alleys; to the south, the Transamerica Pyramid rises from the Financial District; San Francisco's "Great White Way" stretches along neon-lit Broadway; and the heart of North Beach lies north on Columbus as far as Fisherman's Wharf.

Literary landmark: On this corner is Lawrence Ferlinghetti's **City Lights Bookstore**, recently named a National Literary Landmark. Founded in 1953, City Lights was the first all-paperback bookstore in the country. Soon after its opening, it began to publish a number of its own titles, most of them works by local writers who were to become the founders of San Francisco's beatnik scene. They were soon joined by such figures as Allen Ginsberg, Neal Cassady and Jack Kerouac.

On October 7, 1955, Ginsberg electrified the community of North Beach poets with his performance of *Howl* at the famed Six Gallery reading. Kerouac deemed the event "the birth of the San Francisco Poetry Renaissance," and Ferlinghetti immediately requested the manuscript for publication.

Howl, the incendiary poem, was printed in England. When Ferlinghetti tried to ship the books back into the United States, customs officials seized them and arrested the shopowner on obscenity charges. Civil libertarians, professors and fellow artists rallied around Ferlinghetti, and City Lights and the beatniks of North Beach were catapulted into the national spotlight almost overnight. Ferlinghetti eventually won his case, setting a precedent for a generation of writers and publishers compelled to test the boundaries of political, social and moral standards.

To this day, City Lights remains one of San Francisco's most important literary centers. Bookstore lovers will find City Lights well worth an afternoon, or even an evening (it's open until midnight on weekdays, 1am on weekends,

Lawrence Ferlinghetti and his City Lights Bookstore.

so you can work it into an evening of dinner and drinks).

The shop is known for its leftist leanings, and accordingly boasts an especially good selection of books on social change. Poetry, of course, is also well-served, with a whole room dedicated to the bards. City Lights also sponsors a full schedule of readings by new and established writers. Check the bulletin boards or ask a clerk for details of upcoming events.

"Mad ones" bar: Next door to City Lights you'll find another classic beatnik haunt, **Vesuvio,** a bar adorned with colorful stained-glass windows and the words "We are itching to get out of Portland, Oregon," painted over the entranceway. In its heyday, Vesuvio was owned by Henri Lenoir, whose collections of exotic bar-room paraphernalia still adorn the delightful but rather cramped bar. Near the front door is a list of names drawn in wet cement, which commemorates a handful of North Beach's "mad ones."

At the bottom of the list, a simple epitaph records their fate: "All 86'd." Before taking over Vesuvio, Lenoir managed **Specs'**, located across Columbus in the tiny Saroyan Place. Specs' was a bohemian hotspot in the 1940s, a famed lesbian bar called 12 Adler Place, a nightclub featuring jazz, belly dancers and Middle Eastern music. Tucked away in the corner of this blind alley, Specs' has somehow managed to maintain a low profile throughout its long tenure as a favorite watering hole for San Francisco's underground.

A few years ago, North Beach alleys took on the names of famous writers. The tiny street that divides City Lights from Vesuvio's became **Jack Kerouac Place**, and Specs insisted that its end of the alley be called **Saroyan Place**, after the late Armenian-American novelist William Saroyan.

The offbeat bar is decorated with an exotic hodge-podge of sailor and dock-worker memorabilia, Eskimo carvings, posters, scrimshaw, wartime propaganda

The beatniks' favorite.

– even a dried whale penis. Graffiti lovers should check out the latest offerings, a testament to North Beach's sustained ability to inspire its residents.

A couple of doors down, **Tosca**, (242 Columbus Ave) a strangely elegant bar decorated in vintage 1940s diner trappings, plays opera from its jukebox. It's said to be a favorite spot for the few Hollywood stars who spend their off-hours in San Francisco. Even if you don't spy Nicholas Cage or Melanie Griffith, try the house cappucino, an alcoholic concoction that, while seemingly a harmless dessert drink, can be quite potent.

Just where North Beach begins to give way to the Financial District, half a block off Columbus, a fashionable restaurant called the **Cypress Club** (500 Jackson) draws the curious as well as genuine customers. Its biomorphic, Gaudí-like decor and excessive brass accessories made it one of the most-talked about restaurants in town when it first opened a few years ago, and it

continues to challenge design buffs to come up with a definition.

Dinner isn't cheap, but a drink at the bar – a surprisingly relaxed, unpretentious affair – is a less expensive way to take in the surroundings. Although some locals feel its flashy decor is more fitting to Los Angeles than San Francisco, it's truly a sight to behold.

The main drag: Columbus Avenue cuts diagonally across Broadway, leading directly into the heart of North Beach. This is the district's main thoroughfare, and every year on Columbus Day hordes of revelers fill the street in a celebration of its namesake – although in recent years, indigenous populations, who have found Columbus' discovery poor cause for rejoicing, have protested against these activities.

On the first Sunday in October, Sicilian parishioners from Saints Peter and Paul Church conduct a procession honoring *Maria Santissima del Lume* (Mary, Most Holy Mother of Light) along Columbus Avenue to Fisherman's Wharf, where the traditional Blessing of the Fleet takes place. Restaurants, delis, pastry shops and cafés line Columbus Avenue. For the most part, the cuisine here is northern Italian with a few Chinese, Mexican, Creole and sushi places mixed in. The atmosphere ranges from no-frills slop houses to first-class dining rooms.

A few of these establishments are so off-the-wall they're difficult to classify without a lengthy description. At the very least, visitors can count on hearty meals at reasonable prices, and sometimes one even enjoys a sublime experience of culinary rapture.

Seafood lovers should keep an eye out for Dungeness crab, a famous and celebrated San Francisco treat. The bay's third-largest commercial catch, the Dungeness crab is as tasty and satisfying a dish as its Maynard cousin or the New England lobster. The season extends from mid-November right through June. During these months, you can find it served in a plethora of mouth-watering ways – shredded in salads, submerged in black bean or tomato sauce (the last of these is called *cioppinos*) flavorfully steamed, or seasoned with garlic and ginger in Asian cuisine. There are far too many restaurants to list individually, but here are just a few of the more noteworthy.

At the **Gold Spike** the first thing patrons notice upon entry are the calling cards and dollar bills tacked up everywhere – on the walls, on the ceiling, even on the moose head. Customers are encouraged to leave their cards anywhere they like, and over the years the place has accumulated several hundred, with addresses from all over the world. In addition to the calling cards, patrons will also find one of the city's better collections of bar-room kitsch, including the heads of moose and deer, antlers, stuffed birds, vintage shotguns, pistols, garlic braids, war memorabilia and a giant sailfish – all of it just dusty enough to conjure up images of an attic or basement.

Close-knit houses reflect North Beach's penchant for community.

The Gold Spike holds the honor of being one of San Francisco's oldest establishments owned by the same family, operated in the same location. The Mechetti family first opened the Columbus Candy Store in this location during Prohibition, but profits from spaghetti and bathtub gin soon outstripped the gumball trade, and by the 1940s the storefront became the Gold Spike. Today, the bar serves a limited but solid choice of regular dishes and specials. It's a great place for cold beer, hot minestrone and a long pleasant evening of shooting the breeze.

Up the hill on Green Street is **Caffe Sport**, one of North Beach's few Sicilian restaurants. Bring along a healthy dose of humor and plenty of patience, because this place can be as maddening as it is enjoyable. Patrons are seated en masse at 6.30pm and 9pm and the place is always crowded. As a rule dinner arrives at least half an hour late, so customers have plenty of time to check out the decor, which, even by North Beach standards, is in a league of its own. Caffe Sport displays a perverse and brightly colored collage of garish baubles and tasteless knick-knacks.

By the time patrons get over their initial bewilderment, the staff begins to call out names and after much shuffling, bumping and general disorder, everybody manages to find their seat. This is not the place for a romantic dinner for two: unless you sit at the counter, you'll find yourself at a huge table with other patrons. Chances are that the whole table will have to share one or two menus, so by the time it gets around to you, you'll have to make a quick decision. But not to fear: whatever you decide, the waiter will inevitably advise against your first selection – cajoling, scolding, haggling and joking until you finally concede defeat and accept the recommendation.

The abuse causes spontaneous emotional bonding between customers, and when the food finally comes, everyone is usually happy that they stayed. Caffe

One of many whistle-wetters.

Sport serves some of the finest seafood dishes in North Beach, heavy on the garlic and very rich. For a more conventional setting, there are at least 15 other restaurants near Columbus that provide excellent food and ambience. **Fior d'Italia** is the oldest Italian restaurant in the city, and after several changes in management it is still one of the finest. Fior d'Italia is located on Union Street directly across from Washington Square and opens onto a view of Saints Peter and Paul's romantic, romanesque spires.

Located off Columbus on Stockton Street, the **North Beach Restaurant** observes a strict home-made philosophy. Not only do the owners cure their own *prosciutto* and make fresh pasta every day, but they also use their own fishing boat to ensure the quality of their ever-changing seafood menu.

Set across from Washington Square in the middle of "Restaurant Alley," the **Washington Square Bar & Grill** attracts well-known literati for dinner, drinks and late-night chatter. Other long-standing family-style restaurants that carry reputations for excellence include **Green Valley**, **Ristorante Firenze**, **Capp's Corner**, **New Pisa** and **Ristorante Grifone**. For a more stylish setting, try **Michelangelo Cafe** or **The Stinking Rose**, whose specialty is garlic with everything.

Pizza, of course, is a favorite in this neighborhood, and a couple of establishments battle constantly for the honor of being called San Francisco's best pizzeria. **North Beach Pizza** offers a casual setting and hearty, inexpensive food. If there's a line at the Grant and Union location, you can stroll down Grant to **North Beach Too**, where the pizza is just as good though the atmosphere is lacking. For a kitschy, colorful experience, keep walking down Grant to **Viva's**, a small cozy restaurant with friendly waiters and outstanding pizza.

There are many outstanding cafés along Columbus. **Caffe Trieste** has been a favorite of artists, writers and musicians since the early days of the Beat **Bohemian rhapsody.**

movement. On Saturday mornings you can hear the owners conducting operatic sing-alongs or catch an impromptu performance by a visiting diva. **Mario's Bohemian Cigar Store**, **Caffe Puccini**, and **Caffe Roma** are also popular hangouts for local artists and the cappuccino and pastries tend to be first-rate at all four of them.

If visitors are looking for something sweet to bring home, try **Victoria Pastry** on Stockton Street for *biscotti* and *zabaglione* or **Stella Pastry** on Columbus for her famous *sacripantina*. If a classic Italian deli is desirable, stop in at **Molinari's Deli** for a king-size sandwich of *proscuitto, provolone, ricotta salata, mortadella* or a thousand other celebrations of cholesterol.

Upper Grant: The shopping continues with far more variety a block east of Columbus on **Grant Street**. The pace is much less hectic here, and the tiny shops are perfect for a leisurely afternoon of browsing or buying. There are still several family-run Italian businesses on Grant including **Figoni Hardware Co**. and the **Panama Canal Ravioli Factory**. In between, browsers will find galleries, boutiques, bars, antique shops, restaurants, cafés and Chinese markets. **The Shlock Shop** is an interesting survivor of North Beach's hippie days. Merchandise here includes antique paraphernalia ranging from 75-year-old eyeglasses to risque Victoriana.

Next door, the **Primal Art Center** maintains an intriguing collection of art from Africa and Oceania, and across the street, **Quantity Postcard's** selection of postcards will please even the most discriminating collector. Clothes boutiques also abound, ranging from the chic women's designs at **Donna** and the high-fashion boots and jackets at **North Beach Leather** to funky vintage shops where you can buy Levi's already worn in for you.

Also on Grant Street you'll find **La Trattoria** and **Cafe Jacqueline** and a dive called the **Lost & Found Saloon**. **Café society.** The **Savoy Tivoli** has plenty of open-air

seating along the sidewalk and attracts a lively crowd of local residents. Its street-side terrace is heated in the winter so you can enjoy its Old World feel all year round, though on a weekend night it feels more like a fashion show than a quaint village café. **Grant and Green**, a rollicking, down and dirty blues club, draws a varied clientele, ranging from college students to Harley hogs.

Washington Square: From Grant, it is a short walk down the steep incline of Union Street to **Washington Square**. This is the center of the neighborhood's social world, and every day here is a celebration of the incongruities that give North Beach its special character.

The sounds of Italian and Chinese mingle together as the old-timers gossip on the park benches. Old Italian patriarchs play *bocce* in the corner of the park reserved for the game, while their Chinese counterparts practice *Tai Chi* beneath the trees along its edge.

Facing Washington Square is the inspiring romanesque facade of **Saints**

Peter and Paul Roman Catholic Church. The inscription above the entrance is from the first canto of Dante's *Paradiso: "La Gloria Di Colui Che Tutto Muove Per L'Universo Penetra E Risplende"* (The glory of Him who moves all things shines throughout the universe).

A sign in the vestibule promises all San Franciscans of Italian descent the right to receive special religious services here; another sign lists schedules for English, Italian and Chinese masses. Soon after it was built, the newly-opened church was the target of several anarchistic bombings, and a closer look shows the scars on its white facade left by the explosions.

In characteristic North Beach fashion, the statue located in the center of Washington Square is not of anyone named Washington but, rather, of Benjamin Franklin. It was a gift to the city from an eccentric pioneer dentist named H.D. Cogswell, who amassed a large fortune by putting gold into miners' teeth – a sign of some status in a town that all but worshipped the glittering stuff.

Cogswell, an avid teetotaler, swore to build one public fountain for every saloon in San Francisco. Famous for his offbeat humor, he labeled the three fresh water spouts at the base of the statue Cal Seltzer, Vichy and Congress. On the west side of the square is a statue dedicated to the city's volunteer firemen. The work was bequeathed to the city by Lillie Hitchcock Coit, who also funded Coit Memorial Tower, the monolith that rises over Washington Square from the summit of Telegraph Hill. "Nobby Owld, Slobby Owld Telegraft Hill!"

From Washington Square, the easiest way to get to **Telegraph Hill** is directly up Union Street, where the sidewalk gives way to stairs to make the climbing easier. From the top of Union, visitors can take one of the several footpaths that wind around the uppermost peak to eventually arrive at **Pioneer Park**. Telegraph Hill has always been a part of, and apart from, North Beach. It was **The Polk Street Fair.**

144

largely ignored by early settlers who preferred to fill in the shallows of the bay rather than build on the hill's steep and inhospitable shoulders.

Irish stevedores were among the earliest to inhabit the hill, although the Italians soon displaced them. San Francisco's bohemian crowd were often seen partying in its clapboard shacks, until the well-to-do figured out what all the fuss was about and swiftly claimed the hill for their own. Today, real estate located on Telegraph Hill is some of the most expensive, and the most sought after, in the city.

Originally named *Loma Alta* by the Spaniards, the hill has gone under a number of names over the years, including Goat Hill, Windmill Hill, Tin Can Hill and Signal Hill. The last name refers to the efforts of two enterprising merchants who constructed a signaling station at the top of the hill to notify townspeople of ships approaching the harbor. Some years later the semaphore was replaced by an electrical telegraph

Folk toys for plain folks.

system. During the Gold Rush, the Chilean prostitutes put up tents in "Little Chile," a shanty town of South American immigrants on the hill's western slope.

On the eastern side of the hill was a similar cluster of ramshackle homes known as "Sydneytown," where Australian convicts called "Sydney Ducks" settled at about the same time. In February 1849, the Ducks clashed with members of a gang that called itself the "Hounds," later renamed the "Regulators," who made a career of extorting from local shopkeepers and harrassing the Chilenos. When a Chilean shopkeeper shot one of their members, the gang stormed Little Chile, killed and wounded several people and raped a number of women.

The attack outraged many upstanding citizens, and a group of 250 vigilantes came together to capture the worst offenders. They arrested 19 people, but only two went to prison; the others got off with little more than a slap on the wrist. Although largely ineffective, this

early display of public action set the stage for the Vigilance Committees of 1851 and 1856, which were both far more aggressive than the earlier 250-member committee.

At the top of Telegraph Hill, **Coit Memorial Tower** stands like a giant Roman column. This simple, fluted monument was erected in 1933 with funds left by Lillie Hitchcock Coit, an extremely eccentric heiress who chased fire trucks for kicks. Many people have noted the tower's resemblance to a firehose nozzle, but historians insist that this wasn't intentional.

As a teenager, Lillie became the official mascot of Knickerbocker Engine Company No. 5, and she spent long hours playing cards and gadding about in the company's uniform – much to the consternation of society ladies throughout the city. In order to show her admiration for these brave fire-fighters, Lillie left enough funds to the city to build a splendid commemorative tower.

Inside are spectacular murals depict-

ing images and themes from American labor in the 1930s. These murals were the vision of a group of local artists who proposed a federally-funded Works Progress Administration project. The plan called for an ensemble of artists to paint the interior of the tower with scenes reflecting their personal understanding of Depression-era California. Inspired particularly by Mexican painter Diego Riviera, some of the artists depicted labor scenes that reflected an overtly left-wing sentiment.

Subsequently, officials who saw the murals as communist propaganda, closed the tower. It was not a timely decision; the longshoremen's strike of 1934 was in full bloom, and the tower's closing lit the powder keg of tensions that erupted in the violence of Bloody Thursday, when two pickets were shot dead and over 100 people wounded.

For those whose legs can stand the arduous workout, there are two other trails along the slopes of Telegraph Hill. At the entrance of Pioneer Park, across the street from Coit Tower, visitors will find the **Greenwich Steps**, a lovely red brick path which winds down the beautifully landscaped hillside past some of the city's oldest, most desirable, and expensive homes.

At the bottom of the steps, turn left on Montgomery Street toward the cul-de-sac and a spectacular glimpse of the East Bay. The giant wood frame building perched on the edge of the cliff is **Julius' Castle**, one of the few restaurants located on Telegraph Hill, which specializes in northern Italian and French cuisine (particularly good are the pastas and seafood).

To return to Pioneer Park, double back along Montgomery and mount the equally stunning **Filbert Steps**. The steps are rather precarious but well worth the effort to see some of San Francisco's oldest buildings. They begin next to **Shadows Restaurant**, and allow you to enjoy the breathtaking views that are wonderfully unavoidable in this part of San Francisco.

Left, Coit Tower mural. **Right**, San Francisco's monument to its firemen: Coit Tower.

146

CHINATOWN AREA

Walking up Grant Avenue as it nears Bush Street, you leave one of the city's many retail shopping areas and arrive at the threshold of what seems like another world. Before you stands the famous imperial **Dragon Gate** – a monument of jade-green tiles, crouching stone lions, dolphins and dragons. At the top, four gilded Chinese characters in raised relief translate: Everything in the World is in Just Proportion.

Welcome to San Francisco's Chinatown, the quintessential city within a city. As you pass through the gate, shop windows beckon with crowded displays of silk, porcelain, teakwood furniture, and hand-wrought jewelry, as well as more mainstream tourist bric-a-brac. Walk a little further along the street and you'll find aromatic open-air markets, glitzy emporiums, bustling alleys, and herbalists' shops packed with jars of exotic roots and spices.

You've just entered the outskirts of one of San Francisco's most famous neighborhoods. Since the Gold Rush days, this dense 24-square-block enclave has served as the hub for the city's Chinese population. And today, as it has for over a century, Chinatown bustles with shoppers and strollers, diners, residents and tourists.

Early Chinatown: At the time that gold was discovered at Sutter's Mill in January of 1848, China was undergoing a period of upheaval. The Manchu Dynasty was corrupt and weakening; floods and droughts throughout China resulted in widespread famine; peasant rebellions were becoming increasingly common and the decade-long T'ai-p'ing Rebellion in the 1850s, severely reduced the population of Southern China.

Many Chinese took the opportunity to leave their homes and come to California's new mining towns in order to seek their fortunes. Of the estimated 30,000 Chinese immigrants in California during the 1850s, half made their homes in San Francisco.

Chinatown grew up around what was then the heart of San Francisco, Portsmouth Square. Many Chinese merchants set up shop near the major hotels and rooming houses. This area became known as "Little Canton" in 1850 and boasted 33 retail stores, 15 pharmacies (Chinese herbal cures were in demand in a city with few doctors), and six restaurants serving Chinese and non-Chinese food. This was the beginning of San Francisco's Chinatown, as it was heralded in the local press in 1853.

Booming business: In 1850, San Francisco's population was predominantly male; only 8 percent of the citizens were women. Simple household work, such as laundering, became a monumental task, and the city's lack of large quantities of fresh water made the problem even worse. There was a large watering hole at the base of Russian Hill known as Washerwoman's Lagoon.

This was the largest "laundry" in the

Preceding pages: Grant Avenue, Chinatown. **Left,** an Asian outlook. **Right,** enter the dragon.

city, and much of the work was done by Native American and Spanish women for extremely low pay. This lagoon, however, was not large enough to service the entire city, and it was not unusual for laundry to be sent by sea to Honolulu or Canton to be washed and then returned by steamer some months later. Obviously, there was a great need for laundries closer to hand.

The Chinese saw this need and filled it. It didn't take much capital to open a laundry. Self-employment was ideal for the early Chinese settlers in San Francisco; they neither had to compete with whites for jobs nor work for them directly. When the Chinese entered the laundry business, the price for laundering shirts plummeted dramatically, from $8 a dozen to $2.

Restaurants became another major business for the Chinese in San Francisco as early as 1849. Restaurants were a necessity because few rooming houses included kitchens, and most Chinese craved their native foods. These restaurants quickly became popular with local white miners, providing a welcome change from their usual diet of starchy breads and potatoes.

During this same period, many Chinese went into service in white households as cooks and servants. Good Chinese cooks were in demand and often earned twice as much as their white or black counterparts. The Chinese in San Francisco were also involved in various trade industries such as boots and shoes, candles and soap, clothing, and cigar manufacturing.

Early Chinatown, as was the case throughout most of the city, was remarkable for its lack of women. According to the US Census of 1890, the ratio of Chinese men to women in San Francisco was roughly 20 to one. This was primarily because the early Chinese immigrants, "sojourners," did not intend to settle in the United States; their goal was to make money and return home as soon as possible.

Some women came as wives to suc-

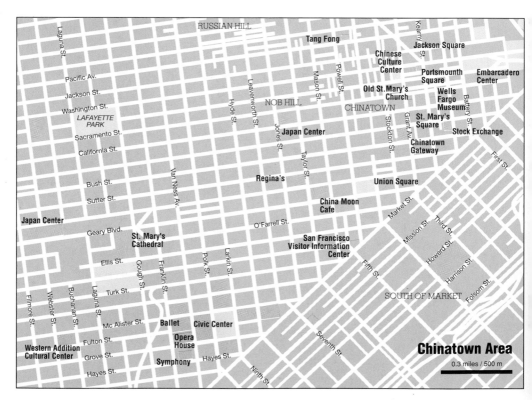

Chinatown Area

0.3 miles / 500 m

cessful Chinese businessmen, but the great majority came as house servants or as prostitutes. Bought for $100 to $300 in China, these so-called "slave girls" sold for double or triple that amount in San Francisco.

In the late 19th century, some Protestant missionaries launched personal crusades to rescue the "poor, helpless" Chinese "heathen" from degrading conditions. As they selectively focused attention on Chinese prostitutes, while ignoring the larger number of white prostitutes plying their trade on nearby Sacramento Street, their efforts were often seen as paternalistic and resented by the Chinese.

Chinese Exclusion Act: In 1882, Congress passed the Chinese Exclusion Act, suspending Chinese immigration for 10 years. The act insured that foreign-born wives and children of Chinese-American citizens would be the only Chinese allowed to enter the country. The Exclusion Act was reinforced (and made even more stringent) by the Scott Act of 1888 and, later, by the Immigration Act of 1924. As a result of these measures, the Chinese population in the United States dropped from 132,000 in 1882 to 62,000 by 1920.

Still, from the 1880s to the 1920s, Chinatown expanded from its six-block length and two-block width until it covered eight city blocks, from Bush to Broadway, and three blocks from Kearny to Powell. The area was completely rebuilt after the 1906 earthquake and again became a busy and thriving community; its narrow streets overflowed with traffic and with tourists.

After the United States and China became allies during World War II, President Roosevelt signed a measure in 1943 repealing the exclusion acts, allowing Chinese to become American citizens and also setting a modest yearly quota for Chinese immigration. This was the first of several acts that opened doors to Chinese students, to women and to refugees from political turmoil. San Francisco's Chinatown flourished

Gateway to the East in the heart of San Francisco.

under these conditions, and today it is estimated that some 70,000 Chinese live within the 24-block radius that makes up the heart of Chinatown.

Grant Avenue is considered Chinatown's main strip. One of San Francisco's oldest streets, it used to be named Dupont Street when it was the main thoroughfare of the Mexican pueblo of Yerba Buena, established in 1834. The street was renamed Grant in honor of Ulysses S. Grant, following the devastating earthquake of 1906.

Grant also remains the major tourist shopping street of Chinatown. Most of the shops are open daily until 10pm. Imperial Fashion and Bargain Bazaar are good places to look for curios and interesting clothes. For jewelry, the China Gem Company is a favorite among visitors with time to spare.

A restaurant that has been an institution for years in Chinatown is the narrow, three-level **Sam Wo** on **Washington Street**, just off Grant Avenue – better known for its charm, cheap fare, and hustling staff rather than top-flight cuisine. What you save on food you should spend elsewhere on drinks: Sam Wo only serves tea, soda and water. You might also look into the **Li Po Bar** at 916 Grant, named for the famous 1st century Chinese poet. Li Po was well-known for his verse celebrating the joys of drunken revelry.

A little heart: You shouldn't visit Chinatown without experiencing *dim sum*, translated as "a little heart." Best as a bruncheon meal, *dim sum* is made up of a broad array of small, delicate pastries which are brought around on trolleys to the tables. Some *dim sum* restaurants provide menus that give a description of each dish, but more often you will find yourself hailing down the trolleys as they roll by, and selecting from small dishes of steaming dumplings, potstickers, and spareribs.

Brunching on *dim sum* is a do-it-yourself meal. Even if you're not entirely sure of the Chinese name for a dish, be adventurous and try it. Some

Food for thought...

lively places to sample delicious *dim sum* include Louie's on Grant and the Hang Ah Tea Room off Sacramento Street just east of Stockton. The larger *dim sum* houses are often noisy and exciting. For a quieter restaurant, you could try Yank Sing, a few blocks outside Chinatown, at 427 Battery in the Financial District.

New Year's festival: *Gung Hay Fat Choy!* means Happy New Year in Chinese. The Chinese New Year is celebrated in February with a colorful and noisy three-hour parade downtown and into the very heart of Chinatown. People from all over the Bay Area flank the streets for the procession, which is tailed by a huge 60-ft (18-meter) dragon carried by at least a dozen men. Often, the ceremonial dragon is made in Hong Kong and shipped over expressly for the New Year's Parade.

The dragon is on display every year after the parade at 383 Grant Avenue. Firecrackers abound during New Year's week in Chinatown, and even four- and five-year-olds can be seen throwing them into gutters and cupping their ears in anxious anticipation of the blast.

Meeting places: The street of day-to-day life in Chinatown is **Stockton Street**. This is the place where most of the produce and fish markets, herbal pharmacopoeias, butchers shops and bakeries are found. Spices are also sold along Stockton Street in large import-export shops.

Yet another important meeting place is **Portsmouth Square** – which was the center of San Francisco in the Gold Rush era and has been the site of rallies, riots and hangings, as well as romantic trysts and countless family picnics. Today, it is somewhat run-down, but still popular with the older generation of Chinese men who gather daily to play *mahjong* at small tables dotted around the square. Many of these men grew up under the shadow of the Exclusion Act: unable to find wives, they grew accustomed to lifelong bachelorhood.

The **Chinese Historical Society**, at

...in the local markets.

650 Commercial Street, has a superb library and a small museum for researchers and people wanting general information about Chinese-American history. Dedicated to tracing the Chinese contribution to the growth of America, and particularly California, its collection includes Gold Rush artifacts, a papier-mâché dragon's head, and an altar from a Napa Valley Taoist temple. The museum is open from Tuesday to Saturday, afternoons only. Admission is free, but donations are welcome.

Next door, at 680 Commercial, is the **Pacific Heritage Museum**, which is located on the site of the old San Francisco Mint, built in 1854. Tours are free and include a look at the old vaults as well as a historical display detailing the building's history. The museum is open from Monday to Friday.

The Six Companies: An important part of Chinatown's commerce and community is made up of what Americans refer to as The Six Companies, also known as the **Chinese Consolidated Benevolent**

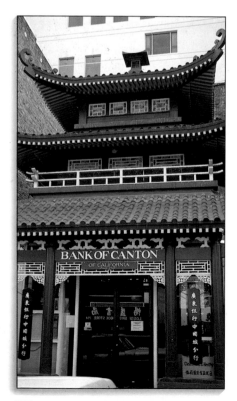

Association. The Six Companies, a far-reaching organization formed around the turn of the century, became the central government of Chinatown, and acted under a coordinating board of control (made up of representatives from disparate organizations, community groups, and clubs).

The Six Companies act as a sort of embassy to Chinese visitors, arbitrate disputes within the community, and operate one of the largest Chinese language schools in the country, as well as playing a major role in organizing the Chinese New Year's Parade.

St Mary's Square is a quiet and peaceful square that rests on top of a large underground parking garage. In the morning, the square is often filled with Chinese and Americans practicing *tai chi*, moving in balletic slow motion.

An impressive 14-ft (4-meter) granite statue of Dr Sun Yat Sen (the first president of modern China) stands at the northeast corner of the square. Dr Sun lived in Chinatown briefly in 1910 and began a revolutionary newspaper. The sculpture in his honour was commissioned by the federally funded Works Progress Administration and was first placed here in 1938. Its renowned sculptor, Beniamino Bufano, also created the statue of St Francis at Taylor and Beach streets.

In the past, this area of Chinatown was known for its rather seedy array of brothels, gambling and opium dens, and often became the setting for violent outbursts between the Chinese and other residents of San Francisco. In the late 1800s, there were a number of attempts to clean up the area around Dupont Street (now Grant Avenue). All of them failed, until the great fire, which came in the wake of the 1906 earthquake, destroyed most of the commercial establishments in the area.

After the fire, St Mary's was decreed a public square. **Old St Mary's Church**, at Grant Avenue and California Street, served as the main Catholic church in San Francisco from 1853 to 1891. Its **Finance with a flair.**

sturdy granite foundation, imported from China, and its walls, brought from the East Coast, survived the devastation of 1906 and another earthquake in 1989. The church's brick tower is engraved with the famous Biblical motto from Ecclesiastes, "Son, Observe the time and fly from evil."

The Chinese Telephone Exchange, located at 743 Washington Street, is where the first San Francisco newspaper, called the *California Star*, was printed in 1846. Currently, this pagoda-like building is home to the Bank of Canton; in earlier years it has been the local office of the Pacific Telephone and Telegraph Company.

Waverly Street, often dubbed "The Street of Painted Balconies," is colorful, noisy, and aromatic. An alley that runs parallel to Grant Avenue between Clay and Washington streets, Waverly Street is the "real" Chinatown – the Chinatown that most visitors don't see. Here, stores sell lychee wine, pickled ginger, rice threads, dried lotus, and powdered antler horns, reputed to restore male virility. Traditional Chinese roofs of turned-up jade and terra-cotta tiles mark the edges of apartment house roofs.

Temples in Chinatown representing Taoism, Buddhism, and other Asian religions, function not only as places of worship but also as providers of community services such as schools, meeting rooms, dormitories and eating places for the old and poor. Most of these lavish temples are located at the top of Chinatown buildings – in order to place them closer to heaven and the gods. They tend to be lavishly decorated with hanging lanterns and other ornaments, and heavy with the scent of incense burned in ceremonial offerings.

The most popular deity is Kuan Yin, a goddess of mercy, or "one who hears prayers." She has a temple dedicated to her in **Spofford Alley**. The **Tin Hou Temple**, dedicated to the Queen of the Heavens and Goddess of the Seven Seas, is a special place to visit and is located at 125 Waverly Place on the second floor. Tin Hou is said to protect travelers, sailors, artists, and prostitutes. This is believed to be the oldest Chinese temple in the United States.

Buddha's Universal Church, which is located at 720 Washington Street (at Kearny Street), was built entirely by volunteers. Once the site of a nightclub, the building was purchased by church members in 1951 for a mere $500, only to have the city condemn the site as being structurally unsound. Volunteers worked together to rebuild it and the temple was finally dedicated in 1963. Free tours of the Universal Church's altar, library and rooftop garden are conducted on the second and fourth Sunday of each month.

Ross Alley: This small alley, which runs above Grant Avenue between Washington and Jackson streets, was once filled with gambling halls and pawn shops. Today, it primarily houses small garment shops, as well as a laundry, a florist and a one-seat barbershop. The sweet aroma of fresh cookies is an invi-

"Urning" her keep.

tation to the **Golden Gate Fortune Cookie Company** at 56 Ross. The job is done in the blink of an eye, as a worker pulls a hot cookie off a rotating press and folds a fortune inside. Samples hot off the press can be bought for a few pennies. They also sell adult versions, called "French" fortune cookies.

Nightlife: At night in Chinatown, the neon and flashing lights give the area a feeling of genuine excitement. While there aren't as many nightclubs here as in the South of Market area, the Palladium on Kearny is a popular spot with young Chinese out for a night on the town. Pearl's, at 256 Columbus, features live jazz nightly.

Not far from Chinatown is San Francisco's theater district, focused on Geary Boulevard. Here, the 1,768-seat **Curran Theater** and the 1,300-seat **Geary Theater** stand side by side. The Geary is the home of the **American Conservatory Theater**, one of the nation's premier repertory companies. It is presently closed for renovation due to dam-age inflicted in the October 1989 earth-quake. The ACT has continued to stage productions at other sites, including the Stage Door Theater at Mason and Geary and the Marine's Memorial Theater on Sutter Street. The Curran Theater offers some of the most successful hits from New York's Broadway.

Also in the area is the **Cable Car Theater** at 430 Mason Street. A little further afield is the **Golden Gate Theater** (6th and Market) – this ornate 2,400-seat theater, formerly a popular movie house, is a frequent host to out-of-town musicals.

San Francisco also has more than 40 cinemas offering almost every kind of visual entertainment – San Franciscans are second only to the citizens of Toronto in their per capita movie attendance.

One of the more interesting neighbor-hood transitions occurring in San Francisco is the creation of a "New China-town" in the **Richmond** and **Clement Street** district. Spilling over into this traditionally Eastern European area, **Chinese spice rack.**

Asians new to America have settled and established a visible ethnic presence. Obviously, this process has created tensions with older residents and disputes over ethnic authority.

The area known as the Richmond was formerly made up of gently rolling sand dunes stretching down to the ocean. The well-known nature photographer Ansel Adams used to play here when he was a young lad growing up in San Francisco, just after the turn of the century. A number of his early photographs give a clear idea of how the area used to look before development.

Many of the early settlers in the Richmond were immigrants from Eastern Europe, but in the 1970s the new wave was largely composed of Asian groups. Second- and third-generation Chinese began moving over from the more crowded downtown Chinatown, followed shortly after by Indochinese and Thai refugees, as well as Koreans. In later years, Japanese immigrants have also moved in.

Today, the Richmond, situated between the Presidio and Golden Gate Park, is made up of family residences, brick and cement row houses, and low-rise apartment buildings. The main street which runs through Richmond is Clement Street, crammed full of restaurants, groceries, clothiers, and bookstores, all oriented towards browsers.

Minh's Garden on Clement near Fourth Avenue specializes in authentic Vietnamese cuisine. Further down on Clement, the **Ocean** restaurant is reputedly the best place for Cantonese food. And for genuine Thai cuisine, **Khan Toke** on Geary Boulevard is highly popular with locals.

Booklovers will find **Green Apple's** irresistible. This two-story, rambling bookstore, located at 506 Clement, houses thousands of new and used titles, all great bargains, and there are no restrictions on browsing time.

Even though traditional Chinatown offers more than enough to see and do, "new" Chinatown is also worth the time.

Proud owners of the family business.

In this city of countless artists, trendsetters, and all-round hipsters, nightlife metamorphoses constantly. In recent years, San Francisco's nightlife has revolved around **South of Market** – or **SoMa**, nicknamed in the spirit of New York's SoHo. An oddly colorless, quasi-industrial neighborhood of warehouses and factory outlets, South of Market seems a rather unlikely place for such a fashionable scene.

During the day, it seems, the only people to be found on its wide, desolate streets are those who patronize the auto centers, pawn shops, factory outlets, and machinery buildings that are sprawled between blocks. At night, the gray landscape is dotted with the lit-up facades of bars and nightclubs, long lines of strikingly-dressed young people waiting to get in, and uncompromising doormen checking IDs.

Redefined: Like the alluring nightlife it supports, the area of SoMa itself has metamorphosed over the years. During the Gold Rush, prospectors and diggers used this marshy area of the city to construct a tent city for themselves. Industrial concerns took over during the Civil War, and by 1900, "South of the Slot" – named after the slotted cable car tracks that lined Market Street – became the new home of 60,000 European immigrants seeking factory jobs.

The 1906 earthquake sent a large part of the population packing to the East Bay, and the Great Depression of the 1930s brought a new flock of lower-income residents back to the area. Since then, South of Market has been one of the city's ethnic underbellies, home to successive waves of immigrants.

Between the Depression and the late 1950s, SoMa even helped San Francisco's claim as a baseball town. The San Francisco Seals, of the old Pacific Coast

Left, bright lights, big city.

League, played in quaint Seals Stadium, located at the corner of 16th and Bryant streets. It was here that one of baseball's all-time greats, Joe DiMaggio (alongside lesser-known brothers Vince and Dominick) got his big-league start.

Soon after, in 1958, Willie Mays and the New York Giants moved to town (and played for two seasons here before moving to Candlestick Park to the south). Seals was eventually done in by a city wrecking ball. Today, the San Francisco Auto Center – where dealers of every stripe hustle new and used cars – stands at approximately the same spot in centerfield where DiMaggio once hustled after fly balls.

Into the night: Nightclubs are not entirely new to the SoMa area. Gay bars began to sprout up here decades ago, and while many still exist – particularly those of the hardcore leather variety – they now mingle with countless other mixed bars and dance clubs.

The main cluster of nightclubs and restaurants is on Folsom and Harrison streets. The pleasant **Café Soma** on 12th and Howard was one of the first art cafés in the South of Market area. This is a good place to sip a cappuccino and see the works of local artists. Café Soma's appeal lies in its decor's Zen-like sparseness, but a random collection of kitsch gives nearby **Hamburger Mary's** its charm. Located at 12th and Folsom, Hamburger Mary's offers a good sandwich or burger at a very reasonable price. Don't be daunted by the sign over the door, "Enter at your own Risk." It's a benign, if overly busy, SoMa stalwart.

Across the street, also at 12th and Folsom, is the **Holy Cow**, a small dance club and bar. Taking its cue from the exclamation, "Holy Cow!" the bar's designer irreverently coupled religious iconography with Old West artifacts; a large ceramic cow sporting a halo hangs above the front door. Top-40 dance tunes play here until the wee hours. A couple of doors down, **The Ace Cafe** is a low-key, yet fashionable spot to get a drink

Relaxing at 20 Tanks; The Paradise Lounge.

or a bite to eat at night. The Ace serves food until 1am on weekends.

What made **Club O' The Oasis** on 11th and Folsom such an attraction when it first opened in the 1980s (as simply The Oasis) was its dance floor – a lighted swimming pool covered by Plexiglas. Dancing on water, however, is only one diversion at the Oasis these days. The large sprawling bar has a basketball hoop, and an outdoor deck for somewhat quieter interludes. Offering a mixture of rock'n'roll and techno-pop, Club O' has evolved into a popular if somewhat suburban haunt.

The Paradise Lounge at 11th and Folsom is always crowded on Friday and Saturday nights as people wait for blues, rock, or pop performers. Its wraparound couch and cozy blue lighting make the Paradise a refuge for those who like nightclubs but tire of endless music and big video screens. **Above Paradise**, i.e. upstairs, features small bands, "spoken word" performances (the latest rage in poetry readings) and per-

formance art. There are also pool tables for the sports-minded.

Nearby on 11th Street is a popular watering hole, the **20 Tanks** microbrewery. The expansive wooden floors and bar, along with industrial bric-a-brac on the walls, give this after-work drinking spot the feel of Monterey's old Cannery Row.

The **DNA Lounge** and **Slim's** (owned by rock'n'roller Boz Scaggs) both jam the nights away with live rock and jazz. DNA clientele are also accustomed to poetry readings, and odd events like "Sluts A Go-Go" and the ever-entertaining "Smut Fest."

SoMa is packed full of dance clubs. Promoters regularly rent some of these clubs, giving them a different name and clientele on certain nights. The **Endup** has two such "specials," one on Friday and one on Sunday.

There are also three large, mostly all-night dance hall operations: **Thunderdome** (175 King), **Pleasuredome** (177 Townsend) and **Tribe** (715 Harrison).

Taking a lunch break Egyptian-style.

These clubs are predominantly gay, but usually quite a mixture of people attend.

You can find conversation and espresso at **Spike's Cafe** (139 Eighth), and **Brainwash** (Folson & 11th St), a chic spot where you can get a bite to eat, or a drink or even do your laundry. Keep an eye open for club "invites," cleverly designed little cards that advertise underground "mobile clubs" – gatherings that happen at different sites every month or so, usually attended by the in-the-know clubbing crowd. Often the invites provide a discount when presented at the door.

Over 20 SoMa art galleries cater to a variety of tastes. Many present the work of unknown artists. The best SoMa museums include the **Cartoon Art Museum** (665 Third St), which exhibits original cells and sketches from animated films. The **Museum of Modern Mythology** presents advertising characters and other artifacts of pop culture – a rare (and somewhat unnerving) collection of polyester shirts, for example.

The **Telephone Pioneer Communications Museum** (140 New Montgomery) offers a large collection of memorabilia and hands-on exhibits tracing the evolution of communications. The **San Francisco Museum of Modern Art** (Third Street), which moved from its previous location on Van Ness Avenue, is the biggest newcomer to the SoMa area.

This state-of-the art building, designed by Swiss architect Mario Botta, has a stepped-back brick-and-stone facade with a soaring, cylindrical skylight and serves as the West Coast's most comprehensive resource center of 20th century art. Over 15,000 exhibits are on display, including many paintings by Henri Matisse, as well as works by Salvador Dali, Francis Bacon, Willem de Kooning, Roy Lichtenstien, Andy Warhol and Diego Rivera.

Yerba Buena Gardens, a 12-block entertainment area set behind the **Moscone Convention Center**, has gardens large enough to include a redwood

Soaring at the Billboard.

grove and a waterfall. The complex also features several museums and restaurants. The nearby **Center For The Arts** has a visual art gallery and a 750-seat performing arts theater.

SoMa by day: Although SoMa has acquired fame for its night-time capers, South of Market never really sleeps. Just as the after-hours dance clubs close, the **Flower Terminal** at Sixth and Brannan opens for merchants and for those visitors who appreciate a warehouse filled with fragrant, colorful and often exotic flowers.

For bargain shoppers, there are several factory outlets South of Market, mostly along Ninth and Tenth streets near Folsom. Get there quite early while the clothing is still on the racks and before the bargain-hungry crowds arrive. Saturday is the busy day at the Center Arcade.

If you have a penchant for teddy bears, don't miss **Woods & Woods** on DeHaro Street – patrons can tour this teddy factory or stuff their own bear. Also on De Haro, near Mariposa Street, is the **Anchor Steam** brewery, home of the city's famous brew. Stop by for a tour or simply a taste.

Another daylight diversion here is the workshop **Neon Neon** on Seventh, a fascinating and original place which reveals how vintage neon is restored and how new pieces are created.

If you are interested in what San Francisco's alley artists are creating, don't miss the art galleries on Folsom Street. Inside unobtrusive warehouses you'll find art spaces full of adventurous works.

Somewhat outside the SoMa's parameters lie a few low-key gems, like **Mission Rock Café** and **The Ramp**. They are among the few places – remarkably few in a city surrounded by water – that have decks and terraces by the bay. With a view of Oakland and the Bay Bridge, Mission Rock and The Ramp cater to a charming mix of dockworkers and young professionals. Small jazz combos entertain at The Ramp almost every night.

State of the art Museum of Modern Art; the Holy Cow.

UNION SQUARE

Though San Francisco is anything but an old-fashioned village, Union Square still fulfils to some extent the role that plazas and public squares once played in small towns. All walks of life gather in and around here: socialites find their gowns for debutante balls, the business-minded plot their corporations' growth, tourists board a cable car for a ride over Nob Hill, and residents come to see plays and to shop. A considerable homeless population congregates alongside street musicians and evangelists.

Air of nostalgia: Despite the area now being primarily a commercial center, the flavor of "Old San Francisco" still prevails. San Francisco's Montgomery Street, for example, is hallowed in city lore. Sam Brannan ran the length of Montgomery Street when he announced the discovery of gold in 1848. Mark Twain found inspiration here in a local fireman named Tom Sawyer. Black Bart, Lotta Crabtree and Jack London have all paced the avenue.

During the Gold Rush, the area was soon overrun by the '49ers, a rugged lot who came in search of gold the year after Brannan's news spread throughout the world. (The city's beloved National Football League team, the 49ers, takes its name from this crew of rough and ready rednecks.)

The original '49ers sailed into the San Francisco Bay, dropped anchor and set off north to pursue their dream of striking gold. It wasn't long before the city's original shoreline began to burgeon, contributing to the birth of today's **Financial District**. Brokers, bankers and insurance agents now pursue wealth on several acres of landfill on and around Montgomery Street, which has been nicknamed "Wall Street West."

What has kept all these entrepreneurial San Franciscans on the go? Several museums in the area provide some of the historical and cultural answers. The

intellectual challenge of the financial world can be explored at the **Federal Reserve Bank** (101 Market St). Inside, the **World of Economics** gallery explains finance principles through hands-on computer games, videotapes, murals and even cartoon stories. Visitors can try their skill at being Board Chairperson; here even stock market crashes and federal deficits can be fun.

Those interested in the aesthetic and historic value of money should be sure to visit the **Museum of American Money from the West** (400 California S). Housed in the **Bank of California** – the oldest banking hall in the district – this cache includes historic coins and currency as well as gold and silver ingots. The value of the exhibits exceeds $1 million.

In a similar vein, the gold nuggets on display at the **Wells Fargo Bank History Room** (420 Montgomery Street) offer insights into San Francisco's financial history. This exhibit includes other interesting artifacts, such as banking articles, miner's equipment, and dioramas from the Gold Rush era. An authentic 19th-century **Wells Fargo Overland Stage**, which was once used on the coach trails of the West and is now seen on the bank's distinctive logo, provides the museum's centerpiece.

Cityscapes: Not all the treasures in this district are gilded. Several historic buildings can be found in the downtown area. Art Deco, Romanesque and the Chicago School are just a few of the styles that contribute to the eclectic architectural kaleidoscope here.

The city's older facades also provide countless surprises. Some of the features to look for are: the Gothic styling of the **Hallidie Building**'s glass wall curtain (130 Sutter Street); the terracotta carvings of ox-heads, eagles and young nymphs on the **Hunter-Dulin Building** (111 Sutter Street); the 21-ft (6.5-meter) high modern sculptures – *Mother Earth* and *Man and His Inventions* – that flank the **Pacific Stock Exchange** (Pine and Sansome); the geometric designs of the

Shell Building (100 Bush Street); and, finally, the winged gargoyles adorning the portico of the **Kohl Building** (400 Montgomery Street).

The **Transamerica Pyramid** (600 Montgomery Street) commands attention because of its great size and unusual shape. The pyramid pierces the sky at 853 ft (260 meters), making it the tallest building in the city which can be viewed panoramically from its 27th floor. It's aesthetic appeal is still being argued, but there's no debate, however, about its most surprising feature: flanking the building is one of the world's few urban Redwood groves.

Visitors will find a stunning bird's-eye view of San Francisco from the 52nd floor of the nearby **Bank of America World Headquarters**, where a cocktail lounge/restaurant opens daily to the public after 3pm. Take a second look at the building's exterior and note the red carnelian granite facade and the outdoor plaza's sculpture *Banker's Heart*, a huge stone of polished granite.

The interiors of many of these buildings are just as remarkable as their facades, and are open for public viewing. **The Garden Court** area of the **Sheraton Palace Hotel** boasts turn-of-the-century opulence (New Montgomery and Market streets). This magnificent dining room is surrounded by 16 ionic marble columns, and an intricate iron framework which supports a leaded glass skylight 48 ft (15 meters) above the floor, as well as 10 crystal chandeliers.

The Garden Court's modern counterpart is the **Hyatt Regency Hotel**. Its dimensions alone make it a micro-world unto itself: the indoor atrium is 20 stories high, and houses over 100 trees and 15,000 hanging ivies. Birds flit about the overhead skylight, while 170 ft (52 meters) below, visitors sink into the plush conversation pits that line the lobby. Even Charles Perry's geometric sculpture – rising only four stories above the pool of water that reflects it – is impressively huge.

The Hyatt Regency is just part of the

Stone and metal tributes to justice and labor.

"city within a city" that John Portman envisioned when he designed the **Embarcadero Center** (*see also Northern Waterfront*). The 8½-acre (3½-hectare) development consists of four high-rise office towers, the **Justin Hermann Plaza**, and an interwoven complex of 45 restaurants and 130 retail stores, all linked by pedestrian bridges and outdoor courtyards filled with displays of sculpture. It is a bit of an anomaly in San Francisco, whose long history has created a hodgepodge of purpose and form in every neighborhood. By contrast, the Embarcadero Center is well-planned, uniform, and self-contained.

The Embarcadero Center's only rival for this kind of variety in the Financial District is the **Crocker Galleria** shopping arcade between Post and Sutter streets (off Montgomery). But truly serious shoppers will venture west, to **Union Square**, a grassy plot at the center of one of the country's most compact and varied retail cores.

Bordered by Geary, Post, Powell and Stockton streets, the square anchors an active commercial area with a colorful history. First deeded for public use in 1850, it acquired its name during the Civil War years when pro-Union sympathizers rallied here. At its center is a 90-ft (27-meter) Corinthian column, topped with a bronze *Victory* commemorating Commodore George Dewey's successful Manila Bay campaign during the Spanish-American War. Neither the 1906 earthquake nor the 1942 installation of the world's first underground parking lot/bomb shelter rattled the column. Today the square is most famous for the glitzy shops and hotels that have grown up around it.

It is framed with several representative institutions. Fronting the west side is the **Westin St Francis Hotel** which since 1904 has provided lodgings for countless dignitaries and celebrities. The plaza of the more modern **Hyatt on Union Square** is adorned with a Ruth Asawa fountain that literally embodies San Francisco. The bronze friezes of

View of the Financial District.

typical city scenes were cast in molds made from bread dough by some 250 schoolchildren and other local residents.

An important part of the scenery here are several of San Francisco's biggest department stores. **Macy's**, **Saks Fifth Avenue**, and **Neiman-Marcus** are the places to find a cornucopia of fashions and accessories under one roof. (The latter institution is crowned by an exquisite stained-glass rotunda which was preserved from the City of Paris, the city's first department store and original occupant of the site.)

All these stores fight to outdo each other's window dressings during the holiday season. Neiman-Marcus erects a Christmas tree that rises up through its three-story atrium, and Gump's, a long-time city landmark, collaborates with the local animal shelter to display adoptable kittens and puppies in its elaborate and hugely popular Christmas windows.

Although San Francisco has never been a center of high fashion, its designers are now beginning to grow in number and reputation. Many of the designs are relaxed and loose-fitting, although the late Roberto Robledo, who lived and worked in San Francisco until his death in 1992, was almost single-handedly responsible for the lycra craze.

The fashions of MAC, Metier, Joe Boxer and Think Tank can all be found in their own boutiques or in the department stores which line the square. **Maiden Lane**, a tiny alley that runs parallel to Post, is home to the Metier store as well as high-fashion hair salons and chic cafés. In the afternoon Maiden Lane is pedestrians only.

Shoppers should also take a walk down the 200 block of Post Street, home to **Cartier**, **Shreve and Co.**, **Gucci**, **Brooks Brothers**, **Eddie Bauer**, and **Alfred Dunhill** and other venerable names. Perhaps most famous of all is **Gump's**. A combination store-and-museum, the best in jade, glassware, Oriental rugs, silks and antiques can be found here. Ironically, Gump's started in business years ago by selling frames **Letter perfect.**

and mirrors to local bars and bordellos.

Civic Center: West on Geary, it's 8 blocks from Union Square to **Van Ness Avenue**, a broad north-south thoroughfare. Abutting Van Ness at McAllister Street is **City Hall**, one of the most beautiful public buildings in the country. Built in 1914, City Hall is honeycombed with municipal offices and both civil and criminal courts. This is the building in which Supervisor Dan White shot Mayor George Moscone in 1978, sparking off a series of demonstrations.

Across the plaza from City Hall is the stately former **Public Library**, built in 1916. The Asian Art Gallery will move here before the century is out. The south end of the plaza is occupied by the **Civic Auditorium** (1913) and the north side by a **State Office Building** (1926). Together, they make up San Francisco's **Civic Center**, a pleasing appearance of order and harmony. Also in the neighborhood are other distinguished buildings, including the **Veterans Auditorium Building** (1932) which houses

the 915-seat **Herbst Auditorium**; the splendid **Opera House**; and, across the street from the Opera House, the lavish **Louise M. Davies Symphony Hall**.

Galleries: The Union Square area is known for its appreciation of the visual arts. The **Circle Gallery** (140 Maiden Lane) is a spiral-ramped showroom, designed by Frank Lloyd Wright in anticipation of his larger Guggenheim Museum in New York City. It is perhaps the first of the many private showrooms that art lovers will want to visit.

The **Allrich Gallery** (251 Post Street) principally supports the fiber arts, while **The Fraenkel Gallery** (55 Grant) is exclusively devoted to photography. **Sergio Old Prints** (50 Maiden Lane) is the city's only dealer in pre-1880 prints and art exhibition posters. Their collection is widely varied and includes oddities such as surgical and stock exchange prints, as well as examples of Americana, Californiana and even Hawaiiana. **Edward Nakhamkin Fine Arts, Inc.** (422 Sutter or 377 Geary) has two gal-

The Embarcadero Center.

leries representing the most important contemporary artists to come out of the Soviet Union.

Further to the west are the **Lone Wolf Gallery** (555 Sutter Street) and the **Rorick Gallery** (637 Mason Street), both of which present almost exclusively the art of Bay Area and California residents – some who are well-known, some who are still undiscovered.

Interspersed with the galleries and stores are the city's best restaurants, with every type of cuisine finding representation. The French food at **Masa's** (648 Bush) is arguably *the* best, as the waiting line will attest (reservations are made 21 days in advance). **Aqua** (252 California), is currently one of the most chic places to eat and be seen in the Financial District.

Two nearby watering holes should provide the perfect sequel to any meal. **John's Grill** at 63 Ellis Street is a good place to play Sam Spade and investigate the *Maltese Falcon* memorabilia that adorn the Dashiell Hammett den. Or try the **S. Holmes Esq. Pub**, on the 30th floor of the **Holiday Inn at Union Square** (480 Sutter Street). It contains a detailed reproduction of the fictional sleuth's Baker Street study.

Several other top-of-the-city nightclubs make it possible to enjoy San Francisco *on high*. There's a piano bar at the **One-Up** (36th floor, Hyatt on Union Square), while the outdoor glass elevators of the Westin St Francis lead up to **Oz**, a 32nd-floor "enchanted" modern music discotheque.

Union Square has also maintained its reputation as the core of the city's theater district. The **American Conservatory Theater (ACT)** at 415 Geary has garnered the most renown since it was born in the '60s, and offers both contemporary and classic works, with a penchant for Molière. The **Stage Door Theater** (430 Mason) is one of the venues that ACT uses. Also in the area, you'll find the **Lorraine Hansberry Theater** (500 Sutter Street), the city's premiere African-American theater company, **The Curran** (445 Geary) and **The Marine's Memorial** (609 Sutter), both of which present Broadway musicals that have made their way to the West Coast from New York.

The square itself offers performances that can't be matched. It's not a bad idea to grab a box lunch and take a seat on one of the park benches to watch the passing street parade. From this vantage, you'll notice the bronze nude atop the memorial to former president William McKinley (who died in San Francisco in 1901), by sculptor Robert Aitken. As his model, Aitken used a teenager, Alma de Bretteville, who become famous at 22 for marrying Adolph Spreckels, a much older and well-to-do president of the San Francisco Parks Commission.

Alma de Bretteville became the richest woman in the West, lived in a vast mansion at 2080 Washington Street, and donated $14 million to various charities while becoming a generous patron of the arts.

Left, Union Square has some of the city's best restaurants. **Right**, the American Conservatory Theater.

CABLE CARS

Only about one out of every 10 riders was a local when the city decided to retire its fleet of cable cars in 1947, but the news galvanized San Francisco. A Citizens' Committee to Save the Cable Cars was promptly set up, its chairman, Frieda Klussman, a doctor's wife, declaring that "any present monetary loss was more than compensated for by the wide publicity they give San Francisco," and, indeed, appeals and protests began to flood in from all over the world.

Landmark: Seven years later the battle was won when an amendment was written into the City Charter perpetuating the system. A decade after that, the cable cars were designated a National Landmark. Although 50 percent of the system had been lost during the lengthy struggle (and 95 other cities had abandoned cable cars as obsolete) three San Francisco lines remained – **Mason-Taylor**, which goes through Chinatown and North Beach to Fisherman's Wharf; **Powell-Hyde**, over Nob Hill and Russian Hill to Aquatic Park; and **California**, which runs from the Financial District to Van Ness Avenue. Today they service 12 million passengers a year, more than half of them local residents. In 1972, the US Post Office issued a postcard (6¢ domestic, 15¢ foreign air mail) depicting a cable car.

Perhaps the most glorious day in the cable cars' history was June 3, 1981, when, after being removed for a $65 million renovation of the system that lasted almost two years, a citywide party celebrated their return. During their absence, the number of visitors to Fisherman's Wharf dropped by 15 percent. "They're Back" read the inscription on thousands of colored balloons, and employees of MUNI, the city-owned transit system that operates above-ground trans-

Right, San Francisco's cable cars cater for around 12 million passengers a year.

portation, served free coffee, brownies, donuts and wontons to lines of customers who had waited since dawn to be among the first passengers.

Three weeks later, singer Tony Bennett turned up for the official party, and the Chinese Chamber of Commerce organized a 120-ft (36-meter) long golden dragon to cavort outside restaurants that were serving sidewalk food. A joyful Frieda Klussman, 30 years after her initial triumph, commented, "They're better than ever."

In a special 28-page supplement, the *San Francisco Examiner* warned freeloaders that it was tacky to try and avoid paying the fare, and ran a feature on cable car etiquette ("If you choose to ride on the running board, it's imperative you face the traffic... don't lean out"), surrounded by ads for engraved knives ($29.95), belt buckles ($18.95), and the usual clutch of coins, posters and T-shirts, all bearing pictures of the famous cable cars.

During the 20-month absence of the cars, San Franciscans had been part-consoled by a substitute Trolley Festival in which were paraded the city's formidable array of ancient vintage streetcars from St Louis, Los Angeles, Australia, Germany, Britain and Mexico. And, of course, the Citizens' Committee had been busy raising money, offering, in return for hefty donations, genuine cable car bells and handcrafted walnut music boxes programmed to play *I Left My Heart in San Francisco*. The fund-raising was necessary because only 80 percent of the important, $65 million for renovations was provided by the federal government.

The renovations were completed on time and under budget, partly because the euphoria spread into the ranks of the workers on the project who donated 5,000 hours of overtime. This kind of sentiment about cable cars has been prevalent since the earliest days of the system, when one family living at Washington and Gough streets used to leave milk and hot apple pie on the stoop of

Fire truck covers the tracks.

their home for the benefit of crews taking a midday break.

In similar fashion, the cable car crews would be indulgent at some stops about waiting for regular passengers to finish their coffee before boarding. And hundreds of San Franciscans have memories of being pulled up the steep hills on their roller skates, as they hung onto the back of ascending cars.

Not everybody was delighted by the the refurbished cable car system in the mid-1980s. One family living at Hyde and Chestnut streets initiated a suit against the noise – "like a dial tone with a sore throat," one columnist wrote – which was measured at 85 decibels at street level. Despite their claim that the sound had made their house almost uninhabitable, the couple lost when a judge ruled that the city was not (in this case) subject to its own noise ordinances.

Back in 1970, in another case, the city was not so fortunate. At that time, 29-year-old Gloria Sykes, described by some newspapers as a buxom, blonde data processor, sued for $500,000 after an accident on a cable car left her with what she described as "an insatiable desire for affection." The press called it nymphomania – but Ms Sykes won her case and was awarded $50,000.

Some critics say that the cable cars, which are of course on a fixed track and thus have no ability to duck potential collisions, are inherently unsafe. Columnist Dick Nolan called the braking system "unimprovable" and "blacksmith shop crudity at its worst." In a typical year, about 12 percent of the injuries sustained by passengers who sue the city's transit system are sustained on or through cable cars. Some exuberant riders lean out too far. Many accidents are due to the unthinking behavior of passing motorists, few of whom are as adept or lucky as Barbra Streisand in the famous scene in *What's Up Doc?* where she maneuvered a Volkswagon between two cable cars that were traveling in opposite directions.

Actually, the cars' braking system is

Market and Powell Street turnaround.

unusually elaborate, based on the timely skill of a "gripman" who applies pressure on the endless wire rope running beneath the track's entire route, passing through the winding machinery in the cable car barn at Mason and Washington streets. The rope has a hemp center braced by steel wire, six strands of 19 wires each in the original version devised by Andrew Hallidie, the English-born inventor usually credited with creating the system in 1873. Seven years before, it's said, he saw a horse slip, causing the chain to break on the overloaded streetcar it was pulling uphill. He was determined to devise a system to eliminate such accidents.

Although Andrew Hallidie and his friends put up the $20,000 to get the cable cars operating, he was anticipated in 1870 by Benjamin Brooks, son of a local lawyer, who had been awarded a franchise to operate a similar system, but had failed to raise the necessary financing. Skepticism was the order of the day. "I'd like to see it happen," said

realtor L.C. Carlson, "but I don't know who is going to want to ride the dang thing." By 1906, the date of the San Francisco earthquake, 600 cars rolled over 115 miles (185 km) of track. But overhead wires strung up to power a fleet of more modern electric trolleys hastened the demise of cable cars. Today, the system has 30 cars and a mere 10 miles (16 km) of track.

Butterscotch: From the earliest days, visitors have been impressed. "They turn corners almost at right angles, cross over other lines and for aught I know run up the sides of houses," wrote Rudyard Kipling, who stopped off in the city for a few days in 1889 on his way to India. President Lyndon Johnson's daughter, Lynda Bird, was less impressed a century later when she was ejected from a cable car by the gripman for eating a butterscotch ice cream cone. (To make amends, the city later made Lynda Bird an "honorary conductor.")

It is the gripmen – there are, as yet, no gripwomen – who have become the stars of the system. With their gentle exhortations to "climb aboard my magic cable car," they have attracted their own brand of groupies who offer them gifts – and sometimes more. Dealing with wedding parties – ceremonies are sometimes conducted while aboard – exhibitionists who suddenly fling off raincoats to pose nude for photographers, and passengers who try to operate the bells, they have become deft at handling almost any situation.

"You've got a much closer relationship here with people than on a bus or a streetcar," explains veteran senior grip Sam McDaniel. "They're happy people… the cable car's a fun thing. The men who work them still have a lot of little boy in them."

And a colleague adds: "The job requires a certain amount of diplomacy. If somebody's blocking the door, I'll say, 'Why don't you step inside, there's a TV in there,' or if they're smoking, 'You got to put that joint out or pass it to the driver first'."

Left and **right**, 30 cable cars are now running.

JAPANTOWN

In the restaurant window, gravity-defying chopsticks lift bright plastic noodles from a bowl next to a neon sushi display. In a café, customers sip Japanese iced green tea *au lait* instead of cappuccino. Above a flickering bank of televisions projecting the news, digital headlines scroll across in Japanese. It's true this is a shopping mall, but it's a mall like no other. This is the megalithic Japan Center in the heart of San Francisco's **Nihonmachi** (Japantown).

Built in 1968 as part of San Francisco's redevelopment project in the Western Addition, the complex is a hub of restaurants, bookstores, and gift shops. The center has become a locus for the community, both economically and culturally, especially during the Cherry Blossom Festival in late April.

Although the 5-acre (2-hectare) **Japan Center** dominates Nihonmachi, there is a vital neighborhood all too easily overlooked outside its walls. Roughly 12,000 Japanese live in San Francisco and many of them make their homes here. The community dwells between Geary Boulevard and California Street to the north and south, and between Octavia and Fillmore streets to the east and west.

Temples and dojos: The best way to visit Japantown is to start in its northwestern corner and make one's way back to the center. An excellent starting point is the corner of Pine and Octavia streets. On the northeast corner is the **St Francis Xavier Roman Catholic Church**, originally a Victorian structure that added Japanese motifs. Diagonally across the street is the **Buddhist Churches of America**'s National Headquarters, which is topped by a *stupa* which holds a relic of the Buddha and with a Buddhist bookstore on its second floor, open daily. A few steps south on Octavia, to the right, is **Morning Star School**, notable for the statue of the Virgin Mary – with Asian features –

standing over the entrance beneath a terra-cotta tiled roof.

Continuing south on Octavia and turning west on Bush, one encounters the **Konko Church** at the corners of Bush and Laguna streets. Founded as a religion in 1859, *Konko-Kyo* (faith) developed as a sect of Shintoism, a form of ancestral worship in Japan. The interior of the church is beautiful, but displays incongruous offerings on its central altar: in a recent ceremony, the ancestors received four six-packs of soft drinks and two six-packs of beer. Housed below the church is the **San Francisco Dojo** (school), where students practice martial arts such as *aikido*, *judo*, and *chi kung*.

One block down Laguna Street, at Sutter Street, is the **Soto Zen Mission's Sokoji**, its austere interior in stark contrast to the upbeat nature of the ceremonies frequently held here, distinguished by chanting, drums and bells. Meditation services are offered in both Japanese and English. *Soko* is the Japanese name for the city of San Francisco.

Tea for two: The **Nichi Bei Kai Cultural Center** at 1759 Sutter Street is the home of the Ura Senke Foundation (the Japanese-American Tea Society), and the site of a *chashitsu* – a specially designed room for tea ceremonies. The interior and the simple ceremony performed emphasize the aesthetic and ethical principles inherent in Japanese thinking. *Chanoyu* is a Japanese tea cult which incorporates the study of etiquette, interior design, ceramics, calligraphy, flower arrangement, and gardening.

This *chashitsu* was designed in Japan according to some 250 precise prescriptions established in the 16th century. Only natural materials, often unfinished or asymetrical, are allowed in the construction. The rooms are purposefully small for intimacy; light is controlled by the careful placement of windows and doors; ornamentation is kept simple and seasonable. The fundamental philosophy of *chanoyu* promotes four principles: harmony, respect, purity and tranquility. For a small fee, the Foundation will lead a ceremony for small groups or individuals.

Turning left out the front door, the traveler heads toward Buchanan Street. At the intersection on the north side of Sutter Street is **Super Koyama Market**. Specializing in fresh, prepared fish, it sells *sashimi*, *gobo*, and *daikon* as well as Japanese snacks and dried goods.

Shops and boutiques: Departing the market and crossing the intersection brings you through the *torii* gate that is the entrance to **Nihonmachi Mall**, a block-long, cobblestoned, pedestrian shopping and eating area. The mall, designed by Ruth Asawa, is meant to resemble a small Japanese village with a meandering stream (this one made of cobblestones) in serpentine pattern. Unfortunately, the two "metal origami" fountains which Asawa designed to create the stream failed to recirculate the flow of water, resulting in monthly water bills too high for the local merchants to pay. As a result, the stream has remained dry for over a decade. **High tea.**

Stepping into **Goshado**, a variety store and bookstore, provides a lesson in Japanese politeness; crossing their threshold triggers a tape-recorded Japanese message: "Welcome" or "Thank you very much," depending on which direction you go. Inside you will find people avidly flipping through Japanese *manga*, serialized newsprint comics, bound into weekly editions hundreds of pages thick. Manga, immensely popular in Japan, range from humorous editions for young kids, action adventures for teenagers, and soap-opera style dime novels for commuters.

When the urge hits to shop, **Nichi Bei Bussan** is a good store for a variety of reasonably priced gifts, while **Genji** is more of a gallery, specializing in kimonos and antique furniture. Genji also has an excellent collection of delicate ceramic Meiji dolls. But the best store of all is **Soko Hardware**, a veritable museum of domestic Japanese culture. Included in the two-story cornucopia are rattan *gonza* mats, cooking utensils, *bonsai* planters and bamboo water spouts. There's lots of hardware too, including Japanese carpentry tools, which differ greatly from their American counterparts.

Of the nearby restaurants, **Iroha** specializes in noodle dishes. The *tempura* dishes at **Sanppo**, on the southeast corner of the mall, are considered the best in the neighborhood. And if it's sushi that whets your appetite, **Akasaka** provides the best value.

When departing the mall toward Post Street, it's best to turn right and stay on the north side of the street. Just at the corner is a set of stairs that leads up to **Kanzaki**, a nightclub that hosts Japanese-American rock and pop groups.

Going west along Post, the musically-inclined may want to stop in at **Sharaku** and purchase Japanese musical instruments such as the flute-like *shakuhachi*, or the zither-like *koto*. The store also offers reasonably-priced instruction in the playing of both intruments. At the end of the block is Webster Street, and

A musical march.

on the right is **Japantown Bowl**, offering round-the-clock bowling on Fridays or Saturdays.

The Japan Center: The **Kinokuniya Building** is a good starting point for exploring the complex's three sprawling buildings. It houses the well-known **Kabuki Hot Springs**. This institution offers communal or private hot baths, saunas, steam rooms and *shiatsu massage*, always in the most immaculate quarters. Upstairs, you'll find the **Kinokuniya Bookstore**, a large, airy store with a wide selection of Japanese paperbacks and magazines, as well as books in English about Japan or by Japanese authors. Across the way, Kinokuniya also has a separate stationery shop which sells origami and beautiful wrapping papers. **Mashiko** specializes in Japanese folk art.

Across the Webster Street Bridge at the **Kintetsu Building**, you'll find the **Kintetsu Restaurant Mall**. All the establishments are elbow-to-elbow, the competition fierce. It's amusing to sit at a circular table in one of the many restaurants and pluck the sushi off miniature wooden boats that float in a trough. Behind them, sushi chefs replenish the tiny vessels with fresh cargo.

The **Japan Information Service** provides a library for public use and shows free educational films about Japan. Across the hall are some of the beautiful flower arrangements of the **Ikenobo Ikebana Society of America**.

At the Laguna Street end of Japan Center is the 14-story high Miyako Hotel, offering luxury accommodation in both Eastern and Western style. In the middle of the complex is the outdoor **Peace Plaza Mall**, its distinguishing feature a 100-ft (30-meter) **Peace Pagoda**, with five tiers (odd numbers bring good luck) donated by Japan.

During *Sakura Matsuri*, the annual **Cherry Blossom Festival**, the plaza is crowded with *Taiko* drummers and dancers wearing brightly colored costumes. Cultural displays of *ikebana* (flower arranging) and *origami* (paper folding) can be seen, as well as demonstrations of martial arts.

Other festivals which draw crowds include the Buddhist *Bon* Festival in July, the *Nihonmachi* Street Fair in August, and *Aki Matsuri* (celebrating the autumn harvest) in September.

Unfortunately, the once-cultivated landscaping of the plaza was uprooted in 1990 when the city waterproofed the garage below it. A non-profit coalition plans to restore the plaza to its former condition, adding a Japanese-style garden, but it will be years before the renovation is complete.

Just south of Japantown at 351 Divisadero Street, in the area known as the **Western Addition**, is the little-known **St John's African Orthodox Church**, probably the only one in the world dedicated to a jazz musician, the late John Coltrane, whose gilded name sits over the entrance. The Sunday morning services draw a mixed crowd to a poverty-stricken area which is anything but touristy during the week.

Left, a fan unfurled. **Right**, Asia in style and song.

MISSION AND CASTRO

The **Mission** and **Castro districts** of San Francisco aren't usually considered tourist attractions, but both are vibrant elements of the city's culture. Their respective Latino and gay populations would seem to have little in common, but a visit to Dolores Park, the geographical meeting point of the two neighborhoods, shows how proximity has bred familiarity: families gather for birthday celebrations alongside sunbathing gay men, from whom the park gets its nickname, **Castro Beach**.

An afternoon spent in either of these neighborhoods is best done with an eye toward people-watching, as it is the residents who give these places their life. These areas certainly boast their share of historic buildings, interesting shops and good restaurants, but the residents reveal its true livelihood.

The Mission: The Mission district is known as San Francisco's Latino neighborhood, and at this point "Latino" is as specific as one can get. In recent years, the demographics of the Mission have changed as have the politics of Latin America; Central Americans joined Mexican immigrants here when political turmoil made them flee their countries. But the Mission has always been a home to San Francisco's newest residents. The **Good Samaritan Community Center**, now boarded up after the Loma Prieta earthquake of 1989 cracked its foundation, served German and Irish immigrants earlier in the century, before turning its attention to the Spanish-speaking population.

Even the deepest corner of the Mission isn't home only to recent immigrants; a thriving Chicano/Latino community that revels in its hybridization has taken root here. The murals on Balmy Alley, for example, are part of a tradition of Chicano political art that came to life in San Francisco in the 1970s. Galería de la Raza, a small adventurous art gallery, sprung up in the wake of the *movimiento*, as it's called, along with the arts and crafts shop next door. The Mission also boasts the intellectual life that exiled academics and politicos have brought with them. In other words, a trip to the Mission isn't just a folklore lesson; it's also a lesson in San Francisco's own culture.

Mission history: The Mission district takes its name from **Mission Dolores**, San Francisco's oldest building and the sixth mission in a chain of Spanish settlements that stretched 650 miles (1,045 km) from San Diego to northern California. Captain José Moraga and Father Francisco Palou founded the mission with a handful of settlers in 1776, just days before the signing of the Declaration of Independence by English colonists on the opposite side of the continent. In 1791 the church was dedicated to San Francisco de Assisi, and became known as Mission Dolores.

Over the centuries this building's 4-ft (1-meter) thick adobe walls have withstood several natural disasters. The original bells, cast in the 1790s, hang from leather thongs above the vestibule, and most of the original craftwork is intact.

By the early 1800s, the Mission was an area of farms and resorts; most of the Castonoan Indians who originally lived here had either died of the Europeans' diseases or fled to the few places left to them. Over 5,000 nameless Castonoans are buried in the small cemetery next to Mission Dolores, along with several notable figures from San Francisco's early days, including the first governor of Alta California and the first *alcalde* (mayor) of Yerba Buena.

After the Gold Rush, a 40-ft (12-meter) wide plank road was constructed, linking the Mission district with the heart of San Francisco. Near the road saloons, dancehalls, gambling houses, a horse-racing track and a bear-and-bullfighting ring soon opened to take advantage of the traffic – much of it spilling over from the Barbary Coast.

As the town expanded westward, a

growing number of Irish families moved into the area surrounding the old church. By the late 1880s the Mission contained the largest group of Irish families in San Francisco, along with a few pockets of Scandinavians, Germans and, after the fire of 1906, Italians from North Beach. The Irish remained until well after World War II, when Mexicans and other Latin American immigrants began to arrive and eventually displaced them.

Melting pot: Today the Mission is San Francisco's Hispanic center, with a large population of Mexicans, Salvadoreans, Bolivians, Guatemalans and Colombians as well as a fair share of non-Latinos, including Samoans, Vietnamese, Koreans and American Indians. It is predominantly a working-class neighborhood with a strong sense of community and social awareness. In addition to the involvement of many residents in Central American politics, a number of political action groups have their headquarters here and an active community of feminists and lesbians has settled along **Valencia Street**. A few cafés tend to attract this crowd – the casual ambiance and heterogeneous clientele make the **Café Picaro** (16th Street between Valencia and Guerrero) especially appealing – and neighborhood bookstores (like **Modern Times Bookstore** on Valencia) are always well-stocked with titles relating to women's issues, liberation, social change and various aspects of Latin America's often stormy history and politics.

Most maps show the Mission extending from about 14th down to Army Street, squared off by Dolores Street and Potrero Avenue. But the other distinct Mission neighborhood, roughly the area surrounding the 16th and Valencia area, was recently deemed San Francisco's New Bohemia, and is home to a mix of ethnicities, students and artists. A boom in the bar scene here is handing the once-prevailing nightlife of South of Market over to the suburbs' bridge-and-tunnel crowd.

Above all, the ties that bind this

Mission has the city's oldest building…

neighborhood are ethnic. The Latino community's identification with *la raza* (the race or the people) is reflected in the many colorful murals scattered throughout the neighborhood, most notably at the **BART station** on 24th and Mission streets, the **Bank of America** on 23rd and Mission, **Good Karma Restaurant** which faces Dolores Park and on countless other school, business, and housing projects.

A similar mixture of art, social commentary and politics is offered on 24th Street at the **Galería de la Raza**, often hailed as the most important Chicano art center in the country, which presents a series of exhibits featuring both local artists and photographers. **Balmy Alley** has gained world recognition for its many political murals.

Ethnic authenticity: The neighborhood's main strip, **Mission Street**, is a bustling commercial avenue lined with discount shops, outlets for inexpensive clothes, pawn brokers, poolrooms, bars, diners and produce stands. This is the place to

check out the *cholos* cruising the neighborhood in low riders or to listen to *salsa* and Mexican folk songs blasting from the bars. Low-budget restaurants are plentiful in this area, and what most places may lack in finesse and ambiance they more than make up for in good humor.

The Mission's primary food product is the *burrito*, and though it's not an authentic Mexican dish, it provides the neighborhood with almost all its economic stature. If you ask a dozen locals about their favorite *taquería* (derived from the word *taco*), you'll get a dozen answers – and there are at least twice that many *taquerías* in the Mission. **El Farolito** and **Taquería San Jose** are a notable couple among the prolific *burrito* joints; **Casa Sánchez** has garnered awards for its *salsa*, which it produces in several forms.

Taquerías, however, are notoriously deficient on ambiance – unless you're charmed by Aztec calendars and posters of scantily clad women draped over

...and most colorful murals.

giant beer bottles. To dine in more comfortable surroundings, check out **Las Guitarras**, **El Norteño** or **La Rondalla**, where the year-round Christmas lights and nightly mariachi bands have made it a local favorite.

Probably every country in Latin America has lent its influence to the culture of the Mission, so distinctions between cultures meld and blur: you can order *pupusas*, heavy, deep-fried Salvadorean tortas, at a lot of Mexican restaurants. **El Tazumel** on 20th Street features a long list of Salvadorean specialties, and **Cuba Restaurant** offers an interesting array of fish dishes prepared Cuban style. For a change of pace, there's **Good Karma Cafe** on Dolores Street, a well-known vegetarian restaurant dating back to the days of the "Summer of Love," when good karma was all-important.

The neighborhood's more interesting shops are also on Mission Street including **Arik Surplus Co.**, **Fashion Uniforms Inc.** and **Felinos**, which stocks

military surplus and vintage clothes ranging from pith helmets to zoot suits.

Four blocks west of Mission Street is **Dolores Street**, a beautiful, palm-lined boulevard bordered by colorful homes with bay windows. Just off Dolores on Liberty Street, between 20th and 21st, are some of the city's most beautifully restored Victorian houses.

Up another block, you'll discover the neighborhood's most coveted possession. **Dolores Park** is a sloping green square fringed at the top with a stately row of Victorian houses. This is one of the sunniest spots in the entire city, with an impressively stunning view of the East Bay. It's a perfect place for tossing a frisbee, picnicking or stealing an afternoon nap. Mission Dolores is two blocks up at 16th Street.

The Castro: San Francisco is often referred to as the gay capital of the world, a title both gays and straights wear with pride. The lesbian/gay community, which has made its home in the Castro, has contributed significantly to every arena of San Franciscan culture: economic, artistic and political.

In a massive campaign of urban restoration, the gay community transformed the Castro's aging Victorian houses into a fashionable, upscale enclave of shops, restaurants and homes. Some straight visitors may feel uncomfortable venturing into the neighborhood, but its residents have few biases. For those who are unacquainted with the gay community, a stroll through the Castro is most likely to challenge many of your pre-existing notions about gay culture.

Some historians trace the origin of San Francisco's gay population to the expulsion of homosexuals from the military during World War II. Since the early 1970s, the gay community has been galvanized by the active politicization of gay issues, a process which transformed this large underground into a lively and influential social force. Thanks in part to the work of people like Harvey Milk, the first openly gay member of city government and the victim of

Castro is home to many all-American boys.

homophobic murder, gays and lesbians in San Francisco recognize themselves and are recognized by others as an active community. In recent years the strength of the community has been challenged and perhaps further galvanized by the ongoing struggle against AIDS. Again, the community has pulled together to support its friends who live with HIV, while pushing legislation that would help find a cure.

Probably the best way to approach the Castro is to spend some time strolling along Castro Street between 17th and 19th streets. This is the neighborhood's compact business section, and in these two short blocks there are plenty of shops and restaurants for an afternoon or two of browsing and gazing.

Whether you want to see a movie or not, be sure to stop by the **Castro Theater**, a beautiful work of Spanish Colonial design built in the 1930s. This revival house features a live organist who plays every evening on an ascending platform, a nostalgic reminder of

The Castro Theater was built in the 1930s.

childhood movie-going for many. You may also want to take a closer look at the **Bank of America building** and the **Hibernia Bank**, both built in the 1920s.

Favorite pubs and cafés in the area include Moby Dick's, The Midnight Sun, a favored cruise joint for men, and Café San Marcos, an essentially mixed bar that nonetheless claims to draw the prettiest women in the Castro.

Castro events: If you time it right, you can catch one of several special events held in the Castro throughout the year. The Gay Freedom Day Parade attracts around 250,000 participants each June. The Castro Street Fair is held in the third week of August, and each year the neighborhood hosts a night-long Halloween parade.

Harvey Milk's birthday is celebrated on May 22, and on November 27 a candlelight march commemorates his murder. The variety of these events, some festive and some outrageous, attest to the lesbian and gay community's strength and pride in its culture.

MANSIONS

Shaped by steep hills and a history of boom or bust, San Francisco's architectural style has always been exuberant. Two years after gold was discovered, in January of 1848, the population exploded from 900 to 25,000. San Francisco became a sprawling, teeming mass of speculators bent on striking it rich.

At first, there wasn't time to build houses. Each day more tents appeared and shacks were put up with whatever materials were at hand. Even the schooners that hauled the precious supplies of food and tools around the Cape were pressed into service. Dragged ashore, doors were cut in the hulls, and the ships were transformed into houses, stores, and even hotels.

But the new-found wealth pouring in from the gold fields created a community that couldn't be satisfied with a "tent-city" status. Houses went up, spreading westward from the bay, at a rate unprecedented for the 19th century – from 15 to 30 a day in 1852. Construction overwhelmingly favored timber, cut and shipped from the virgin pine forests of the Oregon Territory in vast quantities. But even the modern advances of balloon framing and manufactured nails could not keep pace with the housing demand, and some homes and hotels arrived as easily assembled prefabricated kits from the East.

Techniques developed for the mass production of ornamental shapes out of wood gave even common house builders a claim to splendor. Every architectural fashion of the day was fair game, from Victorian Gothic to St Anne, from French Renaissance to Turkish towers. The result is a bedazzling architectural eclecticism. In San Francisco, Moorish cupolas can be found on an Italianate facade, perhaps accompanied by an Egyptian column or two. For the very rich, no expense was too great, no splendor too excessive.

Preceding pages and left, several mansions have been turned into grand hotels. Right, Spreckels Mansion greets the dawn.

Nob Hill: From a historic perspective there is no better place to start a relationship with San Francisco's gracious homes than at Nob Hill. The cable car lines cross at **California** and **Powell** streets. From here there is a magnificent view of the bay, crossed by the Oakland Bay Bridge and framed by the pagodas of Chinatown and the pyramidal spire of the Transamerica Building. The climb up California Street ends atop what writer Robert Louis Stevenson called the "hill of palaces." In a fevered rush to outdo each other in opulence, the robber barons of the last century built their palatial homes on Nob Hill. Many of the homes that remain have now been converted into condos or multi-dwelling apartment buildings.

The best-known landmark on the hill today is the **Mark Hopkins Hotel** which occupies the site of the former Mark Hopkins mansion, whose original stables boasted rosewood stalls with silver trimmings and mosaic floors covered with Belgian carpets. Hopkins, one of

the "Big Four" railroad magnates of the time, saw much of this luxury destroyed in the fire that raged for five days and nights following the earthquake of 1906. The **Pacific Union Club**, built for silver magnate James Flood in 1855, is just about the only survivor of the fire. Today the sturdy brownstone structure with its pine-framed entrance is a private club.

The **Stanford Court**, **Mark Hopkins** and **Huntington** hotels were built on the ashes of the great mansions and retain an aura of the original splendor, especially the **Fairmont Hotel** with its gilded lobby and faux-marble pillars. Have a cocktail in the lounge or enjoy a swank meal with a view at the original **Top of the Mark**, the revolving restaurant atop the nearby Mark Hopkins Hotel. The **Big Four** bar at the Huntington celebrates Messrs Crocker, Hopkins, Huntington and Stanford, the tycoons who built the transcontinental railroad, and evokes the robber baron era with its woody, masculine interior.

During the Christmas season, the Nob Hill hotels host free choral concerts in festively decorated lobbies. And, of course, the rich folk on the hill descend downtown for the city's renowned opera season, although even at the opera, the Snob Hill residents find themselves pushed aside every now and then by ordinary people. "Opera-throwers," as they are called, are fans who hurl bouquets at beloved divas during encores. Sometimes they brusquely push aside ushers and patrons alike to take advantage of the mere 30 seconds during which they can perform their self-appointed task of homage.

It requires more than a little skill to send flowers 35 ft (10 meters) over the heads of the orchestra so that they land perfectly at the desired singer's feet. A loosely organized group of about 50 throwers – mostly men – called the Opera Standees Association, is tolerated by, but not formally associated with, the San Francisco Opera. The Standees' record most successful "performer" is Robert Parks, who hurled

The Pacific Union Club.

some 300 bouquets in a single season, each one hitting the mark.

Huntington Park, one of the best maintained and most pleasant public spaces in the city, occupies the central block of Nob Hill. Above the park is **Grace Cathedral**. Built of concrete and consecrated in 1964, it is not particularly remarkable for its architecture, but the doors are worth a closer look, for they are cast from Lorenzo Ghiberti's original *Doors of Paradise* in Florence.

On Sacramento Street, the Beaux Art extravagance of the **Chambord Apartments** at 1298 demonstrates San Francisco's love of the exotic. Two blocks up, take Leavenworth Street or Hyde Street and wander toward **Russian Hill**. Take this jaunt at a leisurely pace, or you'll miss the tiny avenue lined with attractive garden apartments on Priest and Reed streets.

Russian Hill is also home to **Lombard Street**, possibly the curviest street in the world. As if lining up for some urban rollercoaster ride, tourists drive up to the top on sunny afternoons and wait their turn to traverse this unique slalom course. Why? More likely than not because they've once seen somebody else do it on film.

Between Hyde and Leavenworth streets, this short stretch of Lombard takes cars on its infamous criss-crossing hairpin turns along a cobblestone roadway. To each side are some of the city's most elaborately landscaped homes, tucked precariously into the slopes of Russian Hill. Those on foot might have an easier time taking a leisurely stroll down Lombard's less famous, but perhaps more scenic footpath.

Pacific Heights: For the most part, Pacific Heights escaped the great earthquake and fire, and an address on the Heights still denotes position, power and wealth. **Alta Plaza Park** is an excellent starting point for a stroll through this majestic neighborhood. The view is magnificent: to the south, Twin Peaks, Buena Vista and Potrero Hill are visible in one commanding sweep and, turning

The Fairmont Hotel.

toward the bay, the ships appear dwarfed by the panorama below.

Across the street, at 2600 Jackson, is the **Smith House**, a Jacobean-style brick structure built by Mr Scott in 1895 for his daughter, who became Mrs Reginald Knight Smith. The fact that the house is built of brick is noteworthy itself. Not indigenous to the area, brick had to be imported to San Francisco, making it a rare and costly material in those days. It is said that when the city was shaken by the earthquake of 1906, neighbors found Dr Smith on his roof clearing away the loose bricks and tiles, in case they fell on refugees from the fires. The mansion was also the first fully electrified house in the city.

Down the street at 2622 Jackson is the **Gibbs House**. This copy of a Roman villa, built in 1894, was the first commissioned work of the celebrated designer, Willis Polk, who was later honored for his architectural contributions to the city by having a street named after him. The bas-reliefs of the muses which decorate the entrance are appropriate to the building's current use as a conservatory of art. During school hours you can view the fine wood panelling of the lobby and the stairway and the original stained glass windows.

At 2421 and 2415 Pierce Street is the **James Irvine Home**. The houses were designed by Edgar Matthews. Notice the signature windows with their graceful pane designs. Inside, the house is brilliantly designed: a piece of architectural trickery makes the building seem to be much larger than it actually is by cleverly reducing the inner scales of the house. In fact, much of San Francisco was built in this manner to overcome spatial restrictions.

To the left along Pacific is the **Monteagle House**, which was designed by Lewis Hobart, the architect of Grace Cathedral. It is French-Gothic in style, and was built in 1923.

The oldest house on Pacific Heights is the **Leale House**, at No. 2475. It was once a farmhouse, set in a 25-acre (10-

The Haas-Lilienthal homestead.

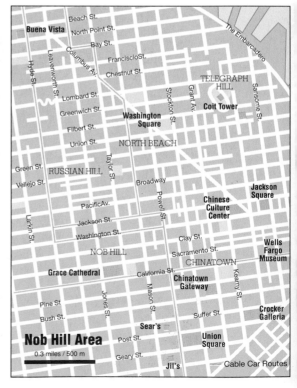

Nob Hill Area
0.3 miles / 500 m

hectare) dairy farm. In time, it became the home of a retired sea captain who wrote a book called *Tule Sailor*.

On the corner of Pacific and Webster there is a gorgeous view of the bay, including Alcatraz and Angel islands. At 2550 Webster is the **Bourn Mansion**. This was the townhouse and office of the richest man in San Francisco during the 1920s and 1930s. William B. Bourn was president of the Spring Valley Water Company and the inheritor of a Mother Lode gold mine.

The large window over the door belonged to his office. It was positioned here so that visitors had to literally walk under his feet in order to visit him. The architect, Willis Polk, added to the power of this window by omitting all but the small windows on the upper floor. The façade is made of cinder brick, a poor-quality brick popular in that era, but it is only a veneer – underneath it is 2 ft (60 cm) of rugged brick.

Broadway and Webster is the heart of Pacific Heights. When the cable car lines were being laid out, they covered the whole of the city, but they didn't run down Broadway. It was believed that the residents of this area were wealthy and resourceful enough to provide for their own transportation.

At 2120 Broadway is the **Flood Mansion**, the palace built by Comstock mine owner James Flood. It is a magnificent neoclassical Revival building, its interior rich with red lacquer, bamboo, a maple library, a walnut and mahogany staircase and Tiffany skylights. After the earthquake, Mrs Flood expressed her fears about the largely wood-built house. Her husband told her not to worry, because "I'll build you a marble house on a granite hill."

There is no granite in San Francisco, let alone a granite hill. So Mr Flood had a granite slab brought in, on which he built the house at **2222 Broadway**. It is a copy of a 3-story Italian Renaissance villa and was completed in 1912, just six years after Mrs Flood first expressed her fears. The house is now a convent.

Lombard Street: the curviest in the world.

After continuing down Broadway for two blocks to Laguna, turn left on Jackson. At 2090 Jackson is the **Whittier Mansion**. From the outside, the house presents an odd conglomeration of styles. The Roman temple entranceway abuts the Queen Anne tower with a harmony that attests to the skill of the architect, Edward Swain. The house is the headquarters of the California Historical Society and is open to the public. It is well worth the modest admission fee for the chance to see the interior of one of these magnificent mansions.

The house was commissioned in 1894 and completed in 1896. It includes several gadgets that Whittier fancied, as well as many of the innovations of the day. The closets light up when the doors open; the reception room includes a fixture for a champagne fountain; and all the floors have snaps to hold the rugs in place. The house also boasted the first central hot water heating system and a ventilation system so efficient that it changed the air every three minutes.

At Jackson and Octavia Street, the back of the **Spreckels Mansion** is visible. This is one of San Francisco's most elegant mansions, commissioned originally by the sugar magnate Adolph Spreckels. The low-rise building behind the mansion houses a covered pool. The gate on the Jackson Street side is the old delivery entrance and behind the window in the wall is where the gate keeper lived.

At 1925 Jackson is the massive and baroque **Grenlee Terrace** apartment. There are few apartment buildings in this area because the residents, alarmed by the appearance of the first high-rise buildings, quickly included a ban on tall buildings in the zoning code.

The **Haas-Lilienthal House**, at 2007 Franklin, is straight ahead and to the right. This huge Victorian house, built in 1886 in the Queen Anne style, is open to the public and furnished with period pieces. You can turn back uphill from here and rest in **Lafayette Park** amid the crisp scent of eucalyptus trees while watching the ships sailing in from the Golden Gate.

Union Street: Just below Pacific Heights is Union Street. Today it is crowded with shops and singles bars, but once this was Cow Hollow and an area in which dairy farms flourished.

A walk down Gough Street leads to an eight-sided oddity, the **Octagon House** at 2645 Gough. Built in 1861, it is one of the few remaining examples of this style. It is furnished with Colonial and Federal period antiques and is open to the public on a limited basis.

Turn left on Green Street to the **Vedanta House** at 2963 Webster. This is Joseph Leonard's tribute to Hindu tolerance, and the effect is spectacular. Mingled together are Queen Anne towers, Moorish domes and medieval turrets. Finally, at 2727 Pierce is the **Casebolt House**. This massive Italianate edifice dates from 1865, quite late in the silver era, and forms a link with the days when San Francisco was a young city with a glittering future.

The Vedanta House has Hindu influences.

(S)NOB HILL

San Francisco lore has it that the contraction of the word "Nabob" — meaning Moghul prince – gave rise to the name Nob Hill, the one-time stomping ground of the city's powerful railroad tycoons, site of San Francisco's premier luxury hotels and turn-of-the-century mansions, and residential enclave of wealthy socialites. Given the concentration of wealth to be found here, and the exclusiveness that such riches have been known to inspire, Nob Hill soon earned itself another nickname, a gift from the city's more down-to-earth population: "Snob" Hill.

The highest of the city's seven hills, it looms over Union Square and the Tenderloin to the south, Polk Gulch to the west, and Chinatown to the east. This was not a desirable residential area until the invention of the cable car in 1873. Only then did the railroad barons build their colossal mansions here, running cable car tracks down California Street to the Central Pacific (now Southern Pacific) headquarters on Market Street. James Ben Ali Haggin, was one of the first to build, with a modest home of no more than 60 rooms.

Banker Ralston, grocer Leland Stanford, hardware merchant Mark Hopkins, and dry goods purveyor Charles Crocker quickly followed suit. The real Gold Rush fortunes, of course, were made not from mining but from the hard-earned dollars of the miners themselves, by those who supplied them with needed goods and services.

But the nabobs (or, if you prefer, snobs) of the late 19th century no longer wield unlimited power in the neighborhood, and while the Pacific Union Club may not be opening its doors to the general public, many of the palaces of yesteryear have been diminished by their conversion into condominiums and hotel penthouses.

Even at the height of their influence, the nabobs were occasionally kept in check. Charles Crocker, for example, the only one of the Big Four not to have a luxury hotel named for him today, owned a sprawling mansion which occupied most of the block on California Street between Taylor and Jones. His desire to own the entire block was thwarted by a Chinese undertaker named Nicholas Yung who declined to sell his corner lot to Crocker, for a generous, even exorbitant price.

Infuriated, Crocker proceeded to erect a 40-ft (12-meter) "spite fence" around three sides of the property. An outraged mob of San Franciscans marched onto Nob Hill in protest, demanding that the fence be torn down and that Charles Crocker be lynched. Neither event actually occurred. Yung never surrendered his property and, when Crocker's mansion was destroyed in the 1906 earthquake, the site was taken over by the Episcopal Diocese. Today it is known as Grace Cathedral (*see page 203*).

As in bygone days, the nabobs still descend from the heights to patronize the opera. Columnist Herb Caen's description of a recent opening night at the impressive Opera House highlights the persistent gap between the city's haves and have-nots. "All the well-worn contradictions of capitalism were very much in evidence," Caen observed. "Limos purring, ladies preening, guys groaning, beggars supplicating from their positions on the icy sidewalks… [but] the really rich carry no cash." ∎

The Mark
Hopkins Hotel.

AROUND GOLDEN GATE PARK

Imagine a place where you can sip tea in a fragrant Oriental garden, row past a cascading waterfall, rollerblade past a herd of buffalo, watch a polo match or ride your own horse (either the real or the wooden carousel variety), or jog along winding, shaded paths on your way to the Pacific Ocean. You may also mingle with the Old Dutch Masters or ogle an El Greco, find out when to plant your favorite roses and enjoy the aroma of a Himalayan rhododendron.

Welcome to San Francisco's **Golden Gate Park**, once a wasteland of sand dunes and now the largest man-made urban park in the world. It has offered outdoor and recreational respite to the city-bound for nearly 120 years.

The park's origins: Adjoining the Haight-Ashbury district, running to the Pacific between the Richmond and Sunset districts, Golden Gate Park – eight blocks wide and 52 blocks long – covers 1,040 acres (420 hectares). This outdoor park of wind-swept dunes was the project of the park's designer, William Hammond Hall. His dream, thought to be outlandish at the time, was to create a park utilizing natural topography rather than imposing artificial forms.

Hall faced some impressive challenges, the most pressing of which was planting in a wind-scoured surface composed largely of sand – hardly conducive to the cultivation of flowers, shrubs and trees. Legend has it that the park got its official start accidentally when Hall neglected to clean up a feed bag of barley that a horse had kicked over and returned to discover a delicate fuzz of green sprouting up through the sand. Inspired to plant barley fields he was eventually able to root trees. It is a good story, but not necessarily a true one.

Nevertheless, Hall persevered. Employing a combination of deep-rooting sea grasses, lupine and trees, he began the arduous task of creating a park by tacking down the sand dunes in the eastern park from the Panhandle to the Conservatory. Credit for his five years of effort, however, eluded Hall – sadly, there is no monument in the park commemorating his contributions – mostly because his work was overshadowed by his dynamic successor, the Scotsman "Uncle John" McLaren.

"Uncle John's rule": From his original lodge at the park's western edge (on the northwest corner of Stanyan Street and John F. Kennedy Drive), the short, gruff Scot managed his magnificent empire with diligence and endurance.

It was through the skill of McLaren's "green thumb" that the park really began to flourish. An estate gardener-turned-supervisor, "Uncle John" lived and worked at the park from 1885 until his death in 1943 at the age of 96. His love of nature, bountiful resourcefulness, and determination to preserve a natural environment underpins almost every aspect of the park.

McLaren had boundless reserves of

Preceding pages: the Palace of Fine Arts. Left, Golden Gate rolls out the red carpet. Right, passion in the park.

persistence and perseverance, planting over one million trees and introducing hundreds of varieties of rhododendron, eucalyptus, conifer, shrubs and flowers to California. In 1931 alone he brought in 700 new species.

Many colorful tales survive about "Uncle John," particularly about the way he repeatedly outwitted both tampering politicians and special interest groups as he shaped dunes into dells and a wasteland into a municipal Eden. His two stipulations for the park were: no "keep off the grass" signs, and his admonition, "You mind the politics, and I'll mind the parks."

McLaren wasn't above a bit of chicanery for the sake of his beloved trees, and had absolute power over park employees. In order to become a gardener under his rule, an applicant had to score better than 90 percent on a test identifying – and spelling correctly – 100 plants found in the park. It was under McLaren's peculiar and forceful charisma that the park blossomed, while misers were turned into philanthropists through his persuasion. From one wealthy benefactor, Collis Huntington, McLaren even wheedled a waterfall.

Off Kennedy Drive as you turn toward the DeYoung Museum, there is, in the Rhododendron Dell, a lifesize statute of McLaren himself, who detested the monuments that the city fathers insisted on placing in the park. Many of the statutes in Golden Gate Park are virtually hidden by foliage.

The sporting life: In addition to the many gardens, lawns and millions of plants, Golden Gate Park offers sports lovers of every kind a satisfying weekend workout. (Main park roads are closed to traffic on Sundays to make this easier.) There are football, baseball and soccer fields; *bocce*, basketball, tennis and handball courts; and lawn bowling greens. There are horseshoe and barbecue pits; marble chess tables; a golf course; a running track; jogging, bike and bridle paths; and hiking trails. Dog owners can even train their pets here. Swarms of in-line skaters take over much of the roadways and hold races here during the summer. After-work or weekend games of "Ultimate frisbee" are usually in progress on the large grass fields, while smaller groups kick around the "hackey sacks." And if fishing lures you, head for the charming, old-fashioned **Fly Casting Pool**. There are pedal and row boats that can be rented and a very pretty lake designed for piloting scores of miniature model boats.

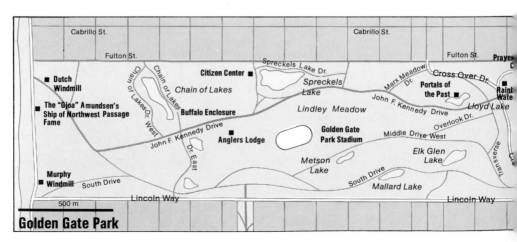

Golden Gate Park

In the less frequented western half of the park, the prevailing aura is of the Victorian era. A rustic **Anglers' Lodge** hidden among the evergreens and eucalyptuses presides over a fly-casting area, and the **Golden Gate Stadium**, with its stables and polo fields, is the scene of cricket and rugby matches.

Also evocative of the past century is the **Buffalo Paddock** off Kennedy Drive. The buffalo here, however, trace their lineage not to the Great Plains, but to the Bronx Zoo of New York City, where the species was bred in captivity and thus saved from extinction around 1900. Admiring visitors find themselves feeding these dignified beasts the bread they brought for the birds.

On a typical Sunday the **events calendar** invites visitors to watch the Morgan Horses Club of Northern California assemble on the Polo Field, attend an art opening, go to a concert by the park band in the Music Concourse or enjoy a ballroom dance for seniors.

Hippie Hill, on the north side of the large field opposite the Children's Playground, was renowned in the Haight-Ashbury heyday for its gatherings of longed-haired young people, playing music and smoking pot, and was the site of the many gatherings and free concerts during the 1967 "Summer of Love."

Haight Street runs into the east end of the park and **Haight-Ashbury** is still a mecca for a particular kind of tourist. It's been over a quarter century since the Summer of Love, when the tie-dyed, the beaded, the bell-bottomed and the barefoot inaugurated a new generation of self-proclaimed freaks and flower children – or hippies, as they were called.

For several hot months in the summer of '67, life became a costume party staged in a wonderland setting of brightly painted Victorian buildings. The neighborhood became a swirl of colors as flower children painted storefronts, sidewalks, posters, cars, vans and, of course, themselves. The days and nights were filled with sex, drugs, and a pot-laced breeze, with music provided by Jimi Hendrix, Janis Joplin, Jefferson Airplane and the Grateful Dead – all of them living in riotous, 24-hour Haight-Ashbury pads.

Things have changed, of course. Today there are more homeless on the streets than hippies, and the color schemes on the old Victorians have been toned down. Bus-riding tourists snatch up Summer of Love t-shirts. Upscale boutiques draw downtown shoppers to avant-garde lingerie and studded black

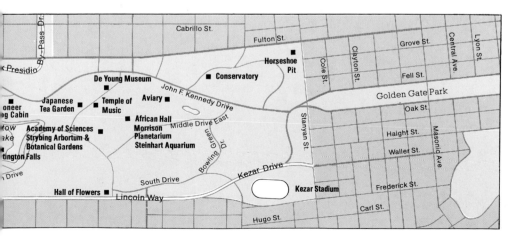

leather. Janis Joplin's old apartment – an elegant, 1878 Edwardian building – was fully refurbished and sold for nearly $1 million, a decent buy for the yuppies who now populate the Haight's hillside neighborhood.

The old Psychedelic Shop, which hawked concert tickets and rolling papers, is now a pizza parlor. Diggers, a street theater commune, is now an organic food café. And at the center of what was once the hippie universe – the corner of Haight and Ashbury streets, where Joplin, the Grateful Dead and others performed – a clothing store and a Ben and Jerry's ice-cream parlor are now the primary attractions, aside from the nonstop sideshow of street people.

Still, the Haight continues to offer in abundance what it proposed in 1967 – tolerance. And the denizens of the '90s owe something to the '60s mind-expansion movement. In addition to a hippie culture all its own, the Haight became in its time a haven for new ideas in alternative medicine, ecological preservation, conceptual art and natural foods. Walking tours of the area are available on certain days.

Back in Golden Gate Park itself, relaxation is still the key-note. One way to experience the park is to cover the terrain on a mountain bike. Start at the **Panhandle** (a narrow strip of parkland at the park's eastern edge bounded by Fell and Oak streets) and end at the ocean a few miles westward. Bicycles as well as in-line skate rentals are available along the park's periphery – and also at the ocean, if you want to start from the other direction.

Kid stuff: The 100-year-old **Children's Playground** off Kezar Drive is the oldest playground in a public park in the country. Attractions here include a Mouse Tower and Troll Bridge. A carousel up the hill is open every day. This 1912 model, besides its richly decorated steeds, features a turning tub, rocker, and two chariots for aspiring Ben Hurs. The Carousel gift shop is open at the same time, so you can buy a

The Haight-Ashbury district...

picture of your favorite horse to take home. There is also a little farmyard full of friendly animals to pet and feed.

A short walk northward brings you to 24 tennis courts, available for open play as well as city-sponsored classes.

Watering holes: There are 11 lakes in the park, the largest of which, **Stow Lake**, is man-made and offers boating, scenic picnicking and hiking. **Strawberry Hill** (459 ft/140 meters), situated in the center of the lake, is the highest point in the park. Those who climb its slopes are rewarded with a spectacular view. On a clear day, you can see the Farallon Islands, 26 miles (42 km) out to sea, and Mount Diablo, 30 miles (48 km) inland to the east. Mt Tamalpais or "Mount Tam," can be seen to the north across the Golden Gate.

West of Transverse Drive is **Lloyd Lake**, celebrated for its Portals of the Past. These six white marble columns formed the portico of the A.N. Towne home on Nob Hill before the big quake and fire of 1906. They mark the end of an era – an age of champagne, gold and privilege. Many of the city's homeless lived here as refugees for up to a year after the catastrophe. This reminder of the earthquake characterized a new start, a fresh hope for devastated San Francisco. A plaque at the foot of one pillar testifies: "This is the portal of the past – from now on, once more, forward!"

Spreckels Lake, between 30th and 36th avenues, is the park's second largest lake. It serves as an ocean to flotillas of model boats. In the morning the power boats predominate, while afternoons are reserved for stately sailing craft. The **San Francisco Model Yacht Club** houses a testing tank, dry dock and several workbenches available for building model yachts and making repairs.

At **North Lake**, west of the Buffalo Paddock, there's a tiny, transplanted Everglades-type area, a swamp replete with water-wading cypresses. A nine-hole golf course and clubhouse are found further west. Horseback riding trails, scenic bike paths and archery ranges are

...still offers music and tolerance.

nearby for enthusiasts of these activities.

Strybing Arboretum, with over 70 acres (28 hectares) of gardens, fountains, a bookstore and a library, is a park within a park. There is a **Garden of Fragrance** dedicated especially to the visually-impaired, a **Succulent Garden** and a **Conifer Garden**. A special garden contains many of the plants mentioned in the Old and New Testaments. Visitors can also learn helpful planting techniques at the landscape demonstration gardens.

A touch of Japan: Only in romantic San Francisco could you find a **Moon-Viewing Pavilion and Garden**. It is a Japanese custom to hold a *tsuki-mi* in the fall when the harvest moon appears. Wildflowers and a bowl of rice dumplings are offered. Brightly colored kimonos billow in the breeze, while music and *sake* flow freely at the garden's festivities, and torches light a ceremonial parasol dance in front of the reflecting pool. Group reservations for your moon-viewing at this unique spot

are welcomed. Classes, lectures and "theme walks" are held at the **Arboretum**, and the public can buy rare varieties of plants which are on sale here.

In the vicinity of **Strybing** is a bucolic blend of horticulture and literature – the **Garden of Shakespeare's Flowers**. Enclosed by hedgerows of English laurel are "lady-smocks," eglantine and rosemary, along with 150 other species mentioned in Shakespeare's writings.

First, find the bust of the bard – one of only two copies cast in 1914 by George Bullock from a bust carved sometime before 1623. It is thought to be the best likeness of Shakespeare known to exist. Then, match flora and folio, comparing your guesses with the botanical quotes on the bronze plaques provided. Or maybe you're not so studious and, like the proverbial lover from *As You Like It*, could be found instead, "sighing like a furnace, with a woeful ballad made to his mistress's eyebrow."

The cultural center of Golden Gate Park surrounds the 20,000-seat outdoor

Lawn bowling green.

Music Concourse, a sunken auditorium with formal groves of oaks set between the park museums. Free concerts are held in the bandshell and additional programs for senior citizens are scheduled weekly during the summer.

Incidentally, the **Palace of Fine Arts Theater**, 3 miles (5 km) north, also offers a variety of events. Built 30 years ago to house an international film festival, the theater is now used for many other activities. This 1,000-seat auditorium is host to a summer dance concert series and music events.

Museums and music: One of the most admired buildings of the 1915 Panama-Pacific International Exposition was the **Palace of Fine Arts** itself, located at the foot of Lyon Street in the marina district. The exposition celebrated the opening of the Panama Canal, the advent of air travel, the development of the car and electric power. It also heralded an age of optimism and progress, beginning in the early part of this century.

The semi-circular palace, with its domed rotunda and lagoon-reflected arches, was designed by Bernard Maybeck and modeled after the mysterious edifice in Bocklin's painting, *The Island of the Dead*. In 1918, at the fair's close, the palace once again housed an art collection, but after 1921 the building was allowed to deteriorate to the point where it really did resemble its painted prototype on fog-shrouded mornings. Reconstruction began in 1964, and the palace was re-opened on September 20, 1967.

But the palace was to go dark (on the outside anyway) once again. Over the years the outdoor lighting – which gives the palace its majestic glow, reflected at night in the glass-like lagoon that surrounds it – fell victim to both vandals and the elements. In 1990, following a $500,000 fund-raising drive, the palace was lit once again, with a city celebration and 365 new outdoor lights.

In 1969, San Francisco's **Exploratorium** was also founded here. This is a collection of exhibits aimed at demon-

The Japanese Tea Garden.

strating the interdependence of science and art. Over 500 "hands-on" exhibits emphasize perception as the means to explore our relation to light, color, sound and hearing, touch and heat, as well as animal behavior. A museum without walls, the cavernous laboratory of discovery is characterized by an atmosphere of playfulness. The only hard and fast rule is "no bike riding."

Aspects of 226 phenomena are explored here, with 12 exhibits on friction, six laser-related demonstrations, and 21 on the production of light. Orange-clad "explainers" show visitors how to work the installations and assist in the building and repair of old exhibits as well as the creation of new ones.

The Exploratorium was founded by Frank Oppenheimer, the brother of J. Robert Oppenheimer, known as "the father of the atomic bomb." The Exploratorium aims to be a place where participation replaces passive learning, providing the student/visitor with experimental opportunities impossible to achieve through school, books or TV. The first thing one sees on entering the Exploratorium is the Sun Painting: interweaving rays of refracted sunlight directed beautifully onto a huge silver screen. Another attraction, **The Shadow Box**, "freezes" dancing and gesticulating participants' shadows for 30 seconds on phosphorescent screens before they dissolve. In the award-winning and ever-popular exhibit called **Everyone is You and Me**, "explorers" observe their features gradually merge with those of their partner, transposing two individuals' separate physical characteristics into one.

The **Vidium** lets inquiring sightseers draw pictures with sound. A miked oscilloscope translates singing, talking, and clapping into wave patterns. In addition, there's a 213-ft (65-meter) long Echo Tube which bounces back sounds with a delay and distorts them according to the component frequencies. A crawl-through **Tactile Dome**, using fingertips in total darkness, makes for a

The "Bay to Breakers" marathon.

fun-filled finale to the Exploratorium.

The Palace remains home to a host of other regular cultural events in the city, such as the Ethnic Dance Festival and the annual Animation Festival.

The De Young Museum: Back in Golden Gate Park, the various cultures of western civilization – from Egypt to the present – are all represented in the De Young Museum. This handsome, rose sandstone museum is fronted by a lily-covered Pool of Enchantment which reflects the 144-ft (44-meter) tower. Several galleries are devoted to American art from colonial times to the present day. The central court of the museum is a reconstructed 12th-century Spanish monastery with Moorish portals and archways. Masterpieces exhibited include El Greco's *St John the Baptist* and Ruben's *The Tribute Money*. **Café De Young**, with its bust of the museum's founder, serves good cappuccino along with snacks and full meals.

The **Avery Brundage Collection of Asian Art** is housed in a 2-story wing of the museum and is replete with Japanese paintings, ceramics and lacquer; Chinese paintings, bronzes, and jade; and sculpture from all over the East, including Korea and India.

Another of San Francisco's fine arts museums is the **Palace of the Legion of Honor** in nearby Lincoln Park, commanding a beautiful view of the bay and ocean. It was designed and built in 1924 as a memorial to California's war dead.

There is a peculiar and moving grandeur to the museum's architecture, with its courtyard and many columns and porticos. One of five original castings of Rodin's *The Thinker* is outside; it is one of a number of his works shown in the **Rodin Gallery** inside, where weekend organ recitals are held. Included in the museum's works is another El Greco, *St Peter*, and Turner's moody *Grand Canal at Venice*.

Situated across the Music Concourse from the De Young is the **California Academy of Sciences**. Walk to the central courtyard past the fine sculpture and the fountain of *Mating Whales*, and enter **African Hall** where life-like dioramas of big game beasts seem tame in comparison to a 30-ft (10-meter) dinosaur unearthed in Utah and on display in **Cowell Hall**.

Adjacent is the **Morrison Planetarium**, open for sky shows and Laserium concerts. In the nearby **Wattis Hall of Man**, *homo sapiens* are depicted in every imaginable environment, from a New Guinea tribesman to an Eskimo hunter. If you want to catch *all* the park's museums and attractions in a day or weekend, you can purchase a "Culture Pass" from the city's convention and tourist bureau – or any of the park museums.

Directly ahead of the Hall of Man is the balustraded swamp pit, where alligators laze in the water and crocodiles lurk. Downstairs from the pit are vipers, huge toads, pythons and boas, lizards of every hue and even poisonous frogs, the venom from whose skin is used by Amazon natives to tip arrows.

The first dark alley you duck into is

A baby and his balloons.

populated by phosphorescent fish. Here also is the **Steinhart Aquarium** with 208 tanks containing phosphorescent fish, giant sea bass, blowfish, sharks, "croakers," and even "talking fish." This tank is bugged so you can eavesdrop on their conversation. Other inhabitants are dolphins cavorting with acrobatic seals, penguins and a manatee.

Among recent additions is the **Fish Roundabout**. Hundreds of fast-swimming, open ocean species of large fish – snapper, yellowtail, sea bass and sharks – encircle the visitor and race past one another in a see-through aquatic donut 204 ft (62 meters) in circumference. The roundabout gives the visitor a real appreciation of the size and power of the ocean and all of its diverse life forms. It's the next best thing to scuba diving, and you don't even get wet.

Japanese village: The exquisite **Japanese Tea Garden** is the most visited 4 acres (1.5 hectares) of the park. Devised by George Turner Marsh, an Asian art dealer, the garden was originally

intended to represent a one-acre Japanese village. Marsh hired a renowned Japanese gardener, Makoto Hagiwara, who planned the garden and planted traditional dwarf *bonsai* conifers, elms and cherry trees. Hagiwara (whose family is said to have invented the fortune cookie) also designed the winding brooks with their moss-covered rocks, irises and carp pond. A large bronze Buddha cast in Japan in the 1790s overlooks the garden. The **Tea House** offers rice cookies and green tea served by hostesses dressed in traditional kimonos. A wishing bridge, a wooden gateway, and a five-story pagoda add to the garden's Japanese aura.

A contrast in moods is created by a visit to the **Conservatory**. This glass building was shipped around the Horn in 1875 and houses wonderful collections of rare palms and other tropical flora. It is believed to have been modelled after a building in London's Kew Gardens, and was imported by a private owner, then acquired from his estate by the city. Here the atmosphere is one of color unleashed and an energetic, vibrant mood pervades.

A seasonal flower bed out front is a living announcement board for local civic events. The grounds around the Conservatory have fine collections of fuchsias and azaleas.

As sunset approaches, plan to end your visit to Golden Gate Park out by the ocean. First, take a stroll by (or around) the Polo Fields, where a polo match might be in progress. The **Polo Fields** have, over the years, been the home to live concerts and events – including the "Human Be-In Gathering of Tribes" during the famous "summer of love" in 1967.

Westward, the renovated **North Dutch Windmill,** complete with tulip garden, and the **Murphy Windmill** in the park's southwest end, stand forlorn in the wind. They onced pumped water from the streams that flowed by; today they stoically face the sun as it sets over the Pacific.

Left, ship's captain. **Right,** *The Thinker* from the Rodin Gallery.

As friendly an invitation as it is – and as much as there is to explore in San Francisco alone – the city might also be considered a convenient launching pad for greater Bay Area and nearby California exploration. The paths out of San Francisco can take you quickly to the dramatic coastline, mist-soaked trails in the foothills, the verdant hills of Napa Valley, the towering peaks of the Sierra Nevada, and beyond. There are shortages in California from time to time – from state water supplies to the state budget – but, barring catastrophe, the state's natural wonders will always be in evidence. Best of all, most are within reach of San Francisco.

Travel is easy: three bridges span the bay, an underground train system links up the East Bay with San Francisco, ferries criss-cross the water, and trains run up and down the peninsula. Getting around by car, however, is still the best way to explore the area. Whatever your means, get out and explore – you'll discover delights far beyond those framed in California postcards.

Marin County: Starting from San Francisco and going north on Route 101, travelers cross the Golden Gate Bridge which links two unlikely shores. The Marin Headlands are formidable cliffs, wild and lonely, that stand in stark contradiction to the metropolis immediately across the bay.

The **California Marine Mammal Center** is also located here. This private, non-profit organization rescues and treats sick or injured marine mammals stranded along the California coastline. Visit one of the world's most unusual wild animal hospitals and get close-up views of seal and sea lion patients.

Not far from the bridge is Highway 1, a windy, scenic drive through eucalyp-

Preceding pages: pool with a view. **Left**, San Francisco's copper cliffs.

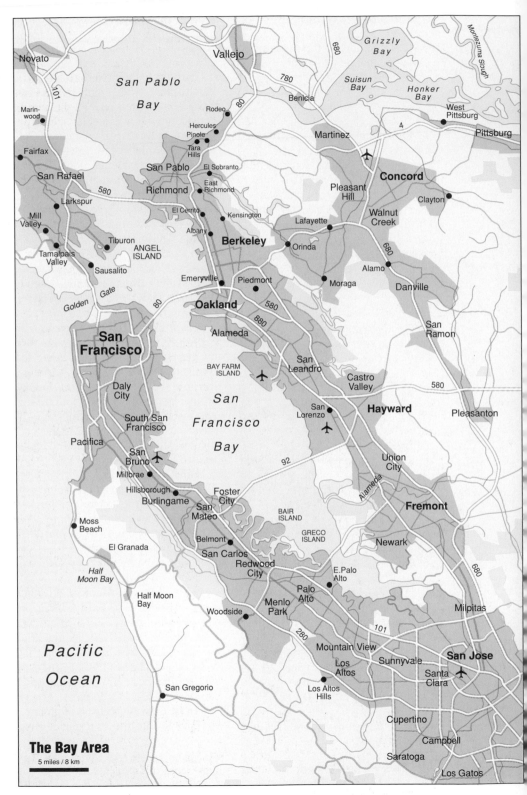

The Bay Area

5 miles / 8 km

tus groves which leads to a view of the shimmering Pacific Ocean. Stop at the **Zen Center**, a meditation community that was founded in the early 1970s when the property was bought from George Wheelwright, co-inventor of the Polaroid Land Camera.

Rustic and peaceful, the center and nearby farm provide a pastoral contrast to the city, only 12 miles (19 km) away. The old hayloft is the Zendo, or meditation room, and the horse stalls next to the milking troughs are private offices. Extensive vegetable gardens, lovingly cultivated by Green Gulch residents, cater for the Zen Center's restaurant, **Greens**, in San Francisco. Visitors are welcome to walk around the grounds, to attend morning instruction or to have some homebaked bread with tea.

Further beyond the Zen Center is **Muir Beach** and **Muir Woods**. A small beach at the foot of a cow pasture, Muir Beach is an open area with sheltered coves for picnicking. Nearby, a public, nude sunbathing area is protected from the wind by a cluster of rocks. After swimming or beach-combing, stop for tea and snacks at the **Pelican Inn**. Near Muir Beach's entrance, Pelican Inn is exquisitely decorated with European antiques and Turkish rugs, making it a pleasant respite.

Both Muir Beach and Muir Woods are named after naturalist John Muir, and are famous for their impressive redwood grove. Home of the *Sequoias*, a slender brand of redwoods that thrive in the damp, foggy climate, Muir Woods can be a wonderful place for rigorous hikes or quiet strolls. A paved walkway winds through the tall, mysterious columns of red-tinted trees.

Trails lead from the parking lot and pass through both redwood and eucalyptus groves to a high, open path that drops to the ocean. **Steep Ravine** is the rocky beach at the foot of the trail. A dramatic sight, for the rock wedges meet the waves straight on, sending a frothy spray high into the air.

While hiking, look out for the unusual albino redwood. The bark on these peculiar trees is a pale, sinewy green, and the needles are actually white. Walking through the woods can be an enchanting experience: certain groves seem untouched, undiscovered.

Just past Muir Woods is **Stinson Beach** (originally called Willow Camp). Today Stinson Beach is the most popular beach in the San Francisco Bay Area. Students come here to get the sun while they study, families picnic and build sand castles, and those who dare the cold water rush in for a swim.

From Highway 1, turn right on Panoramic Highway and follow the signs that will lead you to **Mount Tamalpais**, once home to the Miwok Indians who never ascended its peak because they believed that their gods lived there. Mount Tamalpais actually has three peaks, though the east one (2,571 ft/784 meters) is always the most popular with hikers because a number of trails lead to its summit, where there is a fire-lookout tower. The **Mountain Theater** is one of Tamalpais' most well-loved landmarks.

Muir Woods.

Three early lovers of the mountain – Garnet Holme, John Catlin and "Dad" O'Rourke – conceived the notion of staging theatrical performances in this natural amphitheater.

At the foot of Mount Tamalpais is **Mill Valley**. On its south side is Old Mill Creek, where John Reed built the country's first sawmill in 1836. The streets of Mill Valley spread out from the old railroad depot and offer lovely, shady avenues for walking.

Point Reyes: "Point Reyes Peninsula… is fastened like a haunted fingerprint to the California coast," wrote Richard Brautigan. Point Reyes can still overwhelm its visitors with awe-inspiring coastal beauty, much as it did Sir Francis Drake, who named the peninsula "New Albion" (New England) because he was reminded of the white cliffs of Dover. From Muir Woods, the drive to **Point Reyes National Seashore Park** is particularly scenic, especially if you take Sir Francis Drake Highway. Drake landed here in 1579 and declared the

peninsula British land, in the name of Queen Elizabeth. In 1603, Don Sebastian Vizcaino gave Point Reyes its name, *La Punta de Los Reyes* (The Point of the Kings), in commemoration of the 12th day of Christmas. Like a blunted arrow, Point Reyes points into the Pacific, the narrow finger of Tomales Bay at its base and Drakes Bay on its southern edge. Flocks of birds, a colony of sea lions, and tidepool creatures as well as greenery flourish in this 65,000-acre (26,000-hectare) natural showcase. Thirty-two thousand acres (13,000 hectares) of the National Seashore are officially designated as wilderness.

During spring and early summer, the hills are a vibrant green, dotted with wildflowers and cattle. During late summer and fall, they are somewhat eerie: toasted beige and wheat-colored, they rise in stark contrast to the ocean.

Start at the **Bear Valley Visitor Center**, for a good introductory hike up to **Arch Rock**. The trail leads to the sea where you can see the strange, rock/statue jutting out of the water. Also visible is **Sculpture Beach** where waves crash into coastal caves and tunnels. A less dramatic hike can be found along the **Limantour Trail** which leads to the *Estero de Limantour*, a quiet wetland. The estuary, protected by a wall of dunes and tall grass, is a perfect spot for a picnic. Further down the coast is **Drake's Beach**, where Drake once grounded his ships for repairs, and which is now a popular visiting place.

Hemmed in by **Tomales Bay** on one side and the park on the other, **Inverness** is a charming stop-off before the drive to **Point Reyes Lighthouse**. The Grey Whale is a pizzeria, where the locals gather in the evenings to sing country songs and old ballads. Further down the road is a Czech restaurant called Vladimir's, always exuding seductive smells from its wood-burning stove. On your way out of town, look out for the miniature royal palace that sits on the dock: it adds a zany twist to Inverness' sleepy atmosphere.

Sailing the Marin coast.

After Inverness, there is another interesting diversion on the way to the point: the **Johnson Oyster Company**. Oysters are sold by the case or – for those who seek instant gratification – in small, inexpensive cocktails. Visitors can walk around the somewhat shabby premises and see how oysters are bred, processed and prepared for eating.

From the oyster company, the drive along the coast is magnificent. Grazed, smooth fields are flanked by the ocean on one side and the surreal, commanding Drakes Bay on the other. At Point Reyes Lighthouse, gray whales can be spotted between December and May. (The best time is the second week in January as they pass Point Reyes in their search for warmer water.) The lighthouse itself is worth exploring. It was constructed in 1872 after 15 ships were destroyed off the point. It was built low on the precipice because winds at the top are commonly 40 miles (64 km) per hour. The lighthouse has a specially designed revolving lens which can cast a powerful beam to vessels in the area. Nearby is **Sea Lion Overlook** where the sleek creatures sunbathe on the rocks.

Bayside towns: Just across the Golden Gate Bridge, follow Alexander Avenue and drive or walk into the town of **Sausalito**. Accessible by ferry and car, the town is called the "French Riviera" of the West Coast because of its Mediterranean climate, expensive art galleries, restaurants, antique and gift shops. It is hard to resist a stroll beneath the palm trees along the curved main street. Visitors can immediately sense the changes that Sausalito has undergone in the past century: the gracious Victorian homes that hug the hill are reminders of a town from a different era. In the 1870s, when California fruit and vegetable produce was needed to feed Europe, English ships often loaded grain in **Richardson's Bay**. Since they spent so much time in the area, English captains often set up homes. Quaint, tree-lined walkways, small, carefully manicured gardens and specialty shops attest to the

Mount Tamalpais.

influence of the British. A tour through the Victorian-style **Sausalito Hotel and Bar** offers a reminder of those days.

When Sausalito became an important shipping link between Northern California and San Francisco, the main street sprouted innumerable saloons, brothels and gambling houses. Sausalito also served as a base for liquor bootleggers who supplied the speakeasies of San Francisco. Sausalito's colorful past is not quite ancient history.

As recently as the 1950s, the late Sally Stanford, restaurateur and madam, came to Sausalito after she shut down her bordello in San Francisco. She started the Valhalla Restaurant, now the Chart House, on Bridgeway Drive. She ran for Sausalito's town council in the early 1960s and was mayor in 1973.

The rebellious spirit of this seemingly quaint area is best appreciated in the **houseboat community** along the northern coastline. Although an old and established sight on the bay, these boats must now be docked in a "civilized" marina with rents and plumbing. **Issaquah Dock**, also known as "Millionaires' Row," displays the most expensive floating homes. **Yellow Ferry** dock holds the quainter but still picturesque homes and the funkier docks; **South Forty** and **Liberty** harbor anything from eccentric to derelict boats. Another site to see: the **Bay-Delta Model** in the Marin shipyard complex, which accurately simulates water levels and flow patterns and shows how the bay was formed.

East of Sausalito and just a ferry ride away, the town of **Tiburon** is famous for its **Ark Row**, a winding street of art galleries, restaurants and specialty shops. Christmas lights line each shop facade and thus add a sparkle to the festive decor of the town. But Tiburon was not always so appealing. Before 1930 the town was a marsh, and people lived in rough and often shabby "arks." When entrepreneur Fred Zelinsky filled in the swampy land, he constructed a street where people once had to paddle to get **Sausalito.**

to the grocery store. Pictures of the old Tiburon are in the **Vintner's Shop** on Ark Row where, incidentally, the only free wine tasting in Marin is offered.

Apart from Ark Row, Tiburon is a developing residential town, interested in attracting San Franciscans who might prefer the 20-minute ferry ride to work instead of unpleasant freeway traffic jams. The idea of using Tiburon to lure city dwellers is not new: in the late 1800s, Dr Benjamin Lyford, a pioneering embalming surgeon, tried to start one of California's first utopian communities. Named after the goddess of health, Lyford's **Hygeia** was designed to draw people away from San Francisco into the "healthful" environs of Tiburon. In his promotional brochure, Doctor Lyford promised a community with "restrictions that will keep out the vices and vampires common to all communities." Interesting landmarks of Lyford's life are his Victorian home and **Lyford's Tower**, which once was the gateway to his Hygeia.

After visiting Lyford's Tower at the northern exit of town, continue on **Paradise Drive** which winds through the protected parkland, **Ring Mountain Preserve**, through eucalyptus trees, before opening onto some great views of the bay. Tiburon has three main centers of visitor interest: downtown and its environs, including Point Tiburon; old St Hilary's church and wildflower preserve; and Richardson Bay Audubon Center. Paradise Drive leads to another bay town named **Larkspur**. A bedroom community for those who commute to San Francisco and the East Bay, Larkspur is a quiet town nestled against the foot of Mount Tamalpais. To escape the crowds of Tiburon and Sausalito, go to Larkspur for the small restaurants and boutiques along **Main Street**.

When asked about their favorite pastimes, townsfolk comment that they like to ride bikes along **Corte Madera Creek** or up onto Mount Tam.

Angel Island: A ferry ride from Larkspur (or from San Francisco) takes visi-

Tiburon.

tors to **Angel Island**, an uninhabited isle and protected parkland. Deer and other wild animals still graze here. This triangular-shaped island draws picnickers for its panoramic view of San Francisco and the Golden Gate Bridge. A stroll around the island's perimeter trails takes only an hour – an ambitious climb up to the top of **Mount Livermore** delivers breathless views of the bay.

Angel Island hides many secrets it will never tell. It has been home to Coast Miwok Indians, Spanish explorers, Russian otter hunters, American soldiers, and many others. In the 1840s Angel Island belonged to Antonio Osio, who grazed his cattle on the island's pastures and cut timber for the presidio at Yerba Buena. In 1853, the United States took the land from Osio and for more than a century the island was put to military use.

Angel Island is clearly a promenade through California history. Isla de los Angeles was the name given the island by the crew of the Spanish ship San Carlos. Yet for thousands of Chinese immigrants interned on the island, this was the dreaded "Ellis Island of the West," the place that often kept them away from Gold Mountain. Notice the buildings near the ferry landing: these were used as a quarantine station in the 19th century when the smallpox epidemic hit San Francisco. On the northeast side of the island are the remains of stations that were used for two purposes: processing immigrants and holding World War II prisoners.

As they proceed to the eastern side of the island, travelers will see **Fort McDowell**. These barracks were used to process soldiers as early as the Spanish-American War. Later the fort was used as a missile base.

One of the most peculiar features on Angel Island is related to events that occurred on its south side, an area called **Point Blunt**, home of the Coast Guard station. This area used to be a favorite dueling spot for San Franciscans, especially when "affairs of honor" were con-

A soldier's barracks, Angel Island.

cerned. A crowd of 1,000 came here to witness a 1858 duel between a state senator and a United States commissioner. Friendlier crowds now come to relax, sail, picnic and ride mountain bikes around the island.

Oakland: Also visible from Angel Island is the East Bay. Originally named *La Contra Costa*, meaning the opposite coast, the East Bay is not just another urban area but an unusual hodgepodge of neighborhoods and industries. **Berkeley** and **Oakland**, the biggest cities in this area, have emerged from San Francisco's shadow. In fact, many people eventually leave San Francisco for the East Bay's better weather, cheaper rents and smaller communities.

Oakland's **Lake Merritt** is a good first stop for travelers to the East Bay. This large body of salt water is located in Oakland's financial center. Along with the geese, ducks and lanky egrets it supports, the lake is ringed by a macadam footpath. At night a "Necklace of Lights" gives the lake a romantic glow.

Awaiting Halloween at Half Moon Bay.

Nearby is the **Children's Fairyland USA**. Built in 1950, the park served as an inspiration for Disneyland, with its colorful depictions of nursery rhymes and fables. Also close to Lake Merritt is the **Oakland Museum**, which is widely held to be the best museum of California history, art and natural science.

Small shopping areas and boutique streets are scattered throughout Oakland. South of Lake Merritt and on the inlet is **Jack London Square**, named after the author of *The Sea Wolf* and *The Call of the Wild*. Once a decrepit waterfront section, the area is now a restaurant and convention center. Stop in for a drink at the **First and Last Chance Saloon** which the author once frequented.

Berkeley: The name was once synonymous with protest, social experimentation and progressive community politics. Famous as the site of student demonstrations in the 1960s, the **University of California at Berkeley** has earned its reputation as one of the country's leading public universities. Noted land-

marks on campus are **Sather Gate** and **Sproul Plaza**. The obelisk **Campanile** – reminiscent of the original belltower in Venice – is especially intriguing for its full view of Berkeley, the bay, San Francisco and the Golden Gate Bridge. It is worth going to the top to hear the hourly bell-ringing.

From here visitors can also look down onto **Telegraph Avenue**. Branching off from the university, this street is a collage of vendors, performers and an endless parade of people who represent a mixture of races, cultures and looks. "Beserkely" some critics have said.

If Telegraph Avenue is Berkeley's advertisement for the ethnic melting pot, then the **Claremont Hotel** is clearly where the aristocrat feels at home. Decorated in British Imperial style, the hotel is surrounded by palm trees and stands pearly white against the Berkeley Hills.

Up **Strawberry Canyon** is the university's **Botanical Garden**, filled with over 25,000 species of South American, South African, European and Australian plants. Further along Centennial Drive is the university's **Lawrence Science Hall** where weekend visitors conduct biology experiments or operate computer terminals. At the "top of the world" (or the campus) is **Tilden Park**. A leisurely and picturesque place to picnic or to hike here is along **Lake Anza**. Walking by the lake, one can listen to the wheezing sounds of the organ music wafting down from the old-fashioned carousel at the top of the hill. Other attractions include the steam trains which pass through fields and eucalyptus groves.

Over the Berkeley ridge and past Walnut Creek is **Mount Diablo**, a central landmark in California. Meaning "mountain of the devil," its name stems from a strange phenomenon which occurred when the United States government tried to usurp the mountains from the Indians. A strange spirit was reported to have intervened on behalf of the Indians to scare off the soldiers. Hence the name: Mount Devil. The

peak's panoramic vista – of the Sierra Nevada mountains and the Central Valley – and the jarring, craggy summits, leave visitors with a deep impression of the endless California landscape.

Wine Country: The state's premium wine grapes grow best in the sculpted, emerald vineyards and valleys northeast of San Francisco in the **Napa** and **Sonoma valleys**. Cabernet Sauvignon and Pinot Chardonnay, the royal couple of red and white wines, thrive throughout the area, as do Sauvignon (Fumé) Blanc, Johannisberg Reisling and Gewurtztraminer, and Zinfandel – California's mystery grape, which has been traced to Italian roots.

Running up and down the verdant Napa Valley are a string of wineries, delicatessens, restaurants, and quaint country inns. The valley is compact, offering a full course of adventure in just a day. This relatively small area made wine-making a world-renowned California trade, and its wineries have lured visitors from all over the world

Portrait of a vineyard.

for the free wine-tasting tours. Sonoma Valley is a more recent destination for wine lovers.

Napa Valley, a 30-mile (48-km) expanse of flatland between the pine-forested Mayacamas Mountains and the buff-colored Howell Mountains, is closed off to the north by majestic **Mount St Helena** – named after a Russian princess who once ascended its peak.

The expanse of vineyards that runs along the valley floor is broken up by the occasional farm house, stone wineries, and a few scattered small towns – all accessible via State Highway 29, "the great wine way." Better yet, visitors can ride the **Napa Valley "Wine Train,"** which takes visitors up and down the valley from one wine-tasting to another. The town of **St Helena**, a favorite spot of writer Robert Louis Stevenson, is home to over 40 wineries.

Sacramento: The state's capital city, located about two hours north of San Francisco, nestled in the middle of California's 500-mile (800-km) long Central Valley, has always lived in the long shadows of the prominence and popularity of its larger rivals. Home to more than a million people, it can be a blazing furnace in summer, and in winter a resting bed for thick tule fog, which, like the summer sun, can last for weeks.

Tucked just below the fork of the Sacramento and Americans rivers is **Old Sacramento**, where the old Pony Express and Transcontinental Railroad stations have been fully restored. An afternoon's stroll will take you to the California State Railroad Museum, where 50 restored engines bring alive the history of railroading in California; the Sacramento History Center, a reproduction of the 1854 City Hall and Water Works building; and the Crocker Art Museum, the oldest art museum west of the Mississippi River. A few blocks from Old Town is the **Towe Ford Museum,** housing the largest collection of a single make of car in the world.

Elsewhere in downtown you'll find the restored **California State Capitol,**

Chardonnay in the making.

HEARST'S CASTLE

William Randolph Hearst is said to have acquired his taste for collecting at 10 years old while visiting European castles and museums with his mother. Certainly, by the time he and architect Julia Morgan began to create the San Simeon "castle" he had the means to satisfy his hobby and provide a suitably grand home for his acquisitions. The task that Hearst and Ms Morgan embarked upon was hardly a conventional building project.

All supplies had to be brought up the coast by steamer, then hauled 5 miles (8 km) up hill. Tons of topsoil were brought up to create flower beds for the 127 acres (50 hectares) of gardens. Half-grown, 3-ton cypresses were also replanted during landscaping. Five greenhouses went up to supply plants for year-round color. To hide a water tank on the adjoining hill, 6,000 Monterey pines were planted, plus an additional 4,000 trees planted each year on the estate.

White marble statues flanked the 104-ft (32-meter) outdoor Neptune Pool. A pair of

tennis courts was sited atop the indoor Roman pool. The main house's 85-ft (26-meter) assembly hall was built around a 400-year-old carved wooden ceiling from Italy.

By the time WR was advised by his doctors to move to Beverly Hills in 1947, the "ranch" had 165 rooms filled with mostly Spanish and Italian art and antiques spread over Casa Grande and three guesthouses.

Hearst moved into San Simeon when the last of his five sons went off to school. Instead of his wife Millicent – whom he had married when he was 39 and she 21 – he installed his longtime mistress, Marion Davies, who had been a teenaged chorus girl when he first wooed her with diamonds.

Almost every weekend San Simeon welcomed moviedom's elite. "The society people always wanted to meet the movie stars so I mixed them together," wrote Marion Davies. "Jean Harlow came up quite frequently. She was very nice and I liked her. She didn't have an awful lot to say… all the men used to flock around her. She was very attractive in an evening dress because she never wore anything under it." Clark Gable was another regular guest. "Women were always running after him but he'd just give them a look as if to say, 'How crazy these people are,' and he stayed pretty much to himself."

A special train from Glendale station with a jazz band and open bar brought the weekend party guests 210 miles (338 km) from Hollywood to San Luis Obispo, where limousines transported them through the estate's grounds, filled with lions, bears, ostriches, elephants, pumas and leopards. On arrival at the floodlit mansion, each was allocated a personal maid or valet and was free to wander – except for a mandatory attendance at the late-night dinner over which WR would preside in the Great Hall, at the head of the 16th-century monastery table. Paper napkins, catsup from bottles and the absence of tablecloths preserved the illusion of "camping out." After dinner Hearst showed a movie, often one as yet unreleased; *Gone With the Wind*, for example, was screened six months before its December 1939 premiere. (*Citizen Kane*, whose hero Orson Welles had based on Hearst, did not receive this accolade.)

In 1957, six years after Hearst's death, the Hearst Corporation deeded the San Simeon property to the state of California. ■ **San Simeon's "castle".**

where daily tours are offered; the old **Governor's Mansion**, an 1877 Victorian house in which 13 California governors lived between 1903 and 1967; and the **Blue Diamond Visitors Center**, home of a Del Monte Packing Plant, the city's last operating cannery.

An annual feature in the city is the Dixieland Jazz Jubilee, the world's biggest celebration of dixieland jazz which features more than 120 bands from around the world. The highlight of the summer is the California State Fair, which runs for 18 days before Labor Day at **California State Exposition**, the city's outdoor exposition facility.

During the fall, the Sacramento Blues Festival draws the biggest names in the business, while a drive up Highway 50 to the east brings you to the Apple Hill Growers Festival, held in the town of **Camino**, to which 43 apple ranches bring their finest fruits and pies.

The Delta: One of California's great adventures is a trip on the **Sacramento River Delta** – a web of lazy, winding channels formed by the confluence, near sea level, of the Sacramento and San Joaquin rivers (head south from the capital on Highway 5 or 99). The most interesting thing to do is to rent a houseboat and bring, or rent, a waterski boat – and every other form of watersports equipment you can muster.

The river here, northeast of San Francisco Bay and accessible by Highway 5, winds through the delta in a thousand tiny threads, like lace. Each of the islands in this web has been walled off by levees and turned to farmland. Many farmers reach their homes by small bridges and roads; others are forced to ride ferries across one or more channels.

A number of swampy areas still play host to migrating birds. In certain seasons, some delta towns are filled with so many raucous geese and ducks that you can scarcely hear yourself talk. These migratory sanctuaries, closed off entirely to hunters, are also popular places to see deer, raccoon and other California land animals.

Pigeon Point Lighthouse.

South of San Francisco: Two roads take you south of the city: Highway 1 and 101. Highway 1 is more popular and if you keep going on it, you will eventually arrive in Los Angeles.

The coastline offers gorgeous vistas all the way south, not the least at **Big Sur**, the clifftop aerie once so beloved of the author Henry Miller. Southbound travelers might want to make plans to stop off at California's number two tourist attraction (after Disneyland), the magnificent **Hearst Castle** at San Simeon, about 150 miles (240 km) south of San Francisco, but less than one-third of the way to Los Angeles.

Long before Hollywood, however, is **Half Moon Bay**, a wonderful town filled with interesting houses. It is a popular departure spot for day fishing trips, especially during salmon season. **Pillar Point** is a nice stop for eating; not far is **Pigeon Point Lighthouse** and Youth Hostel. A worthwhile stop or stay, the hostel has a hot tub on the ocean cliff for the use of its guests. The lighthouse is

still in use and its light continues to warn ships of the perilous rocky shore.

Finally, no trip is complete down the coast without a stop at **Año Nuevo State Preserve**, the seasonal home of the elephant seals. These ungainly beasts share the spot with three other species of seals, sea lions and unusual shore and land birds. This park is a rewarding stop for animal lovers. Here, amidst the charms of nature and the sounds of an untamed earth, it is difficult to imagine that San Francisco is just a few miles away.

Santa Cruz: Where else can one find a surfing museum than in the laid-back, sea-swept confines of Santa Cruz? Off Highway 1 south of San Francisco (accessible from the peninsula via Highway 17), the city of Santa Cruz is at once one of the country's surfing meccas, and home of one of nine **University of California** campuses. The traditional Santa Cruz daytrip – from San Francisco, it is only a 1½-hour drive – means a day spent at one of several state beaches, but there's much more to see.

The **Santa Cruz Beach Boardwalk**, also off Highway 1, is a renovated casino built in 1907. The Giant Dipper rollercoaster, almost 70 years old, still thrills its passengers, as do plenty of other rides. The **Surfing Museum**, on the ground level of the Mark Abbott Memorial Lighthouse on West Cliff Drive, exhibits surfboards and surfing photography from the 1930s onwards. Explore the creature-filled tidepools – or witness the vast migration of monarch butterflies in late fall – at nearby **Natural Bridges State Beach**.

Downtown you can visit a half-scale replica of the city's 1791 founding mission, destroyed in an 1857 earthquake. Many of the downtown buildings, you will also notice, are either new or being rebuilt – the city was very close to the epicenter of the 1989 Loma Prieta earthquake that shook most of Northern California. Santa Cruz was hit hard, and is still recovering.

Monterey: Further south on Highway 1 is Monterey, known once as the state's capital under the Spanish and Mexican flags, and known now as a playground for golfers, sea- and sun-seekers, and a friendly, if elite, group of locals. If you want just a glimpse of Monterey beauty, take the **17-Mile Drive** on Highway 1 from Pacific Grove south to the town of **Carmel**. Along the way are some stunning vistas: Seal Rock, Cypress Point, and the expansive views from the seaside **Pebble Beach** golf course.

If you have more time, a visit to the **Monterey Bay Aquarium** is worth the long wait in line. Located on **Cannery Row**, the locale for John Steinbeck's novels *Cannery Row* and *Sweet Thursday*, the old fish canneries that once flourished here have been replaced by eateries and art galleries. The aquarium shows off nearly 600 species of marine life, a large recreation of Monterey Bay, a two-story sea otter exhibit and a three-story kelp forest. Another exhibit features live video transmissions from a deep-sea-diving robot, at a depth of nearly 3,000 ft (915 meters).

Left, ripe for restoration. **Right**, California's giant redwoods.

INSIGHT GUIDES
TRAVEL TIPS

FOR THOSE
WITH MORE THAN
A PASSING INTEREST
IN TIME...

Before you put your name down for a Patek Philippe watch *fig. 1*, there are a few basic things you might like to know, without knowing exactly whom to ask. In addressing such issues as accuracy, reliability and value for money, we would like to demonstrate why the watch we will make for you will be quite unlike any other watch currently produced.

"Punctuality", Louis XVIII was fond of saying, "is the politeness of kings."

We believe that in the matter of punctuality, we can rise to the occasion by making you a mechanical timepiece that will keep its rendezvous with the Gregorian calendar at the end of every century, omitting the leap-years in 2100, 2200 and 2300 and recording them in 2000 and 2400 *fig. 2*. Nevertheless, such a watch does need the occasional adjustment. Every 3333 years and 122 days you should remember to set it forward one day to the true time of the celestial clock. We suspect, however, that you are simply content to observe the politeness of kings. Be assured, therefore, that when you order your watch, we will be exploring for you the physical—if not the metaphysical— limits of precision.

Does everything have to depend on how much?

Consider, if you will, the motives of collectors who set record prices at auction to acquire a Patek Philippe. They may be paying for rarity, for looks or for micromechanical ingenuity. But we believe that behind each $500,000-plus

bid is the conviction that a Patek Philippe, even if 50 years old or older, can be expected to work perfectly for future generations.

In case your ambitions to own a Patek Philippe are somewhat discouraged by the scale of the sacrifice involved, may we hasten to point out that the watch we will make for you today will certainly be a technical improvement on the Pateks bought at auction? In keeping with our tradition of inventing new mechanical solutions for greater reliability and better time-keeping, we will bring to your watch innovations *fig. 3* inconceivable to our watchmakers who created the supreme wristwatches of 50 years ago *fig. 4*. At the same time, we will of course do our utmost to avoid placing undue strain on your financial resources.

Can it really be mine?

May we turn your thoughts to the day you take delivery of your watch? Sealed within its case is your watchmaker's tribute to the mysterious process of time. He has decorated each wheel with a chamfer carved into its hub and polished into a shining circle. Delicate ribbing flows over the plates and bridges of gold and rare alloys. Millimetric surfaces are bevelled and burnished to exactitudes measured in microns. Rubies are transformed into jewels that triumph over friction. And after many months—or even years—of work, your watchmaker stamps a small badge into the mainbridge of your watch. The Geneva Seal—the highest possible attestation of fine watchmaking *fig. 5*.

Looks that speak of inner grace *fig. 6*.

When you order your watch, you will no doubt like its outward appearance to reflect the harmony and elegance of the movement within. You may therefore find it helpful to know that we are uniquely able to cater for any special decorative needs you might like to express. For example, our engravers will delight in conjuring a subtle play of light and shadow on the gold case-back of one of our rare pocket-watches *fig. 7*. If you bring us your favourite picture, our enamellers will reproduce it in a brilliant miniature of hair-breadth detail *fig. 8*. The perfect execution of a double hobnail pattern on the bezel of a wristwatch is the pride of our casemakers and the satisfaction of our designers, while our chainsmiths will weave for you a rich brocade in gold *figs. 9 & 10*. May we also recommend the artistry of our goldsmiths and the experience of our lapidaries in the selection and setting of the finest gemstones? *figs. 11 & 12*.

How to enjoy your watch before you own it.

As you will appreciate, the very nature of our watches imposes a limit on the number we can make available. (The four Calibre 89 time-pieces we are now making will take up to nine years to complete). We cannot therefore promise instant gratification, but while you look forward to the day on which you take delivery of your Patek Philippe *fig. 13*, you will have the pleasure of reflecting that time is a universal and everlasting commodity, freely available to be enjoyed by all.

Should you require information on any particular Patek Philippe watch, or even on watchmaking in general, we would be delighted to reply to your letter of enquiry. And if you send u

fig. 1: *The classic face of Patek Philippe.*

fig. 4: *Complicated wristwatches circa 1930 (left) and 1990. The golden age of watchmaking will always be with us.*

fig. 6: *Your pleasure in owning a Patek Philippe is the purpose of those who made it for you.*

fig. 9: *Harmony of design is executed in a work of simplicity and perfection in a lady's Calatrava wristwatch.*

fig. 10: *The chainsmith's hands impart strength and delicacy to a tracery of gold.*

fig. 2: *One of the 33 complications of the Calibre 89 astronomical clock-watch is a satellite wheel that completes one revolution every 400 years.*

fig. 5: *The Geneva Seal is awarded only to watches which achieve the standards of horological purity laid down in the laws of Geneva. These rules define the supreme quality of watchmaking.*

fig. 7: *Arabesques come to life on a gold case-back.*

fig. 11: *Circles in gold: symbols of perfection in the making.*

fig. 3: *Recognized as the most advanced mechanical regulating device to date, Patek Philippe's Gyromax balance wheel demonstrates the equivalence of simplicity and precision.*

fig. 8: *An artist working six hours a day takes about four months to complete a miniature in enamel on the case of a pocket-watch.*

fig. 12: *The test of a master lapidary is his ability to express the splendour of precious gemstones.*

PATEK PHILIPPE
GENEVE
fig. 13: *The discreet sign of those who value their time.*

your card marked "book catalogue" we shall post you a catalogue of our publications. Patek Philippe, 41 rue du Rhône, 1204 Geneva, Switzerland, Tel. +41 22/310 03 66.

A Wise Man Never Thinks How Far He's Come. He Thinks How Far He Can Still Travel.

REMY XO BECAUSE LIFE IS WHAT YOU MAKE IT

TRAVEL TIPS

Getting Acquainted

Unless otherwise stated, all telephone numbers are preceded by the area code (415). Any call made to another area code must be preceded by a 1. Numbers beginning with 800 are toll-free if dialed within the United States.

The Place

City Song: Official – "San Francisco"; Unofficial – "I Left My Heart in San Francisco".
City Nickname: The City. (Word to the wise: "Frisco" won't impress the natives.)
City Flower: Dahlia.
City Motto: Gold in peace, iron in war.

Time Zones

California is within the Pacific Time Zone, which is two hours behind Chicago and three hours behind New York City. On the last Sunday in April, the clock is moved ahead one hour for Daylight Savings Time. On the last Sunday in October, the clock is moved back one hour to return to Standard Time. (Spring forward, Fall back, is one way to remember the changes.)

Using Standard Time, when it is noon in California, (note: it depends on daylight savings) it will be:
10am in Hawaii.
2pm in Chicago.
3pm in New York and Montreal.
8pm in London.
9pm in Bonn, Madrid, Paris and Rome.
11pm in Athens and Cairo.
Midnight in Moscow.
3am (the next day) in Bangkok.
4am (the next day) in Singapore and Hong Kong.
5am (the next day) in Tokyo.
6am (the next day) in Sydney.

For local time telephone the talking clock, tel: POP-CORN (767-2676).

Size & Topography

The city of San Francisco encompasses 129 sq miles (335 sq km) including 83 sq miles (216 sq km) of water. Although often referred to as the City of Seven Hills, there are actually over 40 hills within the city limits.

Climate

San Francisco has two kinds of weather – wet and dry. Generally, the wet season is winter (October–March), and the dry season is summer (June–September). However, the fog interferes with this schedule. It hovers around the Golden Gate, the entrance to the bay, and obscures the bridge. In summer, the morning fog appears to pour in through the Gate and over the coastal hills. For the daily weather forecast, tel: 936-1212.

The sun usually burns off the fog by midday. Daytime temperatures average in the mid-50°F (10°C–15°C). Unlike the rest of the country, there is no traditional summer with high temperatures. September and October are the warmest months, when temperatures occasionally reach 80°F.

The average daily highs in San Francisco are:

Month	(°C)	(°F)
January	12.8	55
February	14.4	58
March	16.7	62
April	17.8	64
May	19.4	67
June	21.1	70
July	22.2	72
August	22.2	72
September	23.3	74
October	21.7	71
November	17.8	64
December	13.9	57

The People

San Francisco is a city rich with ethnic diversity. Here's the breakdown in total population of 730,000 people; Whites: 46 percent; African Americans: 11 percent; Hispanic: 14 percent; Asian/Pacific Islanders: 29 percent.

Government & Economy

The mayor and the 11-member Board of Supervisors govern the city. San Francisco continues to be one of the most expensive cities in the US. Among the economic mainstays of the Northern California economy are agriculture, travel and tourism, finance and commerce, and high technology.

Planning The Trip

What To Bring

Maps

City maps are available at the Visitor Information Center, Lower Level, Hallidie Plaza, 900 Market Street. Maps are readily available at bookstores, convenience stores, and supermarkets.

Visas & Passports

Canadians may enter the US without a visa. Most Dutch, French, Italian, Japanese, Spanish, Swedish, Swiss, UK and West German citizens do not need a visa for travel of 90 days or less if they enter the US on an airline or cruise line which participates in no-visa travel and have a return or onward ticket. Citizens from these visa-exempt countries who first enter the US may then visit Mexico, Canada, Bermuda, or the Caribbean Islands and return to the US without a visa by any mode of transportation. Citizens of other countries require a visa and a health record if they are from (or have passed through) an infected area. For enquiries, contact the nearest American Embassy or Consulate.

What To Wear

San Francisco is a city best explored on foot, so remember to bring a comfortable pair of walking shoes. Also keep in mind: San Francisco's infamous fog and wind conspire to make

THOMAS COOK
MASTERCARD
TRAVELLERS CHEQUES...

...HOLIDAY ESSENTIALS

Travel money from the travel experts

THOMAS COOK MASTERCARD TRAVELLERS CHEQUES ARE
WIDELY AVAILABLE THROUGHOUT THE WORLD.

American Express offers Travelers Cheques built for two.

Cheques *for Two*^{SM} from American Express are the Travelers Cheques that allow either of you to use them because both of you have signed them. And only one of you needs to be present to purchase them.

Cheques *for Two* are accepted anywhere regular American Express Travelers Cheques are, which is just about everywhere. So stop by your bank, AAA* or any American Express Travel Service Office and ask for Cheques *for Two.*

Travelers Cheques

even summer days wintery. Even if you're visiting during summer, you should bring warm clothes, a windbreaker, and an outer coat.

Entry Regulations

Animal Quarantine

Note to foreign travelers: The US has no quarantine for pets, but does require a rabies certificate which shows that the shot was administered either 30 days to one year prior to arrival, or 30 days to three years before disembarking. Some airlines require health certificates. California has its own regulations. Certain animals are prohibited. Check first with the California Department of Fish and Game, tel: (916) 653-7664.

Customs

If you are 21 or over, you are allowed to bring in 200 cigarettes, 50 cigars or 3 lb (1.3 kg) of tobacco, 1 US quart (1 liter) of alcohol and gifts up to a value of $100. You are not allowed to bring in food items, seeds, plants or narcotics. Customs officials are strict, particularly about food and narcotics.

Extending Your Stay

A foreign visitor who comes to the US for business or pleasure is admitted initially for a period of not more than six months. Extensions of stay are likewise limited to six months each. Visitors may not accept employment during their stay. Check with your consulate for more details.

Currency

Traveler's checks: Since visitors to California may face problems changing foreign currency, it is better to use American-dollar traveler's checks. When lost or stolen, most traveler's checks can be replaced and they are accepted in most stores, restaurants and hotels. Banks readily cash large traveler's checks, although a passport may be required. Smaller denomination traveler's checks (provided you have adequate identification) are usually accepted for major purchases in large stores and supermarkets.

Exchange: The airport is the best place to change currency, since only certain banks perform this service for customers who do not have accounts. In the city, you can exchange currency at Bank of America, 345 Montgomery Street (tel: 622-2451); Foreign Exchange Limited, 415 Stockton Street (tel: 397-4700); and Thomas Cook Currency Services, 100 Grant Avenue (tel: 362-3452).

Cash: Most banks belong to a network of ATMs (automatic teller machines) which dispense cash 24 hours a day.

Credit cards: Not all credit cards are accepted at all places, but most places accept either Visa, American Express, or MasterCard. Major credit cards can also be used to withdraw cash from ATMs. (Look for an ATM that uses one of the banking networks indicated on the back of your credit card, such as Plus, Cirrus, and Interlink.)

Taxes: In most states, a sales tax is added to retail goods. In San Francisco County, the sales tax is seven percent. Sales tax applies primarily to non-food purchases.

Public Holidays

Most government agencies close during the holidays listed below. Local banks and businesses may also be closed. And since schools are often closed for these holidays, you may want to consider whether to avoid the extra crowds during these periods:

New Year's Day: January 1
Martin Luther King's Birthday: January 15
Abraham Lincoln's Birthday: February 12
Presidents' Day: third Monday in February
Memorial Day: last Monday in May
Independence Day: July 4
Labor Day: first Monday in September
Admission Day: September 9
Columbus Day: second Monday in October
Veterans' Day: November 11
Thanksgiving: fourth Thursday in November
Christmas: December 25

Festivals: The Bay area has many different festivals. Check the pink pages of each Sunday's *San Francisco Examiner & Chronicle* newspaper to get information on the current ones (see *Diary of Events*).

Getting There

By Air

San Francisco International Airport (SFO), just 14 miles (23 km) south of the city, is the major gateway for foreign travel. There are approximately 36,000 flights a month and an average of 1,400 a day. Most of the international airline companies that serve Northern California land at SFO. Clearing customs has been facilitated so that 1,200 passengers can be processed hourly. Some 15 international carriers serve the airport. There is no airport tax. Free airport shuttle service operates between airlines.

Several major carriers also operate from **Oakland International Airport** (tel: (510) 839-7488), from which a shuttle bus transports passengers to BART (Bay Area Rapid Transit), and a 10-minute trip to downtown San Francisco. One hour south is **San Jose International Airport** (tel: (408) 277-4759).

By Sea

Cruising into San Francisco Bay is a luxurious and expensive way to arrive. "Vagabond" cruises, which feature a limited number of passengers on cargo steamships, are less common than they once were. Check first with the **San Francisco Port Authority** (tel: 274-0400) or your travel agent to determine which line has a current scheduled stop. However, cruise ships representing five major lines dock regularly at Pier 35 in San Francisco. These are Cunard, Holland America, Princess Cruises, Royal Viking, and Crystal.

By Rail

Amtrak is the passenger line that offers leisurely service from coast to coast. All trains come into a depot in Oakland. Free bus service is provided into San Francisco. Passes for unlimited travel on Amtrak are available only from a travel agent in a foreign country. Information about Amtrak's train services is available by calling (415) 982-8512 or toll-free: 800-321-8684.

By Bus

Greyhound-Trailways provides bus services to San Francisco. Buses load at the Transbay Terminal, First and Mission streets (tel: 495-1551). Bus systems using this terminal include ac Transit (East Bay), SamTrans (San Mateo County and the peninsula) and several city tour-bus lines, including Greyline.

Keep in mind: the bus terminals are located in downtown areas which require caution for personal safety. Bus travelers should avoid walking alone at night, and use taxis or city buses to get to and from the terminals.

By Car

Major land routes into San Francisco are: US Highway 101, over the Golden Gate Bridge, from the North; Interstate 80 over the Oakland Bay Bridge from the East; and US Highways 1, 101, and 280 up the peninsula, from the South.

North-South travelers who are in a hurry use Interstate 5 to connect with I-80. Travelers from Los Angeles can cut three hours off their trip to San Francisco by taking I-5. The slower coastal routes are more scenic and pass through small towns.

The official speed limit is 55 mph (88 kpm), and 65 mph (105 kpm) on marked sections of I-5. Most federal and state highways are well-maintained and policed. Roadside rest and refreshment areas and service stations are well-marked and placed at regular intervals. Bridge tolls are charged.

Special Facilities

People With Disabilities

The US Welcomes Handicapped Visitors is a 48-page booklet available from the Advancement of Travel for the Handicapped, 1012 14th street, No. 803, Washington DC 20005. Or you can write Consumer Information Cen-

ter, Pueblo, CO 81109, Colorado for travel tips.

There is a **Recreation Center for the Handicapped** at 207 Skyline Boulevard (tel: 665-4100). The facility includes an adapted gymnasium, sports/physical fitness area, therapeutic warm water swimming pool, three outdoor parcourses, weekend overnight respite facilities, dining facility, arts and crafts.

Senior Citizens

If you are a senior citizen (over 65 for men, over 62 for women) you are entitled to many benefits, including reduced rates on public transportation and museums. Some restaurants also give a discount. Seniors who want to be students should write Elderhostels, 80 Boylston Street, Suite 400, Boston, MA 02116, Massachusetts for information on places that provide both accommodation and classes. The Bay Area has a number of Elderhostel locations.

Students

If you have an international student ID or can prove that you are a student you are entitled to discounts to museums, theaters, etc. Always ask if there is a student discount.

Useful Addresses

When in doubt, use the telephone if you cannot find a specific place. If a telephone directory is not available, the fastest way to obtain assistance in finding a telephone number is to dial 411 for local information.

The **San Francisco Visitors' and Convention Bureau** is extremely helpful. Their services include a 24-hour events information line recorded in several languages (for the telephone numbers, see *Diary of Events*). You can call or visit the centrally located offices at Hallidie Plaza, Powell and Market streets, Monday–Friday from 9am–5.30pm, Saturday 9am–3pm, Sunday 10am–2pm. Tel: 974-6900.

The **International Visitors' Center** (tel: 986-1388) provides professional appointments and tours for guests of the US Government. Their services include home hospitality, sightseeing

suggestions and translation assistance. Open: Monday–Friday 9am–5pm.

Primarily a business association, the **San Francisco Chamber of Commerce** at 465 California Street (tel: 392-4511), can provide information and referrals to Chamber member businesses and professionals.

Practical Tips

Emergencies

Security & Crime

In general, it is safe to walk the streets during the day in any part of San Francisco, but use special caution in these areas: the Western Addition (bordered by Gough, Divisadero, Geary and Golden Gate streets – between Golden Gate Park and Civic Center); Hunter's Point (the peninsula just north of Candlestick Park); the small streets of the Mission District (unlit passages between Dolores, Potrero, 10th and Army streets); the Tenderloin (bordered by Bush, Powell Market and Polk streets – near the theater district); South of Market from the Embarcadero to Church Street. (South of Market – SoMa – is quickly becoming fashionable, but it's not safe for late-night strolling.)

Whenever possible, travel with another person while sightseeing or shopping, particularly at night. Do not walk in deserted or run down areas alone. If driving, lock your car and never leave luggage, cameras or other valuables in view. Put them in the glove compartment or trunk to avoid any break-in. Try to park your car under a street light.

In regard to your personal belongings, never leave your luggage unattended. While waiting for a room reservation, for example, keep your property in view. Rather than carrying your bags around with you, ask the hotel captain, the restaurant waitress or the department store security guard if you can check your luggage. Never leave money or jewelry in your hotel room, even for a short time. Always turn in your room key at the desk when going out. Report any loss to the nearest police station or tel: 911.

Try to carry only the cash you need. Use credit cards and traveler's checks whenever possible and avoid displaying large amounts of cash. Automated teller machines (ATMs) provide a convenient way to withdraw cash around the clock, but travelers should be careful when using ATMs after dark. Most outlets are equipped with security cameras but are otherwise unattended. Avoid using ATMs alone, or in poorly lighted areas.

Medical Services

American medical care is expensive. It's a good idea to make sure you are covered by medical insurance while traveling in the San Francisco Bay Area.

Most hospitals have emergency rooms with doctors on staff 24 hours a day. For non-emergency services, there are clinics and physician offices listed in the *Yellow Pages* of the telephone directory.

To contact the San Francisco Medical Society Referral Service, tel: 561-0853; the Dental Society Referral Service, tel: 421-1435. An additional free Physician Referral Service is available at tel: 885-7777. General assistance and referrals can be obtained from:
Dept Social Services, tel: 557-5584.
American Red Cross, tel: 202-0600.
Catholic Social Services, tel: 864-7400.
Salvation Army, tel: 861-0755.
Traveler's Aid Society, tel: 255-2252.

Hospitals: Some of the larger hospitals with 24-hour emergency services are:
Children's Hospital, 3700 California Street, at Maple. Main telephone number and information: 387-8700.
Kaiser-Permanente Medical Center, 4131 Geary Boulevard, at Baker Street, tel: 202-2000.
Marshall Hale Hospital and Medical Center, 3700 California Street, at Maple, tel: 387-8700.
Mount Zion Hospital and Medical Center, 1600 Divisadero Street, at Post Street, tel: 567-6600.
California Pacific Medical Center,

2333 Buchanan Street, at Clay Street, tel: 563-4321.
Ralph K. Davies Medical Center, Castro Street, at Duboce Avenue, tel: 565-6000.
St Francis Heights Convalescent Hospital, 35 Escuela Drive, tel: 755-9515.
St Luke's Hospital, 3555 Army Street, at Valencia Street, tel: 647-8600.
St Mary's Hospital and Medical Center, 450 Stanyan Street, at Hayes Street, tel: 668-1000.
San Francisco General Hospital, 1001 Potrero Avenue, at 22nd Street, tel: 821-8200.
Shriners Hospital for Crippled Children, 1701 19th Avenue, at Moraga Street, tel: 665-1100.
Medical Center at the University of California-San Francisco, 500 Parnassus Avenue, tel: 476-1000.

Out-patient Clinics: Low-cost outpatient clinics provide good care but the wait can be long. These include:
Haight-Ashbury Free Medical Clinic, 558 Clayton, tel: 431-1714.
St Luke's Hospital Neighborhood Clinic, 3555 Army, tel: 641-6500.

Pharmacies: Certain drugs can only be prescribed by a doctor. Most drugstores stock a variety of drugs and have a pharmacist on duty. These stores are open long hours or 24 hours:
Rexall Reliable Drug, 801 Irving, tel: 664-8800. Monday–Saturday to 9pm.
Walgreen Drugs, 498 Castro at 18th Street, tel: 861-3136; or 3201 Divisadero at Lombard Street, tel: 931-6417.

Other Services
Child Abuse Reporting, tel: 665-0757.
Drug Abuse Information, tel: 752-3400.
Customs, tel: 705-4440.
Legal Aid Society, tel: 864-3273.
Senior Citizen Information, tel: 626-1033.
Consumer Fraud – check the phone directory for its extensive listings.

Business Hours

Business hours are 9am–5pm, Monday through Friday. Banking hours vary and some bank branches offer limited

Saturday service. The biggest banks in San Francisco are the Bank of America, First Interstate and Wells Fargo. International bank branches are numerous including the Algemene Bank Nederland, Banco Central SA, Banco de la Nacion Argentina, Bangkok Metropolitan, Bank of Canton of California, Bank of the Orient, Bank of Guam, Barclay's, Dai-Ichi Kangyo, Hong Kong and Shanghai Banking Corp., Lloyds, Mitsubishi, Mitsui Manufacturing, Sanwa, Swiss Bank Corporation and Sumitomo Bank.

Tipping

It is courteous to show your gratitude for assistance given to you. This is most appreciated in the form of a tip. The accepted rate for porters at the airports is $1 or so per bag. Hotel bellboys and porters usually expect the same. A doorman should be tipped if he unloads or parks your car. Tip your chambermaids if you stay several days in a small hotel.

Depending upon the quantity and quality of service rendered, 15 to 20 percent of the bill before tax is the going rate for most other help such as taxi drivers, barbers, hairdressers, waiters, waitresses and bar persons. In restaurants, check your bill carefully (or ask), then add the tip to the total. In some restaurants, the tip or a service charge is included in the bill if it is for a large group.

Media

Newspapers, magazines

The major daily newspapers in San Francisco are the *San Francisco Chronicle* in the morning and the *San Francisco Examiner* in the afternoon. The two papers combine into one large edition on Sunday. This weekend paper includes special sections, such as the "Pink Section," which highlight the various sports, entertainment, cultural and artistic events the city has currently scheduled.

The free weekly papers include *San Francisco Bay Guardian* and the *SF Weekly*, both featuring coverage and commentary on everything from arts to city politics. The monthly *City Sports* includes every spectator and participant sport – including running events – scheduled in the Bay Area. All are available in most cafes or from sidewalk boxes. *San Francisco Focus* is the city's premier magazine.

Besides the English language newspapers and magazines, the various communities publish daily and weekly papers in at least 20 foreign languages. They are available at a number of places: Harold's, 599 Post Street (tel: 441-2665); Dave's Smoke Shop, 2444 Durant Street, Berkeley (tel: (510) 841-7292); and De Lauer News Agency, 1310 Broadway, Oakland (tel: (510) 451-6157).

Radio

Two commercial broadcast frequencies, AM and FM, offer a wide variety of radio programming. Generally, the FM stations feature less commercial interruption, and stereo reproduction. Formats often change but the most popular local stations include:

AM

560	KSFO (oldies, talk, sports)
610	KFRC (big band, standards, classic shows)
680	KNBR (NBC) (news and sports)
740	KCBS (CBS) (news and sports)
810	KGO (ABC) (news, talk, sports)
910	KNEW (country-western)
960	KABL (adult contemporary)
1050	KOFY (Spanish)
1100	KFAX (religious)
1220	KDFC (classical)
1260	KOIT (adult pop)
1310	KDIA (urban contemporary, oldies)
1450	KEST (new age)
1550	KKHI (classical)

FM

88.5	KQED (PBS) (classical, talk, news)
89.3	KPFB (news, talk, politics, music)
89.5	KPOO (salsa, reggae, blues, soul, gospel, rap)
90.3	KUSF (University of SF) (public affairs, rock, foreign language, news)
90.7	KSJS (San Jose State University) (rock, news, talk, jazz, gospel)

91.7	KALW (SF Unified School District) (Public Radio programs, British Broadcasting Company, Canadian Broadcasting Company, talk, jazz, classical, big bands)
92.7	KJAZ (jazz)
93.3	KYA (oldies)
94.1	KPFA (talk, classical, community affairs)
94.9	KSAN (modern country)
95.7	KKHI (classical)
96.5	KOIT (adult contemporary)
97.3	KRQR (album rock)
98.1	KABL (easy listening)
99.7	KFRC (oldies)
100.3	KBAY (adult contemporary, oldies)
102.1	KDFC (classical)
102.9	KBLX (adult contemporary)
103.7	KKSF (adult, soft rock)
104.5	KFOG (rock)
104.9	KBRG (Spanish)
105.3	KITS (modern rock)
106.1	KMEL (Top-40 rock)
106.9	KEAR (religious)

Television

The major TV stations in the San Francisco area include Channels 2 (KTVU), 4 (KRON-NBC), 5 (KPIX-CBS), 7 (KGO-ABC), and 9 (KQED-Public Television). There are also a variety of foreign-language stations. Dozens of other cable channels are available through the city's local cable company, Viacom. Complete television listings appear in each day's newspapers.

Postal Services

The General Mail Facility is at 1300 Evans Avenue (tel: 550-5247). Many of the city's 50 postal stations are open extended hours and on Saturday. For current postal rates and other information, tel: 550-6500. Stamps may be purchased from the post office or from vending machines in hotels, stores, supermarkets, transportation terminals, and the lobbies of post office stations.

If you wish, you can have mail addressed to you care of "General Delivery" at the post office station. You will need the zip code of the station and you must pick up your mail in person.

In addition to postal service, there are delivery and messenger services

listed under those designations in the telephone directory (*Yellow Pages*).

Telecoms

Telegram & Telex: Western Union (tel: 800-225-5227) will take your messages by phone. Many smaller, local message and wire transfer service companies are listed in the telephone directory.

Telephone: Public telephones are located in hotel lobbies, drugstores, restaurants, garages, bars, sidewalk booths and many other places. Long distance rates vary but discounts are available during specified calling times. Check the local telephone directory or dial "0" for operator assistance for both local and international calls.

Toll-free numbers for various services or businesses are indicated by an 800 prefix. The Toll-Free Information number is 800-555-1212. The San Francisco area code prefix is (415). The area code for Berkeley, Oakland, and other East Bay cities is (510). The directory or the operator can provide the correct prefix for long-distance dialing. To call the Information Operator in another area, dial 1, then the area code, and 555 1212.

Embassies

Argentina: Suite 1083, 870 Market Street, tel: 982-3050.
Australia: 1 Bush Street, tel: 362-6160.
Bolivia: 870 Market Street, tel: 495-5173.
Brazil: 300 Montgomery Street, tel: 981-8170.
Canada: 50 Fremont Street, tel: 495-7030.
Chile: 870 Market Street, tel: 982-7662.
Colombia: 595 Market Street, tel: 495-7195.
Costa Rica: 870 Market Street, tel: 392-8488.
Dominican Republic: 870 Market Street, tel: 982-5144.
Ecuador: 455 Market Street, tel: 957-5921.
El Salvador: 870 Market Street, tel: 781-7924.
France: 540 Bush Street, tel: 397-4330.

Don't be overcharged for overseas calls.

Save up to 70% on calls back to the U.S. with WorldPhone.®*

While traveling abroad, the last thing you need to worry about is being overcharged for international phone calls. Plan ahead and look into WorldPhone – the easy and affordable way for you to call the U.S. and country to country from a growing list of international locations.

Just dial 1-800-955-0925 to receive your free, handy, wallet-size WorldPhone Access Guide – your guide to saving as much as 70% on phone calls home.

When calling internationally, your WorldPhone Access Guide will allow you to:
- Avoid hotel surcharges and currency confusion
- Choose from four convenient billing options
- Talk with operators who speak your language
- Call from more than 90 countries
- Just dial and save – regardless of your long distance carrier back home

WorldPhone is easy. And there's nothing to join. So avoid overcharges when you're traveling overseas. Call for your free WorldPhone Access Guide today – before you travel.

Call 1-800-955-0925.

THE TOP 25 WORLDPHONE COUNTRY CODES.			
COUNTRY	**WORLDPHONE TOLL-FREE ACCESS #**	**COUNTRY**	**WORLDPHONE TOLL-FREE ACCESS #**
Australia (CC)♦		**Japan** (cont'd.)	
To call using		To call anywhere other	
OPTUS■	008-5511-11	than the U.S.	0055
To call using		**Korea** (CC)	
TELSTRA■	1-800-881-100	To call using KT■	009-14
Belgium (CC)♦	0800-10012	To call using DACOM■	0039-12
China (CC)	108-12	Phone Booths+	Red button 03,
(Available from most major cities)			then press*
For a Mandarin-speaking		Military Bases	550-2255
Operator	108-17	**Mexico** ▲	95-800-674-7000
Dominican Republic	1-800-	**Netherlands** (CC)♦	06-022-
	751-6624		91-22
El Salvador♦	195	**Panama**	108
France (CC)♦	19▼-00-19	Military Bases	2810-108
Germany (CC)	0130-0012	**Philippines** (CC)♦	
(Limited availability in eastern		To call using PLDT■	105-14
Germany.)		To call PHILCOM■	1026-12
Greece (CC)♦	00-800-1211	For a Tagalog-speaking	
Guatemala♦	189	Operator	108-15
Haiti (CC)+	061-800-444-1234	**Saudi Arabia** (CC)+	1-800-11
Hong Kong (CC)	800-1121	**Singapore**	8000-112-112
India (CC)	000-127	**Spain** (CC)	900-99-0014
(Available from most major cities)		**Switzerland** (CC)♦	155-0222
Israel (CC)	177-150-2727	**United Kingdom** (CC)	
Italy (CC)♦	172-1022	To call using BT ■	0800-89-0222
Japan♦		To call using	
To call to the U.S.		MERCURY■	0500-89-0222
using KDD■	0039-121		
To call to the U.S.			
using IDC■	0066-55-121		

(CC) Country-to-country calling available. May not be available to/from all international locations. Certain restrictions apply.
+ Limited availability.
▼ Wait for second dial tone.
▲ Rate depends on call origin in Mexico.
■ International communications carrier.
♦ Public phones may require deposit of coin or phone card for dial tone.

WORLDPHONE℠ From MCI

Let it take you around the world.

Swatch. The others just watch.

seahorse/fall winter 94-95

shockproof
splashproof
priceproof
boreproof
swiss made

swatch+
SCUBA 200

Germany: 1960 Jackson Street, tel: 775-1851.
Great Britain: 1 Sansome Street, tel: 981-3030.
Greece: 2441 Gough Street, tel: 775-2102.
Honduras: 870 Market Street, tel: 392-0076.
India: 540 Arguello Boulevard, tel: 668-0683.
Ireland: 655 Montgomery Street, tel: 392-4214.
Israel: 220 Bush Street, tel: 398-8885.
Italy: 2590 Webster Street, tel: 931-4924.
Japan: 50 Fremont Street, tel: 777-3533.
Luxembourg: 1 Sansome Street, tel: 788-0816.
Mexico: 870 Market Street, tel: 392-5554.
Netherlands: 1 Maritime Plaza, tel: 981-6454.
Norway: 20 California Street, tel: 986-0766.
People's Republic of China: 1450 Laguna Street, tel: 563-4885.
Peru: 870 Market Street, tel: 362-5185.
Philippines: 447 Sutter Street, tel: 433-6666.
Portugal: 3298 Washington, tel: 346-3400.
Spain: 2080 Jefferson Street, tel: 922-2995.
Sweden: 120 Montgomery Street, tel: 788-2631.
Switzerland: 456 Montgomery Street, tel: 788-2272.
Venezuela: 455 Market Street, tel: 512-8340.

Getting Around

On Arrival

From the Airport

Located 14 miles (23 km) south of downtown San Francisco on the shore of the Bay, near San Mateo, the journey from San Francisco International Airport (SFO) takes about 25 minutes, depending on the traffic conditions.

Transportation to and from SFO is provided by a variety of vehicles and companies. The best way to find transportation is by calling 800-SFO-2008, or by visiting one of the information booths in the baggage claim area.

The door-to-door shuttles (Airport Express, Lorrie's, Super Shuttle and Yellow Airport Service) compete for passengers on the upper level of the terminal at specially marked curbs. Although this is somewhat inconvenient if you have luggage (the baggage claim areas are on the lower level of the terminals), commuters and others who travel light prefer the door-to-door service with its low rates. Both Super Shuttle (tel: 558-8500) and Yellow Airport Shuttle (tel: 282-7433) operate 20 hours a day, with vans circling the upper terminal area every 20 minutes or less at peak periods. Call from the terminal or simply walk out to the roadway island and wait.

The vans are hard to come by late at night, particularly after 1am. It's safer to call a cab after midnight. Be sure to ignore hotels suggested by the drivers and have the fare quoted up front. Taxis also wait at the lower level in an area marked with yellow columns. Limousine service is available by using the toll-free white courtesy phones in the terminal.

The Marin County Airporter Coach (tel: 461-4222) services are more expensive than the shuttles. SamTrans, San Mateo County's bus system, makes several stops between the airport area and downtown San Francisco and is very cheap. No luggage may be taken on the "F" Express but may be put aboard the "7B" Local.

The telephone numbers for the various airport transportation services are as follows:
Airport Connection (limousine), tel: 885-2666.
Airport Express (van), tel: 775-5121.
Airporter Bus Service, tel: 495-8404.
Lorrie's (van), tel: 334-9000.
Good Neighbors Shuttle, tel: 777-4899.
SamTrans (bus), tel: 800-660-4287.
Santa Rosa (Sonoma) (bus), tel: (707) 545-8015.
Super Shuttle (van), tel: 558-8500.
Yellow Airport Shuttle (van), tel: 282-7433.

Free shuttle service is provided throughout the airport facilities to all airlines. The airport parking garage, valet parking, long-term parking (more than six hours in lower-priced lots away from the airport) and shuttle service from distant parking lots to the airport are available for those who drive.

The airport shuttle buses run every 5–7 minutes on the upper level of the terminal roadway, except between 12am and 6am when the 24-hour service runs every 10–15 minutes.

The 24-hour parking availability hotline number is 877-0123.

Airport Buses: These buses connect SFO and Hyatt Regency Hotel at Market and the Embarcadero. Board on lower level every 20 minutes from 6am–11pm. SamTrans buses also run south – 7F (no luggage) to Palo Alto and 7B (with luggage) to Redwood City. 7F runs from about 7am–12.30am and 7B from 6am–1am.

Oakland International Airport: Six carriers serve the Oakland Airport (tel: 577-4015) from two terminals. These include Alaska, America West, American, Continental, Delta, United and United Express. There are also cargo lines. A shuttle takes passengers to the Bay Area Rapid Transit (BART) station for a 30-minute ride through the underwater Transbay Tube to downtown San Francisco. Airport coaches, taxis, shuttles and AC Transit provide transportation as well.

San Jose International Airport: Alaska, America West, American, Continental, Delta, Mexicana, Morris Air, NorthWest, Sky West, SouthWest, twa, United, United Express, and cargo lines serve this airport (tel: (408) 277-4759) located about an hour south from downtown San Francisco.

Domestic Travel

Bus: The Greyhound-Trailways bus terminal (tel: 433-1500) is located at Seventh and Mission streets. Greyhound also shares the Transbay Terminal (tel: 558-6789) at First and Mission streets with other bus companies. Other Bay Area bus lines include:
AC Transit, East Bay, tel: 839-2882.
Golden Gate Transit, Marin and Sonoma counties, tel: 332-6600 or 453-2100.

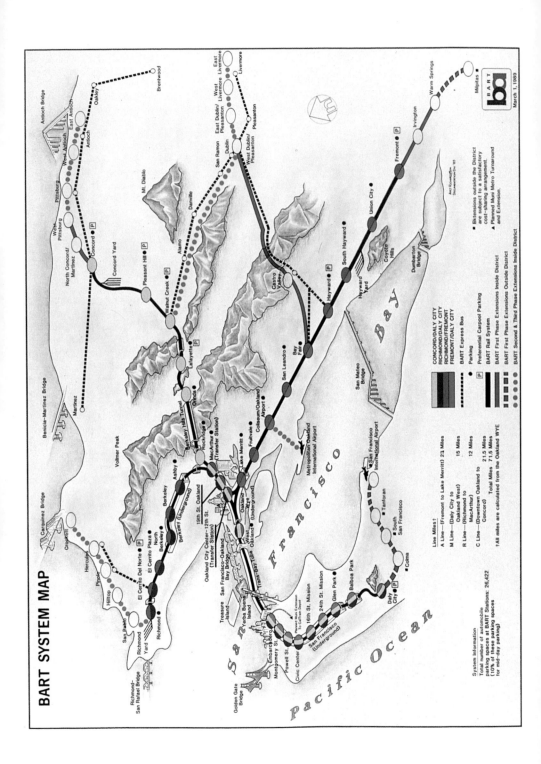

BART SYSTEM MAP

Line Miles†

A Line — (Fremont to Lake Merritt) 23 Miles

M Line — (Daly City to Oakland West) 15 Miles

R Line — (Richmond to MacArthur) 12 Miles

C Line — (Downtown Oakland to Concord) 21.5 Miles

Total Miles 71.5 Miles

†All miles are calculated from the Oakland WYE

System Information

Total number of automobile parking spaces at BART Stations: 26,422 (10% of these parking spaces for mid-day parking)

CONCORD/DALY CITY
RICHMOND/DALY CITY
RICHMOND/FREMONT
FREMONT/DALY CITY

BART Express Bus

P Parking

P Preferential Carpool Parking

BART Rail System

BART First Phase Extensions Inside District

BART First Phase Extensions Outside District

BART Second & Third Phase Extensions Inside District

● Extensions outside the District are subject to a satisfactory cost-sharing arrangement.

▲ Planned Muni Metro Turnaround and Extension.

March 1, 1989

ba B.A.R.T.

MUNI, San Francisco, tel: 673-6864. SamTrans, San Mateo County, tel: 800-660-4287.

Train: Amtrak, which runs state and national passenger trains, makes daily stops in Martinez, Richmond and San Jose. Service may be ended at Oakland's 16th Street Station where a free bus service is provided to the Transbay Bus Terminal in San Francisco. For information, tel: 558-6789.

State-owned CalTrain runs passenger trains between San Francisco and San Jose with several stops along the peninsula. Used by many commuters, the service is most frequent northbound in the morning and southbound in the afternoons. CalTrain operates from a terminal at Fourth and Townsend streets. To receive information, tel: 800-660-4287. Since the terminal is served by many muni bus lines, it is easy to take the train for a sightseeing excursion down the peninsula.

Ferry: For commuters and sightseers alike, ferry boats are a convenient and scenic way to cross the Bay. Golden Gate Ferry services are offered from the original Ferry Building at the foot of Market Street to Sausalito and Larkspur. Two lines run from the Fisherman's Wharf area. The Red & White Fleet offers tours around the Bay as well as ferry service to Sausalito, Tiburon, Angel Island and Alcatraz Island. The Blue & Gold Fleet also operates narrated Bay cruises from the Wharf. Information can be obtained at these numbers:
Golden Gate Ferry, tel: 332-6600.
Blue & Gold Fleet, tel: 800-426-8687.
Red & White Fleet, tel: 546-2896.
Alcatraz Island Tour, tel: 546-2896.

Public Transportation

Visitors to San Francisco should have little problem getting around. Besides public buses and taxis, there are a number of other transportation options which are economical, clean and comfortable.

Cable Cars

There are three cable car lines: California, Mason and Hyde. The latter two travel up and around from the downtown area to Fisherman's Wharf.

The California takes a steep but straight line from the Financial District over Nob Hill to the Van Ness corridor. Your ticket is transferable among the routes and is also good on the MUNI system. MUNI bus tickets are good on the cable system, but since the cable fare is more expensive, you must give the cable conductor the extra amount when you board.

The conductor will give change, but it's easier on everybody if you use the sidewalk cable car ticket vending machines to get your ticket. You can ride on one ticket on as many routes as you can squeeze into the time period indicated. Be forewarned, however, that the Mason and Hyde lines in particular are usually crowded. Plan your time to allow for a wait in line coming back from Fisherman's Wharf – free entertainment is provided by street musicians – or plan to ride the bus to return.

Stop off on your way and see the **Cable Car Barn Museum** at 1201 Mason (tel: 474-1887). Open: daily 10am–6pm (to 5pm in winter). Admission: free. Watch a film, see the moving cable itself, view relics of the earliest transit system and see the very first cable car on display.

Stops are marked with signs mounted on poles displaying a cable car symbol. For information about fares and rates, tel: 673-6864.

AC Transit

To travel east from San Francisco, AC Transit (Alameda-Contra Costa Transit) provides daily service from the Transbay Terminal to most cities in the East Bay area. Fares vary according to distance traveled and exact fare is required when you board. Many buses are wheelchair-accessible. For information, tel: 839-2882.

Golden Gate Transit

To travel north of the city, Golden Gate Transit buses and ferries connect San Francisco with Marin and Sonoma counties. Buses stop where green, blue and white signs are posted on the bus line poles. Exact fare is required and fares vary according to distance traveled. Golden Gate Transit buses are wheelchair-accessible. For information, tel: 332-6600.

Municipal Railway

For getting around in the city, San Francisco MUNI is your best bet. MUNI is responsible for all buses, streetcars, trolley cars (during vintage festivals), and cable cars in San Francisco. Along Market Street, streetcars are underground and are boarded from the bart stations. You must have exact change.

Discounts are available for children, the disabled, and people over 65. Commuter "fast passes" are available for unlimited use during a one-month period. Transfers are free for all and riders may use them for two additional rides during the time period indicated on the transfer slip. Transfers must be requested at the time you board the bus.

Bus stops are marked by the words "Coach Stop" on the street; by a long rectangle of wide, white lines, or by a bright yellow marking on a telephone or light pole, and/or by an orange and brown route sign mounted on a bus stop pole. Service is frequent and some muni lines run 24 hours. For information, tel: 673-6864. Be ready with your starting point, your destination and the time of day of travel, and the MUNI operator will plan your route for you. Some buses are specially equipped for wheelchairs. (See *Motoring Advisories* for map details.)

Some of the buses are electric, and are quiet and clean. On all buses, especially electric-powered ones, hang on to the handholds and bars as you move to your seat or stand; the jerky starts can almost throw you to the floor.

Samtrans

To travel south of San Francisco, SamTrans buses run seven days a week, connecting with AC Transit and Golden Gate Transit at the Transbay Terminal. SamTrans also connects with BART at the Daly City and Hayward stations. Stops include the San Francisco International Airport, Southern Pacific Caltrain station, and the Greyhound Depot. Fares vary according to distance traveled and exact fare is required when boarding. Most buses are wheelchair accessible. For information, tel: 800-660-4287.

Bay Area Rapid Transit

BART is one of the more modern, efficient, and most automated regional transportation systems in the world. The sleek, clean, air-conditioned cars carry hundreds of thousands of commuters each day over 70 miles (113 km) of electric track at speeds approaching 80 miles (129 km) an hour.

Often compared to the super-subways of Europe and Russia, BART serves 34 stations in three counties, from San Francisco to Daly City and throughout Alameda and Contra Costa (the East Bay), Monday–Saturday, 6am–midnight, Sundays 9am–midnight. Some of the bart tracks are underground, while others are surfaced or elevated. Among the underground tracks are those inside the Transbay Tube between San Francisco and Oakland. At 3.5 miles (6 km), this tube is one of the world's longest underwater tunnels.

The trains carry drivers, but are essentially controlled by trackside relays and a $40-million computer center at the Lake Merritt BART station in Oakland. There are no cashiers (only vending machines), no ticket-takers (only automated entrance and exit gates) and no conductors (all incoming trains are announced on computerized bulletin boards).

All stations have wall maps showing nearby tourist attractions, shopping areas, and connecting bus lines. There are displays of printed information explaining station locations, fares and ticket-buying procedures. Fares vary according to the distance traveled. (A typical San Francisco-to-Berkeley trip will cost $2–$3.) Children under the age of five travel free. Discounts are available for youths, senior citizens, handicapped persons and regular commuters.

Tourists can ride BART for a special reduced fare which entitles you to stay on board for up to three hours. You must enter and exit BART from the same station. Commuters crowd the cars from 7am–9am and 4pm–6pm on weekdays. Plan your fun ride during off hours or you may never find a seat.

BART stations are marked with blue and white signs ("ba"). Along Market Street, look for the escalators going down to the underground boarding points. For current information, tel:

788-BART. Outside of San Francisco, local information numbers are listed in the area telephone directory under "Bay Area Rapid Transit."

Taxis

San Francisco is so compact that taxis are a convenient alternative to walking or public transportation when you're in a hurry and going just a few miles. In busy downtown areas, taxis can be hailed from the sidewalk. Use the telephone directory and the numbers below to call in advance. San Francisco cab drivers are known for their helpfulness.

Central, tel: 468-7215.
City Cab, tel: 468-7200.
DeSoto, tel: 673-1414.
Luxor, tel: 282-4141.
Veteran's, tel: 552-1300.
Yellow Cab, tel: 626-2345.

Smaller taxi services include:
American, tel: 775-3377.
Arrow, tel: 564-6911.
Diamond, tel: 781-1138.
Pacific Cab, tel: 776-7755.
Sunshine Cab, tel: 776-7755. (Chinese translation available)
United, tel: 468-7215.

Private Transportation

Car Rentals

There are dozens of automobile rental agencies at the airports and in San Francisco. Rates vary; insurance is extra and varies in price and coverage. Check your own auto policy before you leave home to make sure you really need the extra coverage. Read the rental agreement before you sign it. Most companies offer unlimited mileage and special weekend rates. Many will pick you up at your hotel. Shop around for the best rates and service. Often, smaller local rental companies offer better deals than national firms. If you fancy driving a dented heirloom, try Rent-A-Wreck. Reservations are advised everywhere.

Most rental agencies require you to be at least 21 years old (sometimes 25) and to hold a valid driver's license and a major credit card. In lieu of a credit card, some companies, like Avis, will take a (large) cash deposit

after a special approval and review of your return flight ticket, passport and International Driver's License. Drivers are required at all times to abide by local and State traffic regulations.

If you are an auto club member in another country, National Automobile Club will extend emergency, information and other services to you. The aaa-California State Automobile Association may extend services – you must check first.

Avis, tel: 800-331-1212.
Budget, tel: 800-527-0700.
Dollar, tel: 800-421-6868.
Hertz, tel: 800-654-3131.
National, tel: 800-328-4567.
Rent-A-Wreck, tel: 776-8700.
Sears, tel: 775-5777.
Thrifty, tel: 259-1313.
AAA-California State Automobile Assoc., 150 Van Ness, tel: 565-2012. Monday–Friday 8.30am–5pm. Emergency Service: 863-3432.
National Automobile Club, 115 Steuart Street, tel: 777-4000. 24-hour Emergency Road Service: 800-622-2135.

Motoring Advisories: If you have an International Driving License or a valid license from a Western country, you may drive in California. The California state speed limit is 55 mph (85 kpm), and 65 mph (100 kph) on some sections of interstate highways. Most city speed limits are 25–35 mph (40–55 kpm).

In addition to street signs advising no-parking hours and special tow-away zones, the color of the curb governs the kind of parking permitted. Red curbs mean no parking at any time. Yellow curbs indicate limited stops for loading and unloading passengers or freight, usually by truck, until 6pm. White curbs, usually found at the entrances to hotels and restaurants, mean limited short-term stopping for passengers or baggage. Green curbs usually indicate short-term parking for 10–20 minutes. Blue curbs and wheelchair symbols mean disabled parking only. Remember to read the signs.

Traffic is congested in the city and laws are strictly enforced – violations are expensive. Police issue tickets to impose fines and call tow trucks to remove vehicles in No Parking zones found blocking driveways. You'll need plenty of cash and a credit card to bail out your car.

Much of San Francisco parking space is on steep hills. It is the law that wheels must be "curbed" on these inclines to help prevent unexpected runaways. Always turn your front wheels into the curb so that the tire rests on it at an angle. Be sure to set the emergency brake. Fines are issued for cars that are not "curbed."

Pedestrians and cable cars have the right of way. If you have questions, call one of the auto clubs or the Department of Motor Vehicles, tel: 557-1179.

Many natives use their cars for trips outside the city only. There are two good reasons for this: the city streets are narrow and congested, and the public transportation network is excellent. To get yourself within easy walking distance of any destination, choose from buses, ferries, trolley cars, cable cars, streetcars and bart. A map some swear by and others never figure out is published by MUNI (San Francisco Municipal Railway) and is available at drug and book store counters all over the city. This map includes all the possible transportation options, with route descriptions, schedules, fares and helpful phone numbers.

On Foot

San Francisco is a wonderful city for walking – if you are not too ambitious. Stick to small areas like Chinatown, North Beach, and the lovely, albeit windy Golden Gate Promenade.

Walking is one way to discover charming neighborhoods tucked away behind hills. And there are plenty of cafés where you can rest your feet and drink something hot and soothing.

Hitchhiking

You will sometimes see people thumbing lifts or standing next to signs that signify their destination. Asking for lifts or stopping your car to give a ride are both risky propositions. Best advice: don't try.

Where To Stay

Hotels

San Francisco offers a variety of accommodations in an ever-expanding variety of locations. The compact nature of the city allows visitors to consider many neighborhoods outside the central business and shopping areas. Information and reservation services are available to assist you in your choice. An 11 percent room tax is added to all rates.

Hotel reservations may be made through services including San Francisco Reservations, 22 Second Street, San Francisco, 94102 (tel: 227-1500). The Convention and Visitors' Bureau (tel: 974-6900) can advise you regarding special needs or general information about their member hotels, motels and inns. Hotel chains like Hilton, Hyatt, Marriott offer toll-free telephone numbers for reservations.

Listed is a selection of hotels which we categorized as follows:

$ = Under $100
$$ = Under $200
$$$ = Above $200

Large Hotels

The large hotels of San Francisco are particularly well-suited to international travelers. Many (for example, the classic old hotels sitting atop Nob Hill) are attractive landmarks in their own right. The Fairmont Hotel was once even the featured "star" in a television series.

Grand hotels are mostly situated in established areas, with easy access to tourist sites and public transportation. A concierge is on duty to arrange theater tickets, tours, telex, seats at sporting events, limousines with bilingual drivers, and airline reservations. He recommends restaurants, can speak foreign languages, and helps exchange currency.

The grand hotels in San Francisco each have at least 200 rooms with air conditioning, color TV, room phones and nearby parking, restaurants, cof-

fee shops and bars. There are seasonal rate changes and special off-season packages. Telephone or write to verify current rates and make reservations.

Fairmont Hotel, 950 Mason Street, San Francisco, 94108, tel: 772-5000 or toll-free 800-527-4727. One of San Francisco's landmarks, located atop elegant Nob Hill. $$$

Four Seasons-Clift, 495 Geary, San Francisco, CA 94102, tel: 775-4700. Two blocks west of Union Square. Old, conservative and elegant. $$$

Hilton, tel: 800-445-8667. Two modern skyscrapers in the city, both have swimming pools. $$.

• **Airport**, Off Highway 101, PO Box 8355, San Francisco 94128, tel: 589-0770 or 800-445-8667. Spacious grounds at the airport entrance.

• **San Francisco Hotel & Tower**, 333 O'Farrell, San Francisco 94102, tel: 771-1400. 1,685 rooms on the edge of Union Square. Great view from Henri's Room.

Holiday Inn, tel: 800-465-4329. Five large hotels, all but Union Square with swimming pools. $$

• **Civic Center**, 50 Eighth Street, San Francisco 94103, tel: 626-6103.

• **Financial District**, 750 Kearny, San Francisco 94108, tel: 433-6600.

• **Fisherman's Wharf**, 1300 Columbus, San Francisco 94133, tel: 771-9000.

• **Golden Gateway**, 1500 Van Ness, San Francisco 94109, tel: 441-4000. A last resort on a busy thoroughfare.

• **Union Square**, 480 Sutter At Powell, 94108, tel: 398-8900. The best of the bunch.

Hyatt, tel: 800-233-1234. The chain runs two of the best hotels in the city. $$$

• **Regency**, 5 Embarcadero Center, San Francisco, tel: 788-1234. Spectacular architecture: the triangular lobby atrium rises 170 feet, lined with interior balconies, cascading plants, and glassed-in elevators.

• **Union Square**, 345 Stockton, San Francisco 94108, tel: 398-1234. Good food and great location.

Mark Hopkins Inter-Continental, No. 1 Nob Hill, San Francisco 94108, tel: 392-3434 or call toll-free 800-327-

0200. The "Top of the Mark" remains a "must see." $$$

Marriott, 55 Fourth Street, San Francisco 94103, tel: 896-1600. 1,500 rooms. Mirrored green-glass exterior, which looks from a distance like a giant juke-box. $$$

Miyako, 1625 Post Street, San Francisco 94115, tel: 922-3200. 218 units in tasty Japanese decor. $$

Parc 55, 55 Cyril Magnin, San Francisco 94102, tel: 392-8000. Part of the Park Lane hotel chain, incorporates a health club. $$$

Sheraton, tel: 800-325-3535. Operates very different types of inns. $$

- **Airport**, 1177 Airport Boulevard, Burlingame 94010, tel: 342-9200. Heated swimming pool and whirlpools.
- **Fisherman's Wharf**, 2500 Mason, San Francisco 94133, tel: 362-5500.
- **Palace**, 2 New Montgomery Street, San Francisco 94105, tel: 392-8600. A historical landmark featuring the famous Garden Court Restaurant.

St Francis, 335 Powell, San Francisco 94102, tel: 397-7000. 1,200 units on Union Square in this 1907 landmark. Part of the Westin hotel chain. $$$

The Stouffer Stanford Court, 905 California Street, San Francisco 94108, tel: 989-3500 or call toll-free 800-227-4726, within California 800-622-0957. Just below Nob Hill. An elegant renovation credited with setting the standard for San Francisco hotel revivals. $$$

Small Hotels

These comfortable accommodations are often renovated hotels in newly popular or changing areas like South of Market (SoMa) and the Tenderloin or in neighborhoods around Golden Gate Park and Russian Hill. They provide services with a personal touch at rates lower than the well-known, centrally located grand hotels. Since rooms are limited in number and word spreads quickly about the good ones, be sure to arrange reservations in advance. Rates vary widely in relation to services offered, location or exclusivity.

Campton Place Kempinski, off Union Square, 340 Stockton, San Francisco 94108, tel: 781-5555 or toll-free 800-

647-4077, within California 800-235-4300. Known for personal service. $$

Hotel Bedford, 761 Post Street, San Francisco 94109, tel: 673-6040 or toll-free 800-227-5642, within California 800-652-1889. Reasonable and popular Café Bedford. $$

Huntington Hotel, 1075 California Street, San Francisco 94108, tel: 474-5400 or toll-free 800-227-4683, within California 800-652-1539. A favorite with opera stars and other celebrities who request their favorite, individually furnished room. Views and gourmet restaurants. $$$

King George Hotel, 334 Mason Street, San Francisco 94102, tel: 781-5050 or toll-free 800-288-6005, within California 800-556-4545. Small traditional rooms and afternoon tea, a favorite with European travelers. $$$

Sherman House, 2160 Green Street, San Francisco 94123, tel: 563-3600. Absolute luxury, very expensive, Golden Gate views and fireplaces. $$$

Stanyan Park Hotel, 750 Stanyan Street, San Francisco, 94117, tel: 751-1000. Listed on the National Register of Historic Places, near Golden Gate Park, the Haight-Ashbury district, and the UC Medical Center. $$

Motels

If you are traveling by car and need only basic accommodations for sleeping, motels offer lower rates and a parking space near your room.

Many motels are situated along the busy streets and the degree and quality of amenities vary. Major motel chains provide toll-free telephone numbers for making and confirming reservations. They also offer standard quality. The major chains include Best Western, Holiday Inn, Ramada, and Travel Lodge.

Bed & Breakfast Inns

Converted from mansions and houses with five to 15 rooms, these inns offer travelers a comfortable home away from home. All serve breakfast – either coffee and pastries or a full meal. Inquire first and make reservations. Some do not accept credit cards.

Specialty accommodation reservation services include:

American Family Inn, 2185A Union Street, San Francisco, 94123, tel: 479-1913.

Visitors' Advisory Service, 1530 Fountain, Alameda, CA 94501, tel: 521-9366.

Information for Napa Valley/Wine Country:

Bed & Breakfast Inns. Toll-free 800-424-0053.

Bed & Breakfast International, 1181 Solano, Albany, 94706, tel: (510) 525-4569.

Bed & Breakfast Inn, 4 Charlton Court, San Francisco, 94123, tel: 921-9784. A restored Victorian, English-style pension on Union Street. $$

The Mansions Hotel, 2220 Sacramento Street, San Francisco, 94115, tel: 929-9444. A unique celebrity favorite in Pacific Heights with magic, nightly concerts and Benjamino Bufano sculptures. $$

Petite Auberge, 863 Bush Street, San Francisco 94108, tel: 928-6000. Gourmet breakfast buffet near Union Square. $$

Queen Anne Hotel, 1590 Sutter Street, San Francisco 94109, tel: 441-2828 or toll-free 800-227-3970. In 1890 a school for girls, later an exclusive men's club. $$

Victorian Inn on the Park, 310 Lyon Street, San Francisco, tel: 931-1830. A Victorian Bed & Breakfast near Haight-Ashbury (and former home of alternative comic guru Robert Crumb, creator of Fritz the Cat). Rates are reasonable to highish.

Washington Square Inn, 1660 Stockton Street, San Francisco 94133, tel: 981-4220. Within walking distance of Fisherman's Wharf, Chinatown, the Financial District, in North Beach. $$

Suites

For extended visits or for business travel, more spacious accommodations are available for rent in apartments and condominiums, fully equipped with kitchens. Most have maid service and require a one-week minimum stay. Locations vary throughout city neighborhoods.

Specialty reservation and information services include:

American Property Exchange, 170 Page Street, San Francisco, 994102, tel: 863-8484.

Hotel Alternative, 1125 E Hillsdale, Foster City, 94402, tel: (510) 429-9700.

Hostels

San Francisco is home to one of the largest hostels in the country. The dormitory-style **San Francisco International Hostel** includes about 170 beds and community kitchens. It is located above the Bay in a century-old Army dispensary at Fort Mason, between the Marina and Fisherman's Wharf. The maximum stay is five nights; international hostel rules are observed. Your International Hostel Pass is honored for credit, or you can pay the night rate which includes a guest pass. Reservations are accepted and limited free parking is provided. Tel: 771-7277 for information about this and other hostels in the area.

Another inexpensive alternative for travelers who wish to stay for a maximum of five days is provided by the **European Guest House** at 761 Minna. Accommodation is dormitory style. For more information, tel: 861-6634.

Two universities also provide dormitory accommodations during the summer months. Twin-bedded rooms with shared bath are available for students. For information, contact San Francisco State University, Housing Office, 800 Font Boulevard, San Francisco, 94132 (tel: 338-1067); or the University of California San Francisco, Housing Office, 500 Parnassus Avenue, San Francisco, 94122 (tel: 476-2231). The USF facilities are located in the Haight-Ashbury neighborhood near Golden Gate Park.

RV Parks

Recreational Vehicles are welcome at two facilities within the city limits. South of Market Street, near the CalTrain Depot, there are 200 sites at San Francisco RV Park, 250 King Street, San Francisco, 94107 (tel: 986-8730). Another 120 sites are also available at the Candlestick RV Park, 650 Gilman Avenue, San Francisco, 94124 (tel: 822-2299) which offers a laundromat and shuttle bus to downtown. These industrial neighborhoods might not suit you, so drive by and check it out first.

In the town of Pacifica, on the coast about 20 minutes from downtown San Francisco, you'll find the Pacific Park RV Resort, 275 sites with pool, spa and laundry at 700 Palmetto Avenue, Pacifica, 94044, tel: toll-free 800-822-1250 outside of California, 800-992-0554 within California.

Eating Out

What To Eat

San Francisco is one of the world's great culinary capitals – rich in ethnic diversity, and offering everything from Chinese to California cuisine.

When you wander down the streets you can't help but take in each neighborhood's fascination with food. Each area of the city features authentic restaurants that cater to discriminating locals and travelers. San Francisco once boasted the only restaurant in America serving pizza. The country's first Northern Chinese restaurant opened here. Irish Coffee and other food and beverage delights were invented in the saloons and cafés of San Francisco.

There's a whole world of food waiting for you between San Francisco's city limits, and you may remember in years to come: you ate it here first.

Where To Eat

The restaurants listed have been recommended by local food writers and are but a sample of what is in store to treat your palate. Make reservations whenever possible to avoid disappointment.

Look for "early bird" meals, discounted before busy hours. Since San Francisco is a tourist town, casual clothes are accepted in most restaurants – with the exception of dinner at the fancier ones.

EXPENSIVE

Amelio's, 1630 Powell, tel: 397-4339. French/Continental.

Campton Place, 340 Stockton, tel: 781-5155. American nouvelle.

Donatello, 501 Post, tel: 441-7182. Northern Italian.

Ernie's, 847 Montogmery Street, tel: 397-5969. French.

Fleur de Lys, 777 Sutter, tel: 673-7779. French.

Masa's, 648 Bush, tel: 989-7154. French.

The Squire, 950 Mason, tel: 772-5211. Continental.

Tommy Toy's, 655 Montgomery, tel: 397-4888. Chinese/French.

Trader Vic's, 20 Cosmo Place, tel: 776-2232. Oriental/Continental.

Yank Sing, 427 Battery Street, tel: 781-1111. Chinese.

MODERATELY EXPENSIVE

Chateau Suzanne, 1449 Lombard, tel: 771-9326. French.

Gaylord India Restaurant, Ghirardelli Square, tel: 771-8822. Northern Indian.

Jack's, 615 Sacramento, tel: 986-9854. French/Continental (since 1864).

Le Castel, 3235 Sacramento, tel: 921-7115. French.

Regina's, 490 Geary, tel: 386-8577. French Creole.

Square One, 190 Pacific, tel: 788-1110. Mediterranean.

The Shadows, 1349 Montgomery, tel: 982-5536. Contemporary French.

MODERATE

Angkor Wat, 4217 Geary, tel: 221-7887. Cambodian.

California Culinary Academy, 625 Polk, tel: 771-3500. Contemporary.

Firenze Restaurant, 1429 Stockton, tel: 421-5813. Italian.

Golden Turtle, 2211 Van Ness, tel: 441-4419. Vietnamese.

Khan Toke Thai House, 5937 Geary Boulevard, tel: 668-6654. Thai.

Kuleto's Italian Restaurant, 221 Powell, tel: 397-7720. Californian/Italian.

La Pergola Ristorante, 2060 Chestnut, tel: 563-4500. Northern Italian.

Osome Restaurant, 1923 Fillmore, tel: 346-2311. Japanese.

Tadich Grill, 240 California, tel: 391-1849. American/Seafood.

Washington Square Bar & Grill, 1707 Powell, tel: 982-8123. Italian/American/Seafood.

INEXPENSIVE

Lilies on Mason, 542 Mason, tel: 391-2401. American.

Manora's Thai Restaurant, 3226 Mission, tel: 550-0856. Thai.

Maykadeh, 470 Green, tel: 362-8286. Persian.

Max's Diner, 311 Third, tel: 546-6297. American.

Tommy's Joynt, 1101 Geary, tel: 775-4216. Haufbrau.

Vicolo Pizzeria, 201 Ivy, tel: 863-2382. Pizza. Also at 900 North Point, Ghiradelli Square, tel: 776-1331. Italian.

BARGAIN RESTAURANTS

Brother Juniper's Breadbox, 1065 Sutter, tel: 771-8929. Breakfast, lunch.

Fisherman's Café, 7001 Geary Boulevard, tel: 751-0191. Early dinner.

Jay's Bee's Pub Club, 2736 20th Street, tel: 824-4190. Steak and hamburger.

Kublai Khan's Mongolian BBQ, 1160 Polk, tel: 885-1378. Korean buffet.

Orphan Andy's, 3991 17th Street, tel: 864-9795. Open all night.

Picadilly, 1348 Polk, tel: 771-6477. Fish and chips.

Ping Yuen Bakery, 650 Jackson, tel: 986-6830. Chinese-American cuisine.

Rose, 791 O'Farrell, tel: 441-5635. Vietnamese.

Tsing Tao, 3107 Clement, tel: 387-2344. Chinese banquet.

HEALTHY

Blue Fox, 659 Merchant, tel: 981-1177. Continental.

Café Mozart, 708 Bush, tel: 391-8480. Continental.

Café Riggio, 4112 Geary, tel: 221-2114. Italian.

Cliff House, 1090 Point Lobos, tel: 386-3330. Seafood.

Empress of China, 838 Grant, tel: 434-1345. Chinese.

Ernie's Neptune Fish Grotto, 1816 Irving, tel: 566-3344. Seafood.

La Barca, 2036 Lombard, tel: 921-2221. Mexican.

Narsai's, cellar at I. Magnin, Geary and Stockton, tel: 362-2100. Continental.

Ronayne's Seafood Café, 1799 Lombard, tel: 922-5060. Seafood.

Yamato Sukiyaki House, 717 California, tel: 397-3456. Japanese.

Yet Wah, 2140 Clement, tel: 387-8040. Chinese.

Drinking Notes

In California, the legal age for purchase and consumption of alcoholic beverages is 21 years old. Identification is usually required. Alcoholic beverages are sold by the bottle or in liquor stores, some supermarkets and many drug and convenience stores. From 6am–2am, alcoholic beverages may be sold by the glass in restaurants, clubs and bars. Some establishments are licensed to sell beer and wine only.

In some cases, for an extra "corkage" fee, you may bring your own bottle of wine into a restaurant, where it will be served by the waiter. International travelers are allowed to bring 1 quart (1 liter) of alcohol into the country when they arrive in the US.

Attractions

Balmy Alley: Off 24th Street. Forty local artists created murals on garage doors and walls to urge peace in Central America.

The Bay Model: Sausalito at 2100 Bridgeway, tel: 332-3871. A free exhibit features a two-acre scale model of the San Francisco Bay and Delta Region. Tidal action, flow and current of the Bay are reproduced in this working hydraulic model. There's a computerized slide show along with interpretive displays.

Cliff House: Tel: 386-3331. Overlooking Seal Rock, the turn of the century complex includes a restaurant, historical displays and the *Musee Mechanique* featuring antique mechanical games. Nearby is the site of the famous long-defunct Sutro Baths.

Coit Tower: At the top of Telegraph Hill. Panoramic views and murals depicting California in the 1930s draw thousands of visitors. A free tour conducted on Saturday describes the history of the murals, created as part of the PWA art program.

Fisherman's Wharf: The northern waterfront is occupied by four shopping complexes, the National Maritime Museum and historic ship exhibits, fine restaurants, street entertainment, amusements, souvenir shops and fresh fish. Beginning at Pier 39, the area spreads north to Jefferson and Taylor and West to Van Ness, including the Aquatic Park. The Hyde and Mason cable cars end their runs in the area; many buses pass by, too.

Golden Gate Bridge: Walk, drive or cycle to the lookout points at either end. Visit Fort Point, a military museum with costumed soldiers who demonstrate cannon firings and other activities on a seasonal schedule. For information, tel: 556-1693.

Golden Gate Park: Gardens, museums, sports facilities, a buffalo paddock, Dutch windmill, Japanese Tea Garden and more, the park is a favorite with natives and visitors alike. Rent bicycles or boats and explore the parts that interest you. Once seen, it is difficult to believe that all this was created from sand. The park extends from Stanyan Street to the Great Highway at the ocean, between Fulton and Lincoln Way. For information, tel: 666-7024.

Grace Cathedral: Atop Nob Hill sits the inspiring Gothic structure with vaulted ceilings and stained glass panels. There is a gift shop and visitors are welcome to tour the church.

Haas-Lilienthal House: Franklin Street at Jackson. For tours, tel: 441-3004. Preserved in the grand style of pre-1906 earthquake and fire, this stately Victorian is the only fully furnished one open for touring. Pacific Heights walking tours to other mansions begin here. Open: Wednesday noon–3.15pm, Sunday 11am–4.15pm, but call first.

Hyde Street Pier: Three historic ships are available for boarding at the foot of Hyde Street. Two others have been restored and are docked here also. The exhibit is part of the National Maritime Museum, located nearby.

Jackson Square: This is the city's first historic landmark. The restored buildings are examples of pre-earthquake architecture. The area was originally called the Barbary Coast and was inhabited by unsavory characters. Enter the square from Jackson or Montgomery streets.

Japantown: The Japanese Cultural Trade Center includes restaurants, shops, movie theaters and Buddhist churches. Outdoor performances take place during summer near the Peace Pagoda.

Lombard Street: Walk or drive "the crookedest street in the world." To go down, get on Lombard at Hyde. There may be a line of cars extending to Van Ness on busy days. To go up, enter from Leavenworth if you're on foot (it's one-way to vehicles). The landscaping features an abundance of flowers and this is a great photo spot.

Marina Green: Runners and walkers love the ocean-side promenade – the views of the Golden Gate and Marin County are unsurpassed. Bring a kite, roller skates, binoculars and enjoy both the water and land activity. The promenade extends from Crissy Field to Fort Mason, along Marina Boulevard.

Mission Dolores: One of the oldest buildings in San Francisco, it has survived earthquakes and 200 years of history. Founded in 1776 by Franciscan Fathers, the building features thick adobe walls and hand-hewn beams. The peaceful grounds and church at Dolores and 16th streets are open 9am–4pm daily. A small donation is requested. For information, tel: 621-8203. Stop in the Cafe Picaro nearby.

Nob Hill: Huntington Park, Grace Cathedral, grand hotels and the Pacific Union Club share the top of this famous peak. The California Street cable car struggles up its steep sides, offering spectacular views of the city to the South and the Bay to the North. The official borders are Leavenworth, Washington, Stockton and Bush streets.

North Beach: Situated between the Wharf and Chinatown, the Italian neighborhood includes Coit Tower and Telegraph Hill, along with restaurants, Beat Generation bookstores and coffee houses, and the burlesque of Broadway night life.

SS Jeremiah O'Brien: The last unaltered Liberty Ship in operating condition is tied up at Pier 3 in Fort Mason, located at Laguna and Marina Boulevard. Open: weekdays 9am–3pm and weekends 9am–4pm. Open Ship Weekend, every third weekend of the month, tel: 441-3101.

Octagon House: 2645 Gough Street, at Union, tel: 441-7512. A museum furnished with Colonial and Federal period pieces that was designed to be a luck house for its owners in 1861. Open: noon–3pm the second and fourth Thursday, and the second Sunday of each month. Donation suggested.

The Old Mint: Fifth and Mission streets, tel: 744-6830. A fine example of Federal classical revival architecture, this storehouse reopened the day after the 1906 earthquake. The survivor held one-third of the country's wealth during the early 1930s. Four million dollars in gold bars is displayed, along with coin collections. Open: Monday–Friday 10am–4pm. Admission: free.

The Presidio: Headquarters of the Sixth Army, this facility served the Spanish and Mexican military until 1846. The National Park Service can provide a trail map for the historic and scenic points of interest. Tel: 556-0560 or visit the Golden Gate National Recreation Area office at Port Mason Center, near the Marina. The Presidio can be entered at Lombard and Park Presidio Drive.

The San Francisco Experience: Tel: 982-7550. Experience the earthquake of 1906 from the safety of a theater seat. The history of San Francisco is a multi-media presentation with 35 projectors, seven screens and Surround Sound. Shows are scheduled every half hour at Pier 39. The soundtrack is also available in Japanese.

San Francisco Zoo: Sloat Boulevard at 45th Avenue, tel: 753-7083. The Primate Discovery Center is one of the innovative features of the 70-acre (28-hectare) zoo. Visitors can pet the animals in the children's zoo, ride the antique merry-go-round, inspect the penguin habitat and make the acquaintance of 38 threatened and endangered species among the 1,000 residents. Tours Saturday and Sunday.

Sheraton Palace Hotel: The Garden Court dining room is one of the most elegant settings for a meal anywhere. Take a look at elegance from a time gone by at New Montgomery and Market streets.

Stern Grove: The 12-acre (5-hectare) site features free concerts from June–August. Classical and jazz music is enjoyed among eucalyptus trees every Sunday. Check the newspaper calendar section for local entertainment.

Strybing Arboretum: Tel: 661-1316. Tours and theme walks from this living museum in Golden Gate Park of over 600 plant and tree varieties.

Television Shows: Local station KGO invites visitors to be part of the audience for its morning talk show. For information, tel: 954-7777.

Gay Activities

For the thriving gay and lesbian communities in San Francisco, the Mission, Castro, and South of Market districts are the locus of activities and nightlife. For information covering gay and lesbian nightclub and entertainment listings, to counseling and health resources, two free weekly publications, *The Sentinel* and the *Bay Area Reporter* offer the most comprehensive coverage and classified ads catering to the gay community.

In addition to the annual Halloween bash that takes place in the heart of the Castro each year – it has become San Francisco's own version of Mardi Gras, and draws thousands who party on the streets into the wee hours – San Francisco also hosts the annual **Lesbian/Gay Pride Celebration** on the last Sunday each June, culminating in a Market Street parade which regularly draws up to 250,000 people. The **Castro Street Fair** is held usually in September or October. A **candlelight march** each November in the Castro area honors former city supervisor Harvey Milk, the gay community leader who was brutally gunned down along with Mayor George Moscone at City Hall in 1979.

Along with the city's plethora of gay bars, cafés and nightclubs (SoMa: The End Up, Dekadence, and Rawhide II; in the Castro: Cafe Flore, The Metro, and many others), there are a growing number of theaters drawing gay audiences to alternative performance, including Josie's Cabaret and Juice Joint (3583 16th Street) and Theatre Rhinoceros (2926 16th Street).

For an on-line bulletin board of gay-community activities, call the **Lesbian/Gay Switchboard**: (510) 841-6224.

The San Francisco Bay Area is a major cultural center, home to the San Francisco Ballet, Symphony, Opera and Museum of Modern Art. Each is a first-rate institution. In addition, galleries, theaters, dance companies, concert halls, museums and bookstores offer choices for every taste – classical to contemporary.

Many writers and artists live in the Bay Area and new works and shows are often tested here. Revivals of shows are also popular, on stage and in ornate movie theaters.

Your best source of current information is the "Datebook" section (the pink section) of the weekend edition of the *San Francisco Chronicle & Examiner*. Other good guides for all events are *San Francisco Focus*, the public television magazine; *SF Weekly* and *San Francisco Bay Guardian*.

Museums

All of the museums listed here feature several changing displays in addition to their permanent collections. Call for current exhibitions, schedules and admission fees or check the weekend paper.

Asian Art Museum, Golden Gate Park, tel: 668-8921. Nearly 10,000 bronzes, sculptures, paintings and porcelain from China, Japan, India, Korea, Tibet, Southeast Asia. It also has windows overlooking the lovely Tea Garden. Open: Wednesday–Sunday 10am––5pm. Admission: free the first Wednesday of the month and first Saturday morning.

Cable Car Museum, on the cable car route at Mason and Washington streets, tel: 474-1887. The restored Cable Car Barn houses a complete model collection of San Francisco cable cars. A viewing platform overlooks the electrically powered wheels that move the cables. A film explains how it all works. Open: 10am–5pm. Admission: free.

California Academy of Sciences, Golden Gate Park, tel: 750-7145. The Steinhart Aquarium, Morrison Planetarium and natural science exhibits offer numerous activities and shows. The Fish Roundabout and other exhibits comprise one of the world's best collections of aquatic life. The Earth and Science Hall features a Safe Quake ride and precious stones are displayed in the Gem and Mineral Hall. Open: daily 10am–5pm. Admission: free first Wednesday of the month.

Morrison Planetarium, tel: 750-7138 (Laserium Show) or 750-7141. Daily Sky Show: Monday–Friday 2pm; weekends 1, 2, 3 and 4pm. "Exploring the Skies of the Season" at noon on weekends and holidays. Shows subject to change, call ahead for shows and time.

The California Historical Society, tel: 775-1111. The Society and its library occupy the Whittier Mansion at Jackson and Laguna streets in historic Pacific Heights. The home is a rare survivor of the 1906 earthquake and fire and contains a collection of late 19th-century furnishing and paintings. After a long closure due to lack of funds, the old mansion was re-opened on a very limited basis early in 1991. It would be wise to call in advance for current hours.

California Palace of the Legion of Honor, in Lincoln Park, overlooking the ocean at Clement and 34th Avenue, tel: 750-3600 or 750-3659 (tape). The art, history and culture of France is represented with paintings and decorative arts from the medieval times to the present. Daily tours. Open: Wednesday–Sunday 10am–5pm and some holidays. Admission: free first Wednesday of the month and Saturday mornings.

Chinese Culture Center, on 3rd floor of the Holiday Inn at 750 Kearny Street, tel: 986-1822. Chinese arts and culture displays; frequent exhibit changes. Open: Tuesday–Saturday 10am–4pm. Admission: free.

San Francisco Crafts & Folkart Museum, located in Building A of Fort Mason in the Marina District, tel: 775-0990. The museum offers witty and elegant exhibits of contemporary craft, folk art and traditional ethnic art. Open: Tuesday–Friday and Sunday 11am–5pm, Saturday 10am–5pm.

The Exploratorium and Palace of Fine Arts. This beautiful structure and idyllic pond is a place to stroll, take photographs or rest. Located near the Marina on Lyon Street, the complex was built for the 1915 Panama Pacific Exposition. One wing of the Palace houses one of the best science museums in the world. Visitors are encouraged to touch everything, including over 500 ever-changing exhibits. Complex principles of light, sound, technology and human perceptions are explained. The Tactile Gallery also explores the sense of touch. By reservation only. This is a "must see." Exploratorium: Tuesday, Thursday–Sunday 10am–5pm, Wednesday 10am–9.30pm. Closed: Monday. Admission: free first Wednesday of the month and every Wednesday from 6pm.

Fort Mason, in the Landmark Building A. Unusual exhibits reflect contemporary society. Open: noon–5pm. Admission: free.

Hyde Street Pier. Restored ships, free. Admission: charge for *S/V Balclutha* square rigger.

M.H. de Young Memorial Museum, Golden Gate Park next to the Asian Art Museum, tel: 863-3600. This is the city's most diversified art museum with 21 galleries of everything from American Indian art to European masterpieces, archaeological treasures of the ancient world, art from Africa and Oceania. Housed in a building created, in part, from a Spanish church dismantled by William Randolph Hearst and shipped to San Francisco. Open: 10am–5pm. Closed: Monday and Tuesday. One admission charge admits (on same day) to de Young, Asian Art Museum and Palace of the Legion of Honor.

Mexican Museum, in Building D of the Fort Mason Center near the Marina (Buchanan and Marina streets), tel: 441-0404. The first of its kind in this country, the bilingual museum features a rotating series of exhibits, educational programs and walking tours of Mission District murals. Open: Wednesday–Sunday noon–5pm. Closed: Monday and Tuesday. First Wednesday of month free.

Museu Italo Americano, Fort Mason Center, Building C near Buchanan and Marina in the Marina District, tel: 673-2200. Dedicated to the display of Italian-American and Italian culture and history. Includes work of many prominent contemporary artists. Open: Wednesday–Sunday noon–5pm. Admission: free.

Museum of Russian Culture, 4th floor of 2450 Sutter Street, tel: 921-4082. The immigration to America is documented from various artifacts, books and 120 archival objects. Open: Wednesday and Saturday 11am–3pm. Admission: free.

National Maritime Museum, at the end of Polk Street at Beach Street, tel: 556-8177. The history of the port of San Francisco is represented with photos, art and displays. Exhibits include the historic ships docked at nearby piers. Open: 10am–5pm, summer 10am–6pm. Admission: free.

North Beach Museum, in a branch of Eureka Federal Savings at 1433 Stockton Street, 2nd floor, tel: 391-6210. Historic photographs and artifacts of the Italian-American community, mostly in the North Beach area. Open: Monday–Friday 9am–4pm. Admission: free.

Presidio Army Museum, near Lincoln Boulevard and Funston Avenue, tel: 561-4115. Focuses on the role of the military in the city's history and development from 1776 to the present. In an old hospital dating from the 1860s. Open: daily 10am–4pm. Closed: Monday. Admission: free.

San Francisco African-American Historical and Cultural Society, tel: 441-0640. A combination museum and gallery; features noteworthy exhibits and library of source material on African-Americans and Black Californians. Open: Wednesday–Sunday noon–5pm. Donation requested.

San Francisco Fire Department Pioneer Memorial Museum, tel: 861-8000. Collection includes horse-drawn fire wagons, leather buckets and photos of firemen in action. Various items were collected by Lillie Hitchcock Coit, socialite and friend of the city's early volunteer firemen. Open: Thursday–Sunday 1pm–4pm, Monday, Tuesday, Wednesday closed. Admission: free.

San Francisco History Room and Archives, on the third floor of the Public Library at Larkin and McAllister streets, in the Civic Center, tel: 557-4567. Photographs, paintings, maps and artifacts represent a miniature history museum of old and new San Francisco. Open: Tuesday and Wednesday 1pm–6pm, Thursday and Saturday 10am–12pm, 1pm–6pm, Friday 1pm–6pm. Admission: free.

San Francisco Museum of Modern Art, 151 Third Street, tel: 357-4000. A major museum of contemporary art, the permanent collections include outstanding American and European paintings, sculpture, photographs and ceramics. The best in the West. Open: 11am–6pm daily (Thursday to 9pm). Closed: Monday and holidays. Admission: free on first Tuesday of the month.

Society of California Pioneers, 456 McAllister Street, tel: 861-5278. Items from the Gold Rush plus early San Francisco silver, 19th-century paintings and a Wells Fargo stagecoach. Open: Monday–Friday 10am–4pm. Admission: free.

Submarine USS Pampanito, tel: 929-0202. This 312-foot ship was built in 1943 and took an active role in World War II. A "must-see" for those interested in submarine fleet. Open: Thursday–Sunday 9am–6pm, Friday–Saturday 9am–9pm, summer open daily 9am–9pm.

Treasure Island Museum, tel: 395-5067. The 1939 Golden Gate International Exposition, the China Clipper flying boats and the history of Sea Services in the Pacific are featured. Exhibits are located in Building 1 on Treasure Island, halfway across the Bay Bridge. Open: daily 10am–3.30pm. Admission: free.

Wells Fargo History Museum, in the Financial District, 420 Montgomery Street at California, tel: 396-2619. A Concord stagecoach, gold nuggets, posters, guns, badges and more represent the Gold Rush era. Open: Monday–Friday 9am–5pm. Closed: bank holidays. Admission: free.

Art Galleries

San Francisco incorporates an active visual arts community. Galleries are located downtown, in the Civic Center, South of Market and on Fisherman's Wharf. The art is for sale and the shows often change. Check the "Datebook" pink pages for what interests you. Additional sources of information are the San Francisco Art Institute's 24-hour event listing (tel: 749-4545); and the San Francisco Art Center for Children at Fort Mason (tel: 771-0292).

FISHERMAN'S WHARF

Art ranges from mass-produced commercial to quality prints. Galleries are located on Pier 39, at Ghirardelli Square, along all the side streets and in the Cannery.

DOWNTOWN

The established dealers are on Maiden Lane, Sutter, Grant and other Union Square area streets. The Circle Gallery at 140 Maiden Lane (tel: 989-2100), is in the landmark Frank Lloyd Wright building. Neighboring dealers include:

Braunstein-Quay, tel: 392-5532.
Conacher Galleries, tel: 392-5447.
Graystone, tel: 956-7693.
Fraenkel Gallery, tel: 981-2661.
Harcourts, tel: 421-3428.
John Berggruen Gallery, tel: 781-4629.
John Pence Gallery, tel: 441-1138.
Kertesz Fine Art Gallery, tel: 626-0376.
Maxwell Galleries, tel: 421-5193.
Paule Anglim, tel: 433-2710.
Pasquale Iannetti Art Gallery, tel: 433-2771.
Richard Thompson Gallery, tel: 956-2114.

CIVIC CENTER

Hayes Street is a good place to view and buy the work of upcoming artists.
Emeric-Goodman, tel: 771-9612.
Vorpal Gallery, tel: 397-9200.

SOUTH OF MARKET

SoMa galleries include:
George Belcher, tel: 543-1908.
Camerawork, tel: 621-1001.
Lawson, tel: 626-1159.
Modernism, tel: 541-0461.
Triangle, tel: 392-1686.

Concerts & Operas

In addition to the San Francisco Symphony, there are chamber music groups, ethnic music groups, visiting groups, and the second largest opera in the United States, the San Francisco Opera. In fact, several opera companies are supported by this opera-loving community.

Audium, 1616 Bush Street in the Civic Center area, tel: 771-1616. Presents contemporary and precedent-setting kinds of music. This is the first theater of sound exploration, experimenting with 136 speakers which move music around you in a kind of sculpture.

The Bay Area Women's Philharmonic, tel: 543-2297. Performs the works of women composers. Also other musical menus here from which to choose.

Golden Gate Park Band, Music Concourse, Golden Gate Park, tel: 666-7035. Each Sunday April to October, 1pm. Pack a picnic and enjoy a traditional brass band, free.

The Kronos Quartet, tel: 731-3533. Unconventional string quartet; includes rock, jazz, blues in its classical repertoire.

San Francisco Conservatory of Music, 1201 Ortega, tel: 564-8086 or 759-3477 (a 24-hour tape recording lists music activities). Offers professional chamber music as well as student recitals. With graduates like Isaac Stern to its credit, the San Francisco Conservatory is regarded as the best West Coast music school.

San Francisco Opera, Grove and Van Ness avenues in the Civic Center Area, tel: 864-3330. Features internationally renowned stars of the opera world. Having entered its 7th decade of annual seasons, 10 operas are presented each year in repertory. Standing room tickets can be purchased two hours before the performance.

San Francisco Symphony, Davies Symphony Hall, Van Ness and Grove avenues in the Civic Center Area, tel: 431-5400. The San Francisco Symphony plays a summer pops series, a Beethoven Festival and the Mostly Mozart Festival each year in addition to its regular season.

The "Datebook" section of the *Sunday Examiner & Chronicle* lists events including new music, early music, baroque, band, harpsichord, orchestra, piano, and chamber music under Classical/Opera/Dance. Popular music concerts and festivals are featured with advertisements throughout the pink page section.

Ballet

San Francisco Ballet, established for over 60 years, continues to delight audiences. Well-known for traditional choreography and consistently excellent productions, the San Francisco Ballet was the first in the country to perform the *Nutcracker Suite* as a Christmas event. Performances at the San Francisco Opera House, Van Ness and Grove in the Civic Center area. Tel: 703-9400 for information. Tickets may be purchased through BASS or at the box office for performances at the Opera house.

San Francisco Dance Theater, 60 Brady Street, tel: 558-9355. Pioneers of dance.

The Joffrey Ballet, **American Ballet Theater** and **Stuttgart Ballet** visit the San Francisco Opera House stage regularly. For information, tel: 703-9400.

Theaters

You can choose from New York hits, local experimental works, classic revivals and more in San Francisco but tickets can be very expensive for the big shows. An alternative to paying full price is to attend a preview showing, a matinee performance or to purchase same day tickets at half price from San Francisco Ticket Box Office/Information tape (TIX) on Union Square, tel: 433-7827.

Other ticket services include BASS, tel: (510) 762-2277. You can use a charge card to order by phone and – as with any ticket service – you pay extra for the convenience. BASS has outlets in many stores. The hotel desk can refer you to other ticket services. Look through the pink section of the newspaper and call the recorded BASS listing at tel: (510) 762-2277 to find out what's in town when you are.

The main theater district is bordered by Taylor, Sutter, Market and Post streets. The **Curran**, **Golden Gate**, **Marine's Memorial Theater**, **Orpheum** and **ACT Playroom** seat from 600 to 2,000 people. Although safe when filled with theater goers, the edge of this district borders the Tenderloin. Do not walk about alone after the show.

Repertory companies use smaller theaters which seat an audience of 50 to 500. Although the highly regarded American Conservatory Theater usually performs known works, many of the smaller groups present new material. All offerings are listed in the newspaper calendars, but you may wish to call the theaters for more information.

Actors' Theatre, 533 Sutter Street, tel: 296-9179. Often does classics by such luminaries as Tennessee Williams and other innovators. Thursday–Sunday at 8pm. An intimate, fun setting.

American Conservatory Theater (ACT), tel: 749-2228. Every kind of material.

Asian American Theatre Company, at 403 Arguello Boulevard, tel: 751-2600. Thursday, Friday and Saturday at 8pm; Sunday 3.30 and 7.30pm. Known for innovative Asian themes and casts.

Curran Theater, tel: 474-3800.

The Eureka, 2730 16th Street, tel: 243-9899. Gay/lesbian-oriented material.

Golden Gate Theater, tel: 474-3800. Life on the Water, Fort Mason, Building B, tel: 776-8999. Experimental Works.

The Magic Theater, Fort Mason, Building D, tel: 441-8822. Innovative and known for premiering plays by Michael McClure and Sam Shepard.

Potrero Hill Neighborhood House, 953 De Haro, tel: 826-8080. Professional and amateurs perform together to present contemporary issues and gritty, urban themes.

Theater Rhinoceros, 2926 16th Street, tel: 861-5079. Gay and lesbian works.

Colleges, universities, cultural centers and churches sponsor theatrical productions on a regular basis. Check "Datebook" listings under Theater for current information.

Movies

In addition to first-run theater complexes, there are many theaters which offer special programs. Independent film making is very active in the Bay Area and some theaters showcase these films. Local newspapers list film events and current movie schedules.

First-run movies are expensive but you can save money by attending bargain matinees. Neighborhood theaters are often cheaper than the fancy complexes in key shopping areas.

There is one drive-in movie, the Geneva, south of San Francisco near the Cow Palace (tel: 587-2884).

Public Libraries

The San Francisco Public Library Main Branch, is on Larkin, in the Civic Center, across from the City Hall (tel: 557-4400). Special services are offered for the blind, deaf and physically handicapped. There are story-telling programs for children. A new main library is scheduled to open in the late 1990s, but until then it's hard to get at millions of books stored in odd places since the 1989 earthquake. Only residents may check out of the library.

Activities for Children

Temporary Tot Tending, 2217 Delvin Way, tel: 355-7377. Offers child care by licensed, respected teachers by the hour or by the day. Open: 18 hours, Monday–Friday.

The Josephine D. Randall Junior Museum, 199 Museum Way, tel: 554-9600. Has a petting corral, a working seismograph, mineral and fossil displays plus nature hikes and classes most Saturdays. Open: Tuesday–Saturday 10am–5pm. Free.

The Golden Gate Recreational Park, tel: 666-7200 for information. A guaranteed kid pleaser.

Toy Town, 2801 Leavenworth, boasts the world's largest Teddy Bear. This Dakin creation, 21 ft (6.4 meters) wide and 31 ft high (9.5 meters) presides over a collection that includes vintage dolls, train sets and toys from around the world. A playroom is stocked with 100,000 Lego pieces, Lincoln Logs, soft pieces for under-fives and high-tech construction sets.

California Academy of Sciences, tel: 750-7145. Science in action is available here.

San Francisco Public Library provides a service by which youngsters can telephone 626-6516 for a bedtime story.

Children's Programs
Children's Zoo, tel: 753-7083. Animals to pet and nature walks.
Exploratorium, tel: 561-0360. Exhibits, shows.
Fort Mason Center, tel: 441-5705. Art, theater.
Golden Gate National Recreation Area, tel: 666-7200. History tours, nature hikes, events, Golden Gate Park, carousel, children's playground, Lake model boat club, Stow Lake boats.
Hyde Street Pier, tel: 556-6435. Ships, exhibits, and books.
Morrison Planetarium, tel: 750-7141. Exhibits, and shows.
Natural History Museum, tel: 750-7145. Discovery room and exhibits.
Public Library, tel: 557-4554. Films, story-telling.

Fisherman's Wharf, Pier 39. Amusements, arcade, carousel, entertainers, fairs.
Randall Junior Museum, tel: 554-9600. Animals, computers, petting corral, playground, etc.
Recreation & Parks Department, tel: 556-0560. Boys and Girls Sports, Tiny Tot Program.
San Francisco Ballet, tel: 703-9400.
San Francisco Opera, tel: 864-3330.
San Francisco Symphony, tel: 431-5400.
San Francisco Visitors' Bureau, tel: 391-2000.
Steinhart Aquarium, tel: 750-7145. Fish roundabout, feedings, touching pool.

Tour Packages

In San Francisco, there are countless tour operators and packages to bring you to your desired destination and to meet your particular interest.

TOURS BY AIR

These tours are expensive but memorable. Your tour can be customized and cover the coast from Monterey to Mendicino, from the Golden Gate to the Sierras. Most require a minimum of two persons to take off. Telephone for current rates.

Commodore Seaplane, tel: 332-4843. Champagne sunset flights by appointment.

CRUISES

Alcatraz, tel: 546-2896 or 800-445-8880. Advance reservations up to two weeks advised for busy periods. Tours include self-guided trail, slide show, audio cassettes. Once on the island, Park Rangers provide guided tours if you wish. Alcatraz is one of the most popular and noteworthy attractions in the Bay Area. Tickets may be purchased in advance through Ticketron outlets. Boats leave half-hourly from Pier 41 near Fisherman's Wharf. Take warm clothes and comfortable walking shoes.

Angel Island, tel: 546-2805. Tel: 546-2896 for information about ferries. For camping information, call 800-444-7275. Pack a picnic and board at Pier 43 or in Tiburon. Angel Island is a State Park once used as a military installation and as a processing station for immigrants. It has balmy weather

even when fog fills the bay, along with hiking, bicycling and panoramic views. Ferries run back and forth from Piers 41 and 43, going directly to the island or connecting with the Tiburon-Angel Island Ferry.

BAY CRUISES

Blue & Gold Fleet, Pier 39, tel: 800-426-8687.
Red & White Fleet, Pier 41, tel: 546-2896.

Dine & Dance
Hornblower Yachts, Pier 33, tel: 394-8900. Dinner and lunch cruises aboard The City of San Francisco, replica of a 1900 steamship.
Blue & Gold Fleet, Pier 39, tel: 800-426-8687. Dinner with live music.
Red & White Fleet, Pier 41, tel: 546-2896. Sunset champagne cruises.

Whale Watching
Blue & Gold Fleet, Pier 39, tel: 800-426-8687. December–April to Point Reyes.

National Seashore
Oceanic Society Expedition, Marina, tel: 441-1104. Seasonal, Farallon Islands bird sanctuary. Grey whale migration during the winter-spring.

BUS TOURS

Several companies offer narrated tours in buses, vans or limousines. The typical tour choice is a half-day city tour combined with a visit across the Golden Gate Bridge to Muir Woods, then to Sausalito, often in combination with a Bay cruise.

The Gray Line combination tour leaves at 9am; the half-day city tours leave at 9am, 10am, 11am, 1.30pm and 2.30pm. Reservations are required.

Most of the tour companies listed here also offer tours to the Wine Country, to Yosemite National Park, to the Monterey Peninsula and other scenic attractions. Unless otherwise noted, these companies will pick you up at your hotel.

AgenTours, tel: 661-5200. Multi-lingual narration.
AMI Tours, tel: 474-8868. Social history, earthquake lore, Indian culture.
Cable Car Charters, Inc., Pier 39, tel: 922-2425. Motorized cable cars depart regularly from Union Square, Pier 39.

Golden Gate Tours, tel: 788-5775.
Great Pacific Tour Co, tel: 626-4499.
MaxiTours, tel: 441-6294.
The Gray Line, Inc, tel: 558-9400. Multi-lingual narration; over 20 tours including night clubs around the city and Alcatraz island.

CAR TOURS

Seagull signs in blue and white mark the 49 Mile Scenic Drive. A free map from the San Francisco Visitor Center at Powell and Market streets details the route. Opened in 1938 to show off the city sights to visitors for the 1939–40 Golden Gate International Exposition, the drive has been expanded in later years.

In a leisurely half-day tour you can complete the drive through the most noteworthy scenic and historic locations in San Francisco. This includes Lombard Street, the crookedest street in the world, spectacular vistas, and important buildings. Once you've completed the 49 Mile Scenic Drive, you'll know San Francisco.

CARRIAGE RIDES

Horse-drawn buggies offer a romantic way to tour Fisherman's Wharf. Carriage Charter at tel: 398-0857 or just hail a buggy in the area.

SPECIALITY TOURS

A Day in Nature, tel: 673-0548. Personalized tours in the Marin Headlands with an experienced naturalist as a guide.
AMI Tours, tel: 474-8868. Small group tours to Muir Woods or the beautiful Wine Country.
California Detours, tel: 282-2801. Historical perspectives, multi-lingual guides.
Chinatown Discovery Tours, Chinese Cultural Center, tel: 982-8839. Historic and culinary tours. Reservations required.
Frisco Productions, 1431 11th Avenue, tel: 681-5555. "Love 'n' Haight: A Walking Tour of Haight-Ashbury" – noon on alternate Sundays.
Jeanette's Tours, tel: 397-2343. Culture and history. Reservations required.
San Francisco Bay Tours Inc., tel: 550-8954. For Japanese speaking visitors.
San Francisco Jewish Landmark Tours, tel: 921-0461 for a visit to Jewish sites.

Wok Wiz, tel: 981-5588. Wok-cooking lovers can join Shirley Fong-Torres, cooking instructor and food writer, on a tour of Chinatown with culinary hints. Includes a cookbook. Reservations required.

GOLDEN BAY PARK

Friends of Recreation and Parks, tel: 750-5105. Free tours with trained guides to point out the flora, fauna and history. May–October.

VICTORIAN BUILDINGS

The California Historical Society, tel: 567-1848.
Haas-Lilienthal House, tel: 441-3004. Pacific Heights tours originate here on weekends.

PERFORMING ART CENTERS

Performing Art Center Tours are available for the Civic Center area. Tel: 552-8338. The complex includes the Louise M. Davies Symphony Hall, San Francisco Opera House, the Museum of Modern Art in the Veterans' War Memorial Building, and the San Francisco Ballet building.

You can tour the Fort Mansion center on your own. Tel: 441-5705. The converted army buildings house many innovative arts and environmental groups. The waterfront center at Laguna and Marina Boulevard is open for visitors most days and many evenings. There are theaters, museums, publication offices, community billboards and a gourmet vegetarian restaurant called Greens.

Walks

It is a good idea to check the daily paper or the "pink section" of the *Sunday Examiner & Chronicle* to see if walks have been added to this list. Some historical walks are free but seasonal. All guided walks are fascinating, relaxed adventures.

Diary of Regular Events

The San Francisco daily newspapers, the weekly *Bay Guardian* and *SF Weekly*, the monthly *City Sports*, and *San Francisco Focus* magazine all list current events. Upcoming events are widely advertised. Call ahead to confirm all listings or call the Visitors' and Convention Bureau. Tel: 974-6900 for

additional information. Here are the listings for 24-hour current-event tape recordings:
BASS, tel: (510) 762-2277
TIX, tel: 433-7827
San Francisco Visitors' Bureau:
Auf Deutsch, tel: 391-2004
En Español, tel: 391-2122
En Français, tel: 391-2003
In English, tel: 391-2001
In Japanese, tel: 391-2101

JANUARY

Golden Gate Kennel Club All-Breed Dog Show. Tel: 469-6065.
MacWorld Exposition. Tel: 974-4000. The latest in home computing.
San Francisco Contemporary Music Players (through May). Tel: 252-6235.
San Francisco Sports and Boat Show. Tel: 469-6065.
San Francisco Symphony (through May). Tel: 552-8011.

FEBRUARY

Bay Area Women's Philharmonic (through May). Tel: 543-2297.
Chinese New Year Celebration, with weekend parade. Tel: 982-3000.
International Motorcycle Show, Cow Palace. Tel: 469-6065.
San Francisco Ballet Repertory Season (through May). Tel: 703-9400.
San Francisco Tribal Art Show. Tel: (310) 455-2886.
Orchid Society Annual Show. Tel: 252-7564.
Volvo Tennis Tournament. Tel: 239-4800.

MARCH

Annual Battle of the Harmonicas. Tel: 826-6837.
Bay Area Music Awards (Bammies). Tel: 388-4000.
Contemporary Crafts Market. Tel: 863-3906.
Fifteenth Annual Tulipmania, Pier 39. Tel: 705-5512.
Junior Grand National Rodeo, Horse and Stock Show. Tel: 469-6065.
National Championship Cat Show. Tel: 469-6000.
St Patrick's Day Parade (Downtown). Tel: 661-2700.

APRIL

Annual Golden Gate International Rugby Tournament. Tel: 556-0560.
Cherry Blossom Festival. Tel: 563-2313. Parades and entertainment.

Festival of Animation (through May). Tel: 563-6504.

San Francisco International Film Festival (through May). Tel: 931-film.

San Francisco Giants Baseball (through October). Tel: 467-8000.

San Francisco Indian Arts and Crafts Show. Tel: 441-5706.

San Francisco Landscape Garden Show. Tel: 750-5108, 750-5105.

Todays Artists Concerts, Herbst Theatre. Tel: 527-3622.

MAY

Antique Show and Sale. Tel: 974-4000.

Carnival Celebration and Parade, in the Mission District. Tel: 826-1401.

Cinco de Mayo Parade and Celebration. Tel: 826-1401.

KQED Annual Wine and Food Festival. Tel: 553-2200.

Mozart and His Time, city-wide celebration. Tel: 431-5400.

San Francisco Bay to Breakers Marathon. Tel: 777-7000. With thousands of runners in and out of costume.

San Francisco Historic Trolley Festival (rides through August on Market Street). Tel: 673-6764.

San Francisco Performances, Herbst Theatre. Tel: 398-6449.

Visitacion Valley Street Fair and Parade. Tel: 467-6400.

JUNE

Antique Show and Sale. Tel: 974-4000.

Ethnic Dance Festival. Tel: 474-3914.

Friends of the Library Book Sale. Tel: 557-4257.

Great San Francisco Bike Adventure, 15-mile tour. Tel: 863-9382.

Haight Street Fair. Tel: 661-8025.

International Street Performers Festival, Pier 39. Tel: 981-8030.

Lesbian and Gay Freedom Day Parade. Tel: 864-3733.

North Beach Fair. Tel: 383-9378.

Midsummer Beethoven Festival. Tel: 781-5932.

Stern Grove Midsummer Music Festival (through August). Tel: 252-6252.

Union Street Fair. Tel: 346-4446.

World Cup Soccer Tournament (through July). Tel: (310) 252-1994.

JULY

Cable Car Bell Ringing Championship. Tel: 923-6206.

Comedy Celebration Day. Tel: 777-7120.

Eleventh Annual KQED Beer Festival. Tel: 553-2200.

Fourth of July Celebration and Fireworks. Tel: 556-0575.

Joffrey Ballet. Tel: 864-6000.

San Francisco Marathon. Tel: 391-2123. One of the largest in the country.

San Francisco Symphony Pops. Tel: 431-5400.

AUGUST

Annual Alcatraz Triathalon Challenge. Tel: 974-6900.

Festival of Performing Arts (through September). Tel: 474-3914. Magic, dance, bands, choral groups.

Japantown Summer Festival. Tel: 922-8700. Performances, flowers and food.

Pacific States Crafts Fair. Tel: 896-5060.

San Francisco Fair and International Exposition. Tel: 703-2729.

San Francisco 49ers Football Season (through December). Tel: (408) 562-4949.

San Francisco Shakespeare Festival (through October). Tel: 666-2221.

SEPTEMBER

Festival de las Americas. Tel: 826-1401. Food and arts.

Renaissance Pleasure Faire, Black Point Forest (through October). Tel: 892-0937.

San Francisco Blues Festival. Tel: 826-6837.

San Francisco Hill Stride, 7-mile fitness walk. Tel: 626-1600.

San Francisco Symphony Season. Tel: 431-5400.

Transamerica Men's Open Tennis Championship. Tel: 469-6065.

Opera in the Park. Tel: 864-3330.

OCTOBER

American Conservatory Theatre (through June). Tel: 749-2228.

Bridge-to-Bridge Run, 8-mile race. Tel: 995-6800.

Castro Street Fair. Tel: 467-3354.

Columbus Day Celebration and Parade. Tel: 434-1492. North Beach's biggest event *bocce* ball tournaments, blessing of the fishing fleet, Columbus' landing.

Exotic Erotic Halloween Ball. Tel: 864-1500.

Festa Italiana food and culture, Pier 35. Tel: 673-3782.

German Fest. Tel: 397-1085.

Great Halloween and Pumpkin Festival, Clement Street. Tel: 346-4446.

Grand National Rodeo. Tel: 469-6065.

Halloween Costume Promenade, Castro at Market Street. October 31.

Octoberfest Bavarian Festival. Tel: 397-1085.

San Francisco Fall Antiques Show. Tel: 921-1411.

San Francisco Jazz Festival. Tel: 864-5449.

NOVEMBER

"Fol de Rol" of the Opera Guild. Tel: 565-6432.

Folk Art International Exhibition and Sale. Tel: 441-6100.

Harvest Festival and Christmas Crafts Market (through November). Tel: (707) 778-6300.

International Auto Show. Tel: 673-2016.

San Francisco Bay Area Book Festival. Tel: 861-BOOK.

DECEMBER

"A Christmas Carol," American Conservatory Theater. Tel: 749-2228.

Hanukkah Celebration, in Union Square. Tel: 391-2000.

New Year's Eve Celebration, at large hotels. Tel: 391-2000.

"The Nutcracker," San Francisco Ballet. Tel: 621-3838.

Pickle Family Circus. Tel: (510) 762-bass.

Santa Claus Parade. Tel: 826-1401.

Nightlife

Cocktails, dancing, entertainment, musical revues and more await the visitor's pleasure. San Francisco is noted for its talented comedians who go on to national fame and fortune after getting experience in local comedy clubs.

The city is also noted as the birthplace of the first pizza restaurant and, later, the first topless club in America. Choose your evening's pleasure from these listings and from the listings in the various entertainment sections of local publications. All clubs have cover charges, which tend to vary with the quality of entertainment.

Dining With a View

Sanae, Parc 55, tel: 392-8000. Fine for photos, nice meditation. Open: from 6pm.

Carnelian Room, Bank of America Building, 555 California Street, tel: 433-7500. Open: from 3pm.

Club 36, Hyatt on Union Square, tel: 398-1234.

Crown Room, Fairmont Hotel, 950 Mason Street, tel: 772-5131. Open: from 11am.

Equinox, Hyatt Regency Hotel, 5 Embarcadero Center, tel: 788-1234. 360° revolving view.

Henri's, San Francisco Hilton & Tower, 333 O'Farrell, tel: 776-0215. Open: from 11am.

S. Holmes, Esq., Holiday Inn Union Square, tel: 398-8900. Open: from 4pm.

Oz, Westin St Francis Hotel, tel: 397-7000. Open: from 9pm. Strict dress code.

Starlite Roof, Sir Francis Drake Hotel, Sutter at Powell, tel: 392-7755. Open: from 4.30pm.

Top of the Mark, the Mark Hopkins Inter-Continental Hotel California at Mason, tel: 392-3434. Open: from 11am.

Drinks & Nibbles

Bix, 56 Gold Street, tel: 433-6300. Favorite after-work place for well-dressed executives.

Dubliner Pub, 3838 24th Street, tel: 826-2279. Friendly neighborhood pub in Noe Valley, run by Dubliner Patrick Kent. London Pride and Bass ales and Blackthorne hard cider on tap.

Hillcrest Bar & Café, 2201 Fillmore, tel: 563-8400. Flutes of California sparkling wines such as Scharffenberger, Chandon or Shadow Creek.

Lascaux, 248 Sutter, tel: 391-1555. Bas-relief replicas of the prehistoric drawings from its namesake cave in southern France.

San Francisco Brewing Company, 155 Columbus, tel: 434-3344. Four types of beer and ale.

Tutto Bene, 2080 Van Ness, tel: 673-3500. This is where the fun, lively crowd prowls. Serves stylish drinks such as Tutto Bene's martini of Bombay Sapphire gin and Cinzano Bianco.

Comedy Clubs

Cobb's Comedy Club, 2801 Leavenworth Street, tel: 928-4320.

Curtain Call, 1980 Union, tel: 474-5918.

Holy City Zoo, 408 Clement Street, tel: 386-4242.

The Improv, 401 Mason, tel: 441-7787.

Morty's, 1024 Kearny Street, tel: 986-6678.

Cabaret Shows

Club Fugazi, 678 Green Street, tel: 421-4222.

Beach Blanket Babylon, at Club Fugazi. San Francisco's most popular show. Reservations are a must. No alcohol is served at Sunday matinees so kids can see the musical comedy revue.

Finocchio's, 506 Broadway, tel: 982-9388. Famous for almost 50 years of female impersonators.

Great American Music Hall, 859 O'Farrell Street, tel: 885-0750.

The Plush Room, York Hotel, 940 Sutter Street, tel: 885-2800.

Dancing

Atrium, Lobby, Hyatt Regency, 5 Embarcadero Center, tel: 788-1234. Tea dancing to music from the 1940s and 50s once a month, usually on Friday. Call ahead.

Avenue Ballroom, 603 Taraval, tel: 681-2882. West Coast swing and Latin.

Big Heart City, 836 Mission Street, tel: 957-1825. Hip-hop and funk among other things.

Bopper's House of Rock, 650 Howard Street, tel: 869-1950. Upscale, high energy place.

Caesar's Latin Palace, 3140 Mission Street, tel: 648-6611. Traditional Latin and salsa music and shows.

Camelot, 3231 Fillmore, tel: 567-4004. Top 40. No cover charge.

Club DV8, South of Market, 55 Natoma, tel: 957-1730. Modern music, live acts.

Firehouse 7, 3160 16th Street, tel: 621-1617. Urban pop house, techno music.

New Orleans Room, Fairmont Hotel, 950 Mason, tel: 772-5259. Hot jazz and swing-era music.

Oasis, South of Market, 11th and Folsom streets, tel: 621-8119. Mecca of dance featuring top 100 hits. Free blues nights, lunch by the pool.

Palladium, 1031 Kearny, tel: 434-1308. Top 40 and special effects.

The Stone, 412 Broadway, tel: (510) 574-1954. A mixed bag of music.

Stud, 399 Ninth Street in SoMa, tel: 863-6623.

Jazz & Country

Kimball's, 300 Grove Street, tel: 861-5555. Celebrity talent.

Pasand Lounge, 1875 Union Street, tel: 922-4498.

Pearl's, 256 Columbus near the center of North Beach, tel: 291-8255. Small groups play all night.

Pier 23 Café, along the Embarcadero, overlooking the Bay, tel: 362-5125.

Last Days Saloon, 406 Clement Street, tel: 387-6343. Top-name country bands.

Shopping

There are 20 distinct shopping areas in San Francisco. Malls, theme shopping centers and neighborhood shopping streets offer everything from designer fashions to local crafts.

Union Square: Perhaps the most famous shopping area in San Francisco, the square includes the charming Maiden Lane with boutiques, galleries and a Frank Lloyd Wright designed building. Union Square department stores, boutiques, and historic buildings are concentrated in a 12-block area between Ellis, Powell, Post and Stockton streets, spilling over between Market and Sutter streets, from Kearny to Mason. Here you'll find Saks, Nordstrom, Neiman Marcus, Macy's, I. Magnin, Gumps and more.

It's worth the walk to view the imaginative window displays, flower stands and, of course, other shoppers. Parking garages are under Union Square and on surrounding side streets.

Crocker Galleria: Over 60 specialty shops, restaurants and services near Union Square. This three-level pavilion is modeled after Milan's Galleria Vittorio Emmanuelle and features a soaring glass dome. Parking is near the Sutter Street entrance.

Embarcadero Center: The Center

offers 175 shops and restaurants in four complexes between Sacramento and Clay streets, in the Financial District. Strolling and people-watching are enhanced by pedestrian bridges, outdoor rest areas, landscaping and entertainment. Discount parking is available (free on Sunday) in underground garages.

Chinatown: Situated between Stockton, Kearny, Bush and Broadway, Chinatown is the center of the largest Chinese-American community on the West Coast. Buses bring daily shoppers in from all neighborhoods to purchase fresh produce, fish and poultry. Traditional pharmaceutical shops, antique stores, jewelry stores and souvenir shops vie for attention. The streets are crowded and flow into North Beach.

"Little Italy": This area offers a mix of book shops, Italian restaurants and delicatessens, vintage clothing and designer boutiques. Bordered by Chinatown, the Financial District and the waterfront, it offers many surprises for the shopper strolling along Columbus and its side streets. Walk or take a bus as traffic is congested and parking difficult.

Fisherman's Wharf: Shopping extends from Pier 39 to Ghirardelli Square. The Cargo Pier at Jefferson Street now offers two levels of shops, restaurants and amusements with a view of a working marina and the Bay. A walking bridge spans the street to a large covered parking garage.

Street performers and vendors line the way to the original Fisherman's Wharf area, The Cannery, The Anchorage and Ghirardelli Square – along Jefferson and Leavenworth streets, up to North Point and to Larkin and Polk streets. **The Cannery** is a remodeled Del Monte peach canning plant. **The Anchorage** is a colorful, modern complex, and **Ghirardelli Square** is a converted chocolate factory. Along with unusual shops and galleries, each complex offers individual landscaping, live entertainment, open-air walkways and breathtaking views of Alcatraz, the Golden Gate Bridge, the Bay, Sausalito and harbor activity.

The two Fisherman's Wharf cable cars end their runs in this area, and several buses are routed along adjacent streets. Look for validated parking in marked structures if you drive. This is one area where even the most dedicated shoppers can bring the whole family.

South of Market (SoMa): This is an industrial area in the process of transformation. Warehouses have been converted into factory outlets for discount designer clothes, furniture and galleries featuring local artists. Shoppers can find great bargains on Mission, Howard, Folsom, and Harrison streets between Ninth and 12th and on Third between Folsom and Townsend streets. The neighborhood shopping areas are just that – a few blocks of business streets surrounded by private residences. This is where you'll get a real feeling for living in the city. The Mission district features as well as stores, the Mission Dolores and a large Latino community. Browse in inexpensive thrift shops, specialty stores, and enjoy Mexican dishes at food stands and restaurants. Adjacent to the Mission is 24th Street, in Noe Valley. This is a good place to enjoy outdoor cafés. The friendly street between Castro and Church streets features clothing boutiques, book and record stores and antique shops.

Castro Area: From 20th to Market, and from Market to Church, is the shopping center for the gay community. This unique area offers specialty shops, cafés and good restaurants. Haight Street, center of the Haight-Ashbury district, is a bargain hunter's delight. Books, vintage and trendy new clothing, records, baked goods and espresso are all available.

The Clement Street area: Sometimes called the "second Chinatown" it stretches from 14th Avenue to Arguello Boulevard. Bibliophiles will find many treasures here and others will find a melting pot of Russian, Japanese, Chinese, Italian, Middle Eastern and European restaurants and shops.

Japan Center: Located in a complex occupying three blocks along Geary Boulevard and Webster Street, Nihonmachi (Japantown) features everything from textiles to sushi and is the site of the annual Cherry Blossom Festival.

Upper Fillmore Street: Shops extend along one end of the Nihonmachi, although it is officially designated as running from Bush to Pacific. Here you will find resale shops with designer clothing donated to benefit the San Francisco Symphony and the Junior League. Contemporary boutiques display the latest fashions for men, women and children. In keeping with the Fillmore's transitions, long-respected restaurants featuring authentic southern cooking have been joined by those with French, Italian and California cuisines.

Sacramento Street: Between Broderick and Arguello, there is a concentration of unusual children's and infant's clothing and toy stores. This area also features designer clothes for mom and dad and fine linens and antiques for the house.

Polk Street shopping and eating area: Up and over the other side of Sacramento, across Van Ness, from the Civic Center to the Maritime Museum near Ghirardelli Square, this is an eclectic mixture of decorator and antique stores, high-tech fashions, chain stores, resale shops, record and book stores. Strollers can view the latest jewelry and fashion trends and sample the inexpensive menus of various ethnic restaurants. Several popular gay bars are also located in this area.

Union Street: A sophisticated example of neighborhood restoration, the area extends from Steiner Street to Van Ness Avenue and was once the dairy and stable area for San Francisco. Union Street boutiques are housed in the restored Victorian homes of "Cow Hollow." Upscale shops with imported wares are located among restaurants and bakeries. Parking is a little easier in the neighborhoods than downtown. Bus transportation will put you in the center of any shopping destination.

Maps of the discount outlets are available in book- and drug-stores. **Shopping tour services** are also available. Access to Fashion (tel: 752-5396); and Shopper Stopper Discount Shopping Tours (tel: (707) 829-1597). Reservations are required for both of these tours.

Duty Free shopping is available to those who are leaving San Francisco for a destination in another country. You must show your flight number and date of departure, then you may purchase retail goods duty free at the San Francisco airport.

Bookstores

It's obvious as you walk about that San Francisco loves books as much or more than opera. Every shopping district has distinctive bookstores, the most famous possibly being **City Lights** in North Beach. It opened in 1953 and became the center for the Beat Generation.

Owned by poet Lawrence Ferlinghetti, the store has an extensive collection of poetry and small press publications. It is open daily from 10am to midnight.

Some specialty bookstores are listed below. "Datebook" lists readings and other special events for readers and writers. The *Yellow Pages* provide a complete list of bookstores and special services.

The Northern California Chapter of Antiquarian Booksellers Association of America operates a rare book and manuscript store. Enter at 278 Post Street, Suite 303, tel: 398-0414.

Automobilia, Auto Center, 2300 16th Street, tel: 626-2300. English and foreign-language auto history.
Banana Republic Travel, 224 Grant Avenue, tel: 788-3087.
China Books, 2929 24th Street, tel: 282-2994.
City Lights, 261 Columbus Avenue, tel: 362-8193. Poetry, small press, literary landmark.
Cookbook Center, 2801 Leavenworth Street, tel: 771-3671.
Drama, 511 Geary Boulevard, tel: 255-0604.
Educational Exchange (children's), 600 35th Avenue, tel: 752-3302.
European, French, German, Spanish, Italian and English books, 925 Larkin Street, tel: 474-0626.
Exploratorium, Marina Boulevard and Lyon Street, tel: 561-0390. Science, Palace of Fine Arts.
Fantasy, Etc., 808 Larkin Street, tel: 441-7617. Science fiction.
Fine Arts Museums, Golden Gate Park, tel: 750-3642; Lincoln Park, tel: 750-3679.
Kinokuniya, Japan Center, tel: 567-7625.
Korean, 5633 Geary Boulevard, tel: 221-4250.
Limelight Film & Theater, 1803 Market, tel: 864-2265.
Maritime Store, Hyde Street Pier, tel:

775-2665. Boat building, history, navigation, wildlife.
Metaphysical, 1540 Union Street, tel: 775-7166.
Modern Times, 968 Valencia Street, tel: 282-9246. Politics, culture, travel.
Nature Company, Embarcadero Center, tel: 956-4911. Natural history and field guides.
Old Wives' Tales Women's Visions, 1009 Valencia Street, tel: 821-4675.
San Francisco Museum of Modern Art, 401 Van Ness Avenue, tel: 863-8800.
San Francisco Mystery, 746 Diamond Street, tel: 282-7444. Detective.
Sierra Club, 730 Polk Street, tel: 923-5600. Maps, trail guides, natural history, San Francisco.
Stacey's, 581 Market Street, tel: 421-4687. Computer, medical, technical.
William Stout Architectural, 804 Montgomery Street, tel: 391-6757. New and out of print.
Thomas Brothers Maps, 550 Jackson Street, tel: 981-7520.
Travel Center, 2801 Leavenworth, tel: 541-0300.
Travelmarket, 130 Pacific Avenue, tel: 421-4080.
Western Christian, 1760 Market, tel: 861-4639. Religious.
Znanie, 5237 Geary Boulevard, tel: 752-7555. Russian literature.

Sports & Leisure

Participant Sports

The vistas and the weather draw people outside rather than in. Climbing hills does keep everyone fit and generally there are as many active sports participants as there are spectators. The City Parks and Recreation Department oversees 52 public areas with a variety of facilities in addition to the Golden Gate Park complex. For information about archery, basketball, baseball, bicycling, boating, fishing, football, golf, horseback riding, photography, target shooting, swimming and tennis, tel: 666-7024.

The **Golden Gate National Recreation Area** encompasses 35,000 acres (14,000 hectare) and 69 sq miles (178 sq km) of waterfront. The facilities for bicycling, birding, *bocce* ball, exercise, fishing, hang gliding, hiking, running, jogging, swimming,

and walking in San Francisco include Fort Mason, Aquatic Park, the Golden Gate promenade and Marina Green, Baker Beach, China Beach, Land's End, Ocean Beach and Fort Funston. For information, tel: 556-0560.

The Golden Gate National Recreation Area office is located in Building 201 at Fort Mason. Special program information is available, tel: 556-0563.

In addition to the vast selection of free public facilities, there are private clubs which issue guest memberships, equipment rental and lesson services and sports touring companies. An excellent up-to-date reference for all of this is absolutely free on just about every corner. Look for the oversized *City Sports* monthly magazine stacked in sidewalk news boxes – tel: 626-1600 if you can't find one.

Bicycling: It is possible to tour San Francisco and never struggle up a hill. There are bike paths in Golden Gate Park, scenic bike routes marked from the Golden Gate Park to Lake Merced and north over the Golden Gate Bridge. Both the park and the bridge designate routes for bicycles only on weekends (tel: 666-7200). Rental shops line Stanyan street, at the entrance to the park, and can be found throughout the Marina area. The shops have route maps as well.

Boating: San Francisco Bay is challenging even for the most experienced sailor. If you're experienced, you can try the windsurfing off Crissy Field, between the Marina Green and the Golden Gate Bridge. Ocean kayaking is popular with men and women of all ages. Some of the best sailing in the world can be enjoyed without ever going beyond the Golden Gate. Lessons, equipment, sail and power boat rentals are listed in the *Yellow Pages*. You also can choose to float in smaller vessels and calmer waters like Stow Lake in Golden Gate Park, tel: 752-0347.

Bowling: *Bocce* ball, lawn bowling and indoor bowling are all popular local sports. For information about the first two, tel: 666-7200.

Rock 'N' Bowl at 1855 Haight Street, tel: 826-2695. Friday/Saturday, 9pm–2am. For your entrance fee you get bowling, shoes, pool games and you can listen/watch rock videos on 25 screens.

Fishing: Deep sea fishing boats leave Fisherman's Wharf on regular schedules. Catches include salmon, seabass, halibut, rock fish, bonito, shark and albacore. You can rent equipment and you need a fishing license. Your catch can be smoked, packed and shipped to most places for you. Plan for wind and some rough seas. Bring along motion sickness preventatives and warm clothing. Check the *Yellow Pages* for sport fishing trips.

Fresh water fishing is available at the Lake Merced Boating and Fishing Company, just south of the city at 1 Harding Road where Skyline Boulevard and the Great Highway that runs along the ocean come together. Large trout are stocked in the 360-acre (146-hectares) lake which is open year-round. Boats, licenses, bait and tackle are available. For information, tel: 753-1101.

Before you go to Lake Merced, you might want to practice at the Fly Casting Pools near the Anglers' Lodge in Golden Gate Park, off Kennedy Drive, near the Buffalo paddock, tel: 666-7200.

Golfing: Golf is a year-round sport and San Francisco boasts four beautiful municipal courses, one with the Golden Gate Bridge as a backdrop. Although it's often possible to pick up a partner, call ahead for reservations. These courses are very popular. Rental equipment is generally available.
The Golden Gate Park Course, 47th Avenue at Fulton, is 9 holes, 1,357 yards (1,234 meters), par 27. Tel: 751-8987 for reservations.
Harding Park, south of the city at Skyline and Harding Park boulevards, includes two courses. Fleming (tel: 661-1865) is 9 holes, 2,316 yards (2,105 meters), par 32 and Harding (tel: 664-4690) is 18 holes, 6,637 yards (6,040 meters), par 72.
Lincoln Park Course, 34th Avenue and Clement Street (tel: 221-9911) is 18 holes, 5,081 yards (4,620 meters), par 68. Situated on a cliff, views of the Bay and the Bridge are spectacular.

Hang Gliding: There's more hang gliding in California than any other state because the good coastal winds are consistent. One of the best spots to watch or participate is the 200-ft (60-meter) cliff at Fort Funston, just south of San Francisco, at the end of the Great Highway near Lake Merced. Computerized up-to-the-minute wind condition information is available, tel: 333-0100. See the *Yellow Pages* of the phone directory for lessons and equipment rentals.

Horse Riding: Rentals are no longer available, but you can take lessons at the Riding Academy in Golden Gate Park, John F. Kennedy Drive and 36th Avenue. For information, tel: 668-7360.

Jogging: Although there are jogging paths designated in Golden Gate Park and along the Marina Green, the entire city seems to be one big joggers' paradise. You can stick to the waterfront and avoid the hills, but one of the biggest events of the year is the Bay to Breakers run in which the most serious and the most silly participate. Check the free *City Sports* magazine, as well as the daily papers, for all kinds of jogging, striding and walking events.

Kite Flying: In the meadows of Golden Gate Park, on the beaches, and especially in the Marina Green area, this is serious stuff. It's also colorful and fun. Specialty shops sell kites, including one on Pier 39 which features demonstrations out front on the Fisherman's Wharf promenade.

Tennis: Tennis is a very popular year-round sport. San Francisco has 142 public courts in 42 locations, including some lighted courts for night play. The courts are free except for the 21 located in the Golden Gate Park Tennis complex. Here, reservations are required on weekdays, but it's first-come, first-serve during busy weekends. Generally, people are polite about observing the time limit rules posted at each court. It is not impolite to inquire about the status of the time or game limits when you approach a court in use. There is an excellent women's tennis program. For general information, tel: 666-7024. For Golden

Gate Park information, tel: 753-7101. For reservations, tel: 753-7001.
There are also private tennis clubs in the downtown and South of Market areas. See the *Yellow Pages* for info.

Spectator Sports

Check the local *Diary of Events* section of this guide's *Travel Tips* as well as the local newspapers to find out what is on. Your choice of professional sports includes baseball, basketball, football and horse racing. All of the activities listed under *Participant Sports* can be observed while you picnic in the various parks and promenade areas of the city.

Baseball: The San Francisco Giants play in newly renovated Candlestick Park, infamous for its winds. Tel: 467-8000 for current admission prices and starting times. Express buses make the trip to the park easier, tel: 673-6864.

Basketball: The Golden State Warriors are really an Oakland team, but some of their biggest fans are in San Francisco. They play at the Oakland Coliseum Arena, tel: (510) 638-6000.

Football: The San Francisco 49ers take over Candlestick Park when the Giants aren't using it. Games are usually sold out. For current information, tel: 468-2249.

Horse Racing: Though not within the city limits, two reasonably close tracks provide excitement for thoroughbred and quarter horse race fans. There is general admission and club house seating. Bets can be placed for as little as around $2.
Golden Gate Fields is in the East Bay, near the water, just off Highway 580. Tel: (510) 526-3020 for information. Bay Meadows is on the Peninsula, south of San Francisco just off Highway 101 at the Hillsdale exit. This is the oldest, busiest and one of the most beautiful ovals in California. There is seating for general admission, plus a club house and Turf Club (dress code enforced). Valet parking is available. Tel: 574-7223 for information.

Tennis: The **Transamerica Men's Open Tennis Championship** is held at the **Cow Palace** each year. Tel: 469-6065 for information.

The **Virginia Slims Women's Tennis Tournament** is held either in San Francisco or Oakland each year. Tel: 296-711 for information.

Further Reading

General

All Around the Bay, a Shoreline Guide to San Francisco Bay, by Ruth A. Jackson. San Francisco: Chronicle Books, 1987.
California, by John W Caughey. Prentice Hall 1982.
Combing the Coast: San Francisco to Santa Cruz, by Ruth A. Jackson. San Francisco: Chronicle Books, 1981.
Everyman's Eden, by Ralph J. Roske. MacMillan, 1968.
The Literary World of San Francisco and Its Environs, by Don Herron. San Francisco: City Lights Books, 1990.
Mirror of the Dream, by T.H. Watkins and R.R. Olmsted. Scrimshaw Press, 1976.
Outdoor Adventures, by Tom Sienstra. Foghorn Press, 1989.
Pier Fishing in San Francisco Bay, by Mike Hayden. San Francisco: Chronicle Books, 1982.
San Francisco Almanac, by Gladys Hansen. Presidio Press, 1980.
San Francisco at Your Feet: The Great Walks in a Walker's Town, by Margot Patterson Doss. New York: Grove Press, 1980.
San Francisco by Cable Car, by George Young. Berkeley: Bookpeople, 1984.
San Francisco: Mission to Metropolis, by Oscar Lewis. San Diego: Howell-North Books, 1980.
Stairway Walks In San Francisco, by Adah Balalinsky. San Francisco: Lexicos, 1984.
Suddenly San Francisco, by Charles Lockwood. California Living Book, 1978.

History

Ambrose Bierce, The Devil's Lexographer, by Paul Fatout. University of Oklahoma Press, 1951.

Citizen Hearst, by W.A. Swanberg. Charles Scribners Sons, 1961.
The Gate: The True Story of the Design and Construction of the Golden Gate Bridge, by John Van der Zee. New York: Simon and Schuster, 1986.
The Hearsts, by Lindsay Chaney/Michel Cieply. Simon and Schuster, 1981.
Inside the Walls of Alcatraz, by Frank Heaney. Palo Alto: Bull Publishing, 1987.
The Madams of San Francisco, by Curt Gentry. Doubleday, 1964.
Superspan: The Golden Gate Bridge, by Tom Horton. San Francisco: Chronicle Books, 1983.

Other Insight Guides

Other *Insight Guides* which highlight destinations in the region include California, Northern California, Southern California and Los Angeles. *Insight Pocket Guides* include Northern California, Southern California and San Francisco.

A beautiful, comprehenisve guide to movies stars, Disneyland and Northern California.

This book captures the energy and glamour of America's movie capital.

Insight Pocket Guides

Insight Pocket Guides are for travelers with limited time. A series of personally selected tours by a local host shows the best in attractions, restaurants and nightlife.

267